Faith at the Intersection of History and Experience

Faith at the Intersection of History and Experience

The Theology of Georg Wobbermin

BRENT A. R. HEGE

WIPF & STOCK · Eugene, Oregon

FAITH AT THE INTERSECTION OF HISTORY AND EXPERIENCE
The Theology of Georg Wobbermin

Copyright © 2009 Brent A. R. Hege. All rights reserved. Except for brief quotations in critical publications or reviews, no part of this book may be reproduced in any manner without prior written permission from the publisher. Write: Permissions, Wipf and Stock Publishers, 199 W. 8th Ave., Suite 3, Eugene, OR 97401.

www.wipfandstock.com

ISBN 13: 978-1-55635-055-9

Manufactured in the U.S.A.

Unless otherwise noted, all biblical passages are from the New Revised Standard Version Bible, copyright 1989, Division of Christian Education of the National Council of Churches of Christ in the United States of America. Used by permission. All rights reserved.

Contents

Acknowledgments vii
Abbreviations and Translations ix

1. INTRODUCTION 1

2. GESCHICHTE UND HISTORIE:
   THE PROBLEM OF FAITH AND HISTORY 15

   The Distinction between Geschichte and Historie
   Wobbermin's Appraisal and Critique of Previous Positions
       Gotthold Ephraim Lessing
           Wobbermin's Appraisal and Critique of Lessing's Position
       Martin Kähler
           Wobbermin's Appraisal and Critique of Kähler's Position
       Wilhelm Herrmann
           Wobbermin's Appraisal and Critique of Herrmann's Position
       Wilhelm Bousset
           Wobbermin's Appraisal and Critique of Bousset's Position
   The Historic Picture of Jesus Christ

3. ERFAHRUNG UND GLAUBE: WOBBERMIN'S RELIGIO-
   PSYCHOLOGICAL CIRCLE AND THE DOCTRINE OF FAITH 78

   Systematic Theology according to the Religio-Psychological Method
       The Religio-Psychological Method
       The Religio-Psychological Circle
   The Doctrine of Faith in Light of the Religio-Psychological Method
       The Reciprocal Relationship of the fides quae creditur and the fides qua creditur
       Fides historica and fides iustificans in Light of the Distinction between Geschichte and Historie
       Word and Faith: Scripture, Revelation, and Experience in the Doctrine of Faith
       Experience and Faith: Toward an Existential Theology

Geschichte and Faith: The Historic Picture of Christ
> The Resurrection of Jesus as the Historic Foundation of the Christian Religion
>
> Experiencing the Historic Christ: Geschichte and the Religio-Psychological Circle

4. ZWISCHEN DEN ZEITEN: WOBBERMIN'S SELF-IDENTIFICATION WITHIN THE HISTORY OF PROTESTANT THOUGHT 115

"Captain of the Liberal Rearguard"
Wobbermin's Understanding of His Place within the "Luther-Kant-Schleiermacher Line"
> Martin Luther
> Immanuel Kant
> Friedrich Schleiermacher

Wobbermin and Post-War Theology
> Karl Barth
> Rudolf Bultmann

5. CONCLUSION 159

APPENDIX 1. Fides Historica and Fides Iustificans in Melanchthon, Luther, and the Lutheran Confessions 163

> Melanchthon: Loci communes theologici (1521)
> Melanchthon: Loci theologici germanice (1555)
> Melanchthon: Loci praecipui theologici (1559)
> Luther: Die ein und dreissigste Predigt, 29. Junij am Tage Petrj und Paulj (1538)
> The Torgau Articles (1530)
> Apology of the Augsburg Confession (1531)
> Augsburg Confession Variata (1540)
> The Leipzig Interim (1548)
> Epitome of the Formula of Concord (1577)

APPENDIX 2. National Socialism and the Aryan Paragraph: The Debate between Wobbermin and Bultmann 169

APPENDIX 3. Georg Wobbermin: A Brief Biography 178

Bibliography 181
Index of Names 203
Topical Index 205

Acknowledgments

Although this book appears under my name alone, many people deserve acknowledgment and a word of thanks for valuable contributions:

First and foremost, my *Doktormutter*, Dawn DeVries, John Newton Thomas Professor of Systematic Theology at Union-PSCE, for her guidance, encouragement, and friendship over the past seven years.

My dissertation readers, Andreas Schuele, Aubrey L. Brooks Professor of Biblical Theology at Union-PSCE, and Brent Sockness, Associate Professor of Religious Studies at Stanford University, for their careful reading and for their insightful and challenging criticisms and suggestions.

B. A. Gerrish, John Nuveen Professor Emeritus at the University of Chicago Divinity School, for first suggesting Wobbermin as a theologian worthy of study.

Pam Wells, Serials Librarian at Union-PSCE, for her tireless work tracking down many obscure texts with patience and good humor.

Michael Aune, Dean of Pacific Lutheran Theological Seminary and Professor of Liturgical and Historical Studies at PLTS and the Graduate Theological Union, for many illuminating email conversations and for providing advance copies of parts III and IV of his series, "Discarding the Barthian Spectacles."

Hobbie Carlson, Acquisitions Librarian at Union-PSCE, for purchasing several rare microfilms from German libraries.

Stephen Crocco, James Lenox Librarian at Princeton Theological Seminary, for granting me full access to the PTS library for initial research during the summer of 2003.

Sara Mummert, formerly of the Lutheran Theological Seminary at Gettysburg, for her assistance during research at the Wentz Library.

Acknowledgments

Eric Crump, Associate Professor of Systematic Theology at the Lutheran Theological Seminary at Gettysburg, for many helpful bibliographic references.

Dirk von der Horst, Ph.D. candidate in Theology at Claremont Graduate University, for reading a draft of this manuscript and for assistance with some difficult translations.

The "Dissertation Writers Support Group" at St. Mark Lutheran Church, Charlottesville, VA – Juli Thompson, Thomas Ridenhour, Jr., Laura Hartman, and Roderick Martin – for reading chapters and for general support and encouragement.

The Lutheran Theological Seminary at Gettysburg, for generous financial support through the Graduate Fellowship program.

The Division for Ministry of the Evangelical Lutheran Church in America, for generous financial support through the Educational Grant Program.

Carrie Wolcott, Jim Tedrick, and the entire staff at Wipf and Stock, for their invaluable assistance in bringing this project to completion.

My students at Union-PSCE, for their goodwill and patience during sometimes lengthy digressions on points of early 20th-century theological and historical interest.

My family, for their love and support.

And finally, to Mandy, for everything.

Abbreviations and Translations

LIST OF ABBREVIATIONS

All abbreviations, unless noted with an asterisk, are given according to the *Theologische Realenzyklopädie Abkürzungsverzeichnis*, 2nd ed., comp. Siegfried M. Schwertner (Berlin and New York: de Gruyter, 1994).

ARG *Archiv für Reformationsgeschichte*

ARPs *Archiv für Religionspsychologie*

BGl *Beweis des Glaubens*

BBKL *Biographisch-Bibliographisches Kirchenlexikon*, ed. Friedrich Wilhelm Bautz, 26 vols. (Hamm, Herzberg, and Nordhausen: Traugott Bautz, 1990–2006).

Cited as *BBKL*, volume, page number.

BOC* *The Book of Concord: The Confessions of the Evangelical Lutheran Church*, ed. Robert Kolb and Timothy J. Wengert, trans. Charles P. Arand et al. (Minneapolis: Fortress, 2000).

Cited as *BOC*, page number.

BR *Biblical Research*

BSLK *Die Bekenntnisschriften der evangelisch-lutherischen Kirche*, 3rd ed. (Göttingen: Vandenhoeck & Ruprecht, 1956).

Cited as *BSLK*, page number.

Abbreviations and Translations

CR
: *Philippi Melanthonis Opera Quae Supersunt Omnia*, ed. Carolus Gottlieb Bretschneider, 28 vols., *Corpus Reformatorum* (Brunswick: C. A. Schwetschke & Sohn, 1834-1860).

  Cited as *CR*, volume, page number.

ChW
: *Die Christliche Welt*

CuW
: *Christentum und Wissenschaft*

DE
: *Deutsch-evangelische Monatsblätter*

Dialog
: *Dialog: A Journal of Theology*

DtCh*
: *Deutsches Christentum*

DtPfrBl
: *Deutsches Pfarrerblatt*

EKL
: *Evangelisches Kirchenlexikon: Internationale theologische Enzyklopädie*, 3rd ed., ed. Erwin Fahlbusch et al., 5 vols. (Göttingen: Vandenhoeck & Ruprecht, 1985-1997).

  Cited as *EKL*, volume, page number.

ET
: *Expository Times*

EvTh
: *Evangelische Theologie*

GuV¹
: Rudolf Bultmann, *Glauben und Verstehen: Gesammelte Aufsätze*, 4 vols. (Tübingen: Mohr Siebeck, 1933-1965).

  Cited as *GuV¹*, volume, page number.

GuV²
: Rudolf Bultmann, *Glauben und Verstehen: Gesammelte Aufsätze*, 2nd ed., 4 vols. (Tübingen: Mohr Siebeck, 1954-1967).

  Cited as *GuV²*, volume, page number.

Jacobs*
: *The Book of Concord: or, The Symbolical Books of the Evangelical Lutheran Church with Historical Introduction, Notes, Appendixes and Indexes*, vol. 2, *Historical Introduction, Appendixes and Indexes*, ed. Henry E. Jacobs (Philadelphia: General Council Publication Board, 1908).

Abbreviations and Translations

Cited as Jacobs, page number.

JHI	*Journal of the History of Ideas*
JR	*Journal of Religion*
KeTh	*Kerk en Theologie*
KuD	*Kerygma und Dogma*
Liebing*	*Die Marburger Theologen und der Arierparagraph in der Kirche: Eine Sammlung von Texten aus den Jahren 1933 und 1934,* ed. Heinz Liebing (Marburg: N. G. Elwert, 1977).

Cited as Liebing, page number.

LexTQ	*Lexington Theological Quarterly*
LuJ	*Lutherjahrbuch: Organ der internationalen Lutherforschung*
LW*	*Luther's Works,* American Edition, ed. Jaroslav Pelikan and Helmut Lehmann, 55 vols. (Philadelphia: Fortress; St. Louis: Concordia, 1955–1986).

Cited as *LW*, volume, page number.

MoTh	*Modern Theology*
NLA	*Nachrichten der Luther-Akademie in Sondershausen*
NeRu*	*Neue Rundschau*
NT&M*	Rudolf Bultmann, *New Testament and Mythology and Other Basic Writings,* ed. and trans. Schubert M. Ogden (Philadelphia: Fortress, 1984).

Cited as *NT&M*, page number.

RE	*Realenzyklopädie für protestantische Theologie und Kirche,* 2. Ergänzungsband (Leipzig: J. C. Hinrichs, 1913).

Cited as *RE*, page number.

Abbreviations and Translations

RGG¹	*Die Religion in Geschichte und Gegenwart: Handwörtenbuch in gemeinverständlicher Darstellung*, ed. Friedrich Michael Schiele and Leopold Zscharnack, 5 vols. (Tübingen: Mohr Siebeck, 1909–1913).
	Cited as *RGG¹*, volume, page number.
RGG²	*Die Religion in Geschichte und Gegenwart: Handwörterbuch für Theologie und Religionswissenschaft*, 2nd ed., ed. Hermann Gunkel and Leopold Zscharnack, 5 vols. (Tübingen: Mohr Siebeck, 1927–1931).
	Cited as *RGG²*, volume, page number.
RGG³	*Die Religion in Geschichte und Gegenwart: Handwörterbuch für Theologie und Religionswissenschaft*, 3rd ed., ed. Kurt Galling, 6 vols. (Tübingen: Mohr Siebeck, 1957–1962).
	Cited as *RGG³*, volume, page number.
RGG⁴	*Religion in Geschichte und Gegenwart: Handwörterbuch für Theologie und Religionswissenschaft*, 4th ed., ed. Hans Dieter Betz et al., 8 vols. (Tübingen: Mohr Siebeck, 1998–2005).
	Cited as *RGG⁴*, volume, page number.
RThPh	*Revue de Théologie et de Philosophie*
S&C*	*Sources and Contexts of the Book of Concord*, ed. Robert Kolb and James Nestingen (Minneapolis: Fortress, 2001).
	Cited as *S&C*, page number.
SThZ	*Schweizerische Theologische Zeitschrift*
SvTK	*Svensk Teologisk Kvartalskrift*
ThBl	*Theologische Blätter*
ThLZ	*Theologische Literaturzeitung*
TJT	*Toronto Journal of Theology*
TRE	*Theologische Realenzyklopädie*, ed. Gerhard Müller et al., 36 vols. (Berlin and New York: de Gruyter, 1976–2004).

Abbreviations and Translations

Cited as *TRE*, volume, page number.

ThR	*Theologische Rundschau*
WA	*D. Martin Luthers Werke*, Kritische Gesamtausgabe, 71 vols. (Weimar: Hermann Böhlaus, 1883-).

Cited as *WA*, volume, page number.

ZEvRU	*Zeitschrift für den evangelischen Religionsunterricht an höheren Lehranstalten*
ZKG	*Zeitschrift für Kirchengeschichte*
ZMR	*Zeitschrift für Missionswissenschaft und Religionswissenschaft*
ZSTh	*Zeitschrift für systematische Theologie*
ZThK	*Zeitschrift für Theologie und Kirche*
ZZ	*Zwischen den Zeiten*

TRANSLATIONS

All translations are mine unless the English translation of the text is cited first. In the case of Wobbermin's works, I have chosen to include the German text in the footnotes because these texts are not readily available in any but the most comprehensive research libraries in the United States. The original German text will be given in italics in the footnotes where my translation appears in the body of the text, and it will appear in italics within brackets in the footnotes where my translation appears in that footnote.

If available, the English translation of a text will be included in brackets, preceded by "ET."

1

Introduction

THE HISTORY OF LIBERAL theology has until very recently been considered predominantly from the perspective of its critics, namely Karl Barth and his students.[1] According to the prevailing wisdom of historians of this period of theology, the First World War signaled an abrupt end to the liberal theological program, ushering in a new era of Protestant theology. As George Rupp notes, "In part because of the influence of Barth's judgment, the voices of the condemned themselves have for several generations too seldom been heard in their own right."[2] Historians of theology have generally considered the period as one of decay, both intellectually and ethically. Barthian dialectical theology was hailed as nothing short of a renaissance of Protestant theology, a return to the Word of God and with it a powerful critique of liberal accommodations of a militant and ethically bankrupt German bourgeois culture. Liberal theology was pronounced dead, slain on the fields of slaughter in France and Belgium.[3] The tragedy of the First World War has, until recently, served as the dominant interpretive key to writing the history of German liberal theology.

But with historical distance and the waning of Barthian hegemony in Protestant theology have come a renewed interest in the liberal theologians of the late nineteenth and early twentieth century. Historians of theology are beginning to approach this period of Protestant thought

---

1. See especially Barth, *Die protestantische Theologie im 19. Jahrhundert* [ET: *Protestant Theology in the Nineteenth Century*].

2. Rupp, *Culture-Protestantism*, 14.

3. This sentiment extended beyond theology to include all aspects of social and cultural life, particularly in Germany. Perhaps the most famous example of this profound sense of catastrophe and pathos in the years immediately following Germany's defeat is Oswald Spengler's *Der Untergang des Abendlandes* [ET: *The Decline of the West*], the first volume of which was published in 1918.

with more objective or at least irenic intentions, discarding what Michael Aune has called "the Barthian spectacles."[4] Where once historians of this period preferred to speak in terms of radical *discontinuity*,[5] a new generation of historians is investigating this period for signs of *continuity* across the supposed chasm of the First World War.

The most comprehensive and influential of these recent studies is Matthias Wolfes's *Protestantische Theologie und moderne Welt*.[6] Wolfes intends to present what he calls a "liberal theological theory of theology"

---

4. Aune, "Discarding the Barthian Spectacles, Part I," 223–32. Timothy Gorringe suggests that it was actually Barth's students and followers who were "vehemently opposed" to liberal theology more so than Barth himself. Gorringe acknowledges that Barth was indeed a vocal critic of theological liberalism, but he questions the image of Barth as a "sour 'neo-orthodox' opponent of liberal theology" who had turned his back once and for all on his theological predecessors. Gorringe, "Karl Barth and Liberal Theology," 163. Barth's own reflections on nineteenth-century theology support Gorringe's conclusion. As Barth put it in his 1957 address on evangelical theology in the nineteenth century, "The 19th century is behind us. So also is the evangelical theology of that century. The breach separating us from the 19th century is perhaps more pronounced in the field of theology than in any other academic discipline, although it is nowhere absent. This is not to say that 19th-century theology is to be dismissed. Such a procedure would be out of order in any academic discipline, but most certainly in theology. . . . In the Church and hence in theology the commandment, 'Honor thy father and thy mother,' is valid, and this commandment remains binding on the children even when they have left their parents' house. To respect and sustain the ties that bind the present to the past, in spite of deep breaches, is therefore imperative." Barth, "Evangelical Theology in the 19th Century," 11–12.

5. This is the judgment of Friedrich Gogarten, for example, who declared in 1920, "Today we are witnessing the collapse of your [liberal theology's] world!" It is also the judgment of many historians of theology, such as Claude Welch, for whom 1914 marks the end of the nineteenth century, and with it liberal theology, and Heinz Zahrnt, who claims that the theology of the nineteenth century ended and that of the twentieth century began with Karl Barth, calling this both the "turning-point" and the "renewal" of theology. See Gogarten, "Zwischen den Zeiten," 96 [ET: "Between the Times," 278]; Welch, *Protestant Thought in the Nineteenth Century*, 1:4; and Zahrnt, *Die Sachen mit Gott*, 13ff. [ET: *The Question of God*, 15ff.]. Barth himself recalls two events of the year 1914 that marked the end of liberal theology for him: the "Aufruf der 93 an die Kulturwelt" and Ernst Troeltsch's decision to leave the theological faculty of Heidelberg for a chair in philosophy in Berlin. See Barth, "Evangelical Theology in the 19th Century," 14. For more on Barth's reaction to the "Aufruf der 93 an die Kulturwelt" and on the complex political and theological history of that document, see Härle, "Der Aufruf der 93 Intellektuellen." For a more detailed evaluation of dialectical theology's relationship to liberal theology, see Geyer, "Die dialektische Theologie und die Krise des Liberalismus."

6. Wolfes, *Protestantische Theologie und moderne Welt*. On the question of discontinuity and continuity see especially pp. 17–28.

Introduction

on the basis of three nearly forgotten post-war liberal theologians: Georg Wehrung, Horst Stephan, and Georg Wobbermin. Wolfes's primary thesis is that the dominant narrative depicting a radical discontinuity between pre-war and post-war theology is unsustainable in light of a thorough historical analysis of the liberal theology of the period immediately following World War I. The rapid ascendancy of dialectical or "Word of God" theology obscures the fact that there was a younger generation of liberal theologians publishing important constructive work during the Weimar era. This younger generation, represented in Wolfes's study by Wehrung, Stephan, and Wobbermin, was not merely recycling pre-war theology in a doomed attempt to repristinate a bygone theological era. Rather, this younger generation applied the basic principles of liberal theology within a new socio-political and intellectual milieu and continued the liberal theological program well beyond what has commonly been deemed its complete demise at the end of the Wilhelmine era.

A significant difficulty in writing the history of theology during this period is the lack of an unambiguous and universally agreeable definition of the term "liberal theology." This difficulty is only compounded by the preference of many historians of this period to use alternative terms, such as "Neo-Protestantism" [*Neuprotestantismus*] or "Culture-Protestantism" [*Kulturprotestantismus*].[7] It is made all the more difficult because so few of the theologians of this period consciously or explicitly referred to themselves as "liberal theologians." Nevertheless, some basic shared characteristics can be noted. The most basic definition of liberal theology is a theology or a theological movement that attempts to reconcile Christian faith and modern thought. Liberal theology is characterized by freedom of thought and inquiry,[8] by an insistence on open dialogue

---

7. See, e.g., Birkner, "Über den Begriff des Neuprotestantismus"; Hübinger, *Kulturprotestantismus und Politik*; Graf, "Kulturprotestantismus: Zur Begriffsgeschichte einer theologiepolitischen Chiffre"; and Rupp, *Culture-Protestantism*. Mark Chapman, among others, rejects the use of the term "Culture-Protestantism" in particular because of its overwhelmingly pejorative use by many dialectical theologians. Chapman, *Ernst Troeltsch and Liberal Theology*, 1.

8. Ward, "The Importance of Liberal Theology," 39. The priority of freedom recalls the original meaning of the term "liberal theology" [*liberalis theologia*] as it was used by Johann Salomo Semler in 1774 to describe purely historical investigations of the New Testament that are unfettered by dogmatic interests or presuppositions. For the German edition, see Semler, *Versuch einer freiern theologischen Lehrart*. See also Graf, "What Has London (or Oxford or Cambridge) to Do with Augsburg?" 25.

with culture, and by a respect for critical scientific methods, particularly historical criticism.

Nevertheless, there is significant debate among historians of this period of theology concerning what the term "liberal theology" actually designates.[9] For example, Eckhard Lessing claims that "liberal theology" is first and foremost a church-political designation, a "party name."[10] Friedrich Wilhelm Graf concludes that the term is in many ways simply an "artifice" and "an extremely vague concept,"[11] while Hans-Joachim Birkner contends that a monolithic "liberal theology" was the invention of anti-liberal theologians of the 1920s who were determined to present a unified liberal tradition in order to eradicate its heresies.[12] Matthias Wolfes suggests that the term serves a historically descriptive purpose while also designating a specific type of constructive theological thought.[13]

The standard critiques of liberal theology by its opponents share a few common themes: liberal theology accommodates the prevailing culture at the expense of the gospel, liberal theology is concerned only with the individual at the expense of the community of faith, liberal theology represents a complete subjectivization of the Christian faith at the expense of the objective reality of God and God's revelation in Jesus Christ, and liberal theology is finally anthropology masquerading as theology.

In light of the difficulties attending a comprehensive and universally agreeable definition of liberal theology as well as the persistent myth of liberal theology's total collapse at the end of the First World War, how is liberal theology now to be understood and defined? If, as Eckhard Lessing has suggested, the history of German theology has been and continues to be the history of *systematic* theology,[14] then, as Graf argues, it is only possible to understand liberal theology on the basis of insights drawn from the theological methods of its representatives.[15] Graf proposes five

---

9. For a thorough overview of this discussion, see Wolfes, *Protestantische Theologie*, 29–71.

10. Lessing, *Geschichte der deutschsprachigen evangelischen Theologie*, 1:23.

11. Graf, "What Has London (or Oxford or Cambridge) to Do with Augsburg?" 29.

12. Birkner, "Liberale Theologie," 33.

13. Wolfes, *Protestantische Theologie*, 11.

14. Lessing, *Geschichte der deutschsprachigen evangelischen Theologie*, 24.

15. Graf, "What Has London (or Oxford or Cambridge) to Do with Augsburg?" 22. Wobbermin makes the same observation in his debates with Barth, suggesting that the debate ultimately concerns competing methodologies. See Wobbermin, "Der Streit um

Introduction

common systematic elements of German liberal theology and maintains that these five elements are the key to understanding liberal theology as a movement.

First, liberal theologians were critical of traditional patterns of authority and preferred to base truth in religious experience. Second, liberal theologians could no longer develop dogmatic systems like those of Protestant scholastic orthodoxy; therefore their task became the elucidation of doctrines, now understood as expressions of faith. In liberal systematic theologies, then, a legalistic understanding of doctrine was replaced by reflections on religious experience and lived religion. Third, basing descriptions of the doctrines of faith on personal religious experience meant that liberal theologians were unable to develop "adequate" understandings of corporate identity.[16] Fourth, this weak regard for community and corporate ecclesiastical identity meant that liberal theologians sought the reintegration of individuals into community in a variety of ways. Finally, liberal theologies were "cultural theologies" rather than "church theologies." The primary goal was not a strengthening of confessional identity but an integration of modern pluralist society on a religious basis.[17]

If Graf is correct that the history of liberal theology is best understood from the perspective of theological methods employed by liberal theologians themselves, then a history of modern theology written by a liberal theologian should be especially instructive.[18] In the introduction to his history of modern German Protestant theology since German Idealism, Horst Stephan describes Protestant theology as standing under two "stars":

> As scientific self-reflection and as a presentation [*Darstellung*] of the Christian faith evangelical theology stands under two differ-

---

Schleiermacher."

16. This fourth element proposed by Graf is contradicted by Wolfes, who claims that liberal theology adopted a positive and necessary relationship to the Christian community. See below, p. 7.

17. Graf, "What Has London (or Oxford or Cambridge) to Do with Augsburg?" 29–31.

18. Such a perspective will be instructive but not necessarily more objective than a history of liberal theology written by a critic or by a theologian with another methodological and ideological perspective. It is good to recall Graf's warning that "to talk about the possible relevance of intellectual traditions says more about the person doing the talking than it does about the tradition itself." Ibid., 32.

ent stars. Theology is a function of the Christian *community* and through its work enables the appropriate leading of the church through changing times. But insofar as it carries out this reflection and representation *scientifically*, theology confronts its historical attestations and formations, despite its intrinsic connection to them, by researching, analyzing, and comparing; it constructs methods that shield its doctrines from the suspicion of randomness or arbitrariness; it incorporates critical statements and decisions; it therefore takes part in the general scientific struggle over the right way, means, and goal of knowledge. With this the nobility as well as the danger of theology is described. It is proper theology only as long as it truly follows both stars. It denies its essence and abandons its claim to leadership when it loses its character of faith or of science.[19]

These "stars" serve as the twin foci of an ellipse, as the ecclesial and scientific anchors of Protestant theology. As Michael Aune puts it, Stephan's two stars concern the articulation of faith's content and consequences for the church on the one hand and the scholarly investigation of the Christian witness in history on the other, always in their interrelation.[20] Or as Stephan himself argued, both stars must be held in view simultaneously to avoid denying theology's essence or abandoning its claim to leadership.

Matthias Wolfes turns to Stephan and his two "stars" as the basis for his own "liberal theological theory of theology" [*liberaltheologische Theologietheorie*], a collection of fifty-nine theses under seven main features. These main features are Theology and Faith, Theology and Church, Theology as *Glaubenslehre*, The Presentation of *Glaubenslehre*, Theology as Scholarship, Theology and Christian Praxis, and Protestant Theology and the Modern World. These seven categories are also related to the three main themes of Wolfes's presentation of the work of his three chosen theologians, themes that correspond to the "central unity" of liberal theology: faith and revelation, faith and theology, and faith and history.[21]

The seven main features of Wolfes's liberal theological theory of theology serve both as a historical description of liberal theology and as a designation of a constructive approach, contributing to what Wolfes calls

---

19. Stephan, *Geschichte der deutschen evangelischen Theologie*, 1. Emphasis in original.

20. Aune, "Discarding the Barthian Spectacles, Conclusion," 154.

21. Wolfes, *Protestantische Theologie*, 2–3.

Introduction

a "comprehensive historical-theological view" that is essential for understanding the theological situation of the inter-war period. These theses also serve to expose the inaccuracy of the prevailing thesis that liberal theology ceased to be a factor within Protestantism after World War I. With these theses Wolfes intends to demonstrate the basic continuity of Weimar liberal theology with Wilhelmine liberal theology, and to outline the possibility of a constructive liberal theological approach in our own time.

The first of Wolfes's "main features" concerns the relationship of theology and faith. In a liberal theological theory of theology, theology's chief task is the conceptual and methodical presentation and interpretation of Christian faith. Faith, its experiences, convictions, and presuppositions are made the object of theological reflection, and theology is understood as a function of faith itself. Theology's presentation and interpretation of faith must consider both the normative expression of faith in Christian doctrines and the historical conditionality and relativity of those expressions.

Theology and church belong in an "insoluble reciprocal relationship" insofar as both are dedicated to the interpretation of Christian faith. Theology, as Stephan maintained, is a function of the Christian community, and the reference to the community means that theology is understood as a way of interpreting the faith with reference to the Protestant confessions. According to Wolfes, this is what makes evangelical theology "Protestant." Faith and church are historic "objects," and both refer back to God's revelation in Christ, which is encountered only within history and in a historic way. Thus theology must be understood as a historic process and must take note of its temporal limitations and conditionality.

Theology, according to the liberal understanding, is not a "*scientia de deo*" but a presentation [*Darstellung*] of statements of faith that have their origin in the consciousness of absolute dependence on God. For this reason theology in the liberal tradition is understood as *Glaubenslehre*. As *Glaubenslehre*, theology is related to two sources: the first source is the convictions and ideas of faith found in the community, and the second source is the treasure of church tradition, the history of its faith and its theology. According to Wolfes, "the dogmatic assertion of an 'absoluteness of Christianity' is replaced by the theological determination of an unconditioned and unsurpassed ultimate significance of the Christian faith for religious subjectivity."[22]

The presentation [*Darstellung*] of *Glaubenslehre* follows what Stephan called "the inner logic of Christian faith." The task of *Glaubenslehre* is to reconstruct the internal structure of Christian faith, to reproduce faith in conceptual form. Christian faith is distinguished from all other forms of religiosity by its foundation in the event of revelation in Jesus Christ.

While theology is a function of faith, it is at the same time a science and a scholarly endeavor [*Wissenschaft*] whose object of reflection is the Christian faith, its internal structures and its social, political, and cultural expressions. Therefore theology belongs to the range of cultural-scientific disciplines [*Kulturwissenschaften*] and must make use of the research methods shared by each if it hopes to be an equal partner in scientific discourse. The formation of a comprehensive methodology is an indispensable theological task, and its chief components are the clarification of the relationship between faith and theology, the analysis of the formal character of theological statements, and a definition of theology's proper object.

The liberal theological attention to ethics and lived religion requires the formal relation of theology to Christian praxis. Theology as *Wissenschaft* does not constitute an end in itself; rather, it serves to promote and inform a Christian praxis beyond a scientific reflection on faith.

Finally, theology is tasked with understanding modern life in its spiritual, ideological, social, and political dimensions and with asserting the "humanizing power" [*humanisierende Kraft*] of the Christian faith in a world that no longer grants a special status to religion without justification. To accomplish this task, theology must recognize and embrace its place within the historic process that has resulted in this modern reality.[23]

With this liberal theological theory of theology Wolfes intends to accomplish two objectives. First, he intends to challenge the prevailing thesis of the radical discontinuity between pre-war and post-war German Protestant theology. Second, he hopes to offer a program for construc-

---

22. Ibid., 575.
23. Ibid., 572–79.

Introduction

tive theological work in the present that acknowledges and embraces its liberal theological roots.

The first of Wolfes's intentions presents a range of possibilities for further work by historical theologians in Germany and elsewhere. If, as Aune suggests, the Barthian appraisal of this period of theology is no longer dominant and no longer sufficient, it is therefore possible to approach this period with fresh questions and goals. The goal of challenging the currently accepted thesis of discontinuity is only one goal among many. It is now possible to approach this period on its own terms and to allow the representatives of inter-war liberal theology to speak in their own words. This is an especially promising area of research for historical theologians in the English-speaking world, where these theologians are not yet widely known.[24]

Among Wolfes's three theologians, Georg Wobbermin was the most widely read and discussed in his time.[25] Wolfes's comprehensive bibliography contains ten pages of secondary sources on Wobbermin, the vast majority of which are book reviews and short essays or articles on specific themes in Wobbermin's theology written by his contemporaries. Relatively little attention has been paid to Wobbermin's work since his death. To date only three book-length studies of Wobbermin have been published, including Wolfes's. Wolf-Ulrich Klünker published his dissertation on Wobbermin as *Psychologische Analyse und theologische Wahrheit: Die religionspsychologische Methode Georg Wobbermins* in 1985, and in 1992 Georg Pfleiderer included a section on Wobbermin in his published dissertation, entitled *Theologie als Wirklichkeitswissenschaft: Studien zum Religionsbegriff bei Georg Wobbermin, Rudolf Otto, Heinrich Scholz und Max Scheler*. Additionally, two unpublished dissertations have been writ-

---

24. None of Wolfes's three theologians is widely known or even recognized in the English-speaking world. They are rarely mentioned in English-language histories of liberal theology or of theology in the early twentieth century. As part of his research for the series of articles on the last generation of liberal theologians, Michael Aune conducted an informal survey of American historical and systematic theologians. Only one of the twelve theologians surveyed could identify one of these three figures. See Aune, "Discarding the Barthian Spectacles, Part III," 389. This unfamiliarity is explained partly by the fact that among these three figures only two of Wobbermin's theological works have been translated into English: the third edition of *Der christliche Gottesglaube in seinem Verhältnis zur heutigen Philosophie und Naturwissenschaft* was translated as *Christian Belief in God*, and the second volume of Wobbermin's three-volume systematic theology was translated as *The Nature of Religion*.

25. For a brief biography of Wobbermin, see Appendix 3.

ten on Wobbermin. The first was, until now, the only study of Wobbermin written in English, a dissertation completed at Boston University in 1931 by Jannette Elthina Newhall, entitled "The Influence of William James on Georg Wobbermin's Psychology and Philosophy of Religion."[26] The second is a dissertation written by Günter Irle at the University of Marburg in 1973, entitled "Theologie als Wissenschaft bei Georg Wobbermin." This present study is the first in English to consider Wobbermin's theology and its place within liberal theology and the Protestant tradition as a whole.

Thanks to Wolfes's groundbreaking study, it is now possible to investigate the liberal theology of the interwar period as a legitimate theological movement rather than the last gasps of a dying era. It is now possible to hear these theologians in their own words and on their own terms. As Wobbermin was the most prolific of these interwar liberal theologians and the most widely discussed in his own time, his work presents many opportunities for study and for testing the theses of continuity and productivity within Weimar liberal theology. Wobbermin also presents significant challenges, particularly in terms of his support of the National Socialists beginning as early as 1930. For this reason, Wobbermin also represents the complexity of theological liberalism, which sometimes coexisted with positions that were anything but politically liberal.

Wobbermin is predominantly remembered for his attempt to construct a systematic theology on the basis of the psychology of religion. This concern led him to an engagement with Friedrich Schleiermacher and with the American philosopher and psychologist of religion, William James. The religio-psychological method that Wobbermin developed in his systematic theology rests on the foundation of a distinction between *Geschichte* and *Historie*, which Wobbermin developed as a response to Arthur Drews and in a series of *Auseinandersetzungen* with previous positions on the relationship between faith and history, all contained in a programmatic essay published in 1911. Finally, more general methodological questions compelled him to understand his work in the broader context of the Protestant tradition, leading him to a prolonged occupa-

---

26. There is some evidence that Wobbermin was better known in the United States in his own lifetime. In the foreword to *The Nature of Religion*, Douglas Clyde Macintosh notes that "Dr. Georg Wobbermin . . . has been well and favorably known to theological teachers and students in the English-speaking world for almost a generation." Macintosh, Foreword to *The Nature of Religion*, by Georg Wobbermin, v.

Introduction

tion with Luther, Kant, and Schleiermacher throughout the 1920s and into the 1930s.

With the end of World War I and the rise of dialectical theology, Wobbermin became an ardent defender of liberal theology against the younger generation, especially against Karl Barth. These two theologians, colleagues for a brief time at the University of Göttingen, held public debates in the church newspapers and theological journals of Germany until Wobbermin's death. Beginning in the late 1920s, Wobbermin began to appreciate the significance of Martin Heidegger's existential philosophy and its theological expression in the work of Rudolf Bultmann, although Wobbermin preferred to follow this new existentialist direction on the basis of what he called Schleiermacher's psychology of religion.

Three themes in Wobbermin's theology are especially significant in terms of the theological history of this period. They are the interrelated themes of history, experience, and faith, which together form the essential components of his "religio-psychological circle" [*religionspsychologische Zirkel*]. Wobbermin's religio-psychological approach serves as an example of a liberal theological method that stands within the long tradition of Protestant thought reaching back to Luther and extending beyond the supposed "great turning-point" of World War I.

The primacy of religious experience in Wobbermin's thought recalls Schleiermacher's method in the *Glaubenslehre*, Kant's epistemology, and Luther's emphasis on the relational character of Christian faith in God, or what Wobbermin calls the three great "Copernican revolutions" of theology, epistemology, and religious thought. Wobbermin's strict distinction between the two German words for history (*Geschichte* and *Historie*) serves as a systematic principle by which he hopes to maintain the Reformation emphasis on justification by faith alone and which recalls Melanchthon's distinction between *fides historica* and *fides iustificans*.

By exploring and developing the intersection of these three themes of history, experience, and faith, Wobbermin intends to maintain a systematic interrelation between subjectivity and objectivity: between the subjective experience of the believer and the objective reality of God, between the subjectivity of the individual Christian standing within history and the objective reality of the historic picture of Christ that transcends mere historicity, and between the *fides qua creditur* and the *fides quae creditur*, the subjective and objective elements of faith. Thus the key to Wobbermin's theology is the interrelation of subjectivity and objectivity, expressed most clearly in his religio-psychological circle, which is rooted in this intersection of history, experience, and faith.

In the present study, this thesis will be explored in three parts. The first part will be an analysis of Wobbermin's distinction between *Geschichte* and *Historie*, which he develops in conversation with recent and contemporary discussions of the problem of faith and history. The distinction serves as the foundation for Wobbermin's religio-psychological method and sets up the primary role of religious experience and the doctrines of Christ, faith, and Scripture for both his systematic theology and his *Streitschriften*. In this sense his 1911 essay, *Geschichte und Historie in der Religionswissenschaft*, can be approached as a prolegomenon to his systematic work. The theme of interrelation is present even in this early work on the distinction between *Geschichte* and *Historie*, particularly in the effort to maintain a positive relationship between historical criticism and *Historie* on the one hand and the historic picture of Christ and the experience of redemption through Christ that occurs within and on the basis of *Geschichte* on the other.

The second part will be a presentation of Wobbermin's religio-psychological method and the religio-psychological circle as he employs it in his systematic theology and in his *Streitschriften*. It will also be demonstrated how the religio-psychological circle, the intersection of history, experience, and faith, recalls classic Reformation positions of Luther and Melanchthon, particularly in terms of the importance of religious experience and the distinction between *fides historica* and *fides iustificans*. The goal of this part is to address the methodology operative in Wobbermin's major works and to clarify the relationship between that method and specific doctrines, particularly Christology, revelation, Scripture, and faith. The theme of interrelation will again be emphasized as the key to Wobbermin's theology.

The third and final part will place Wobbermin within the broader context of Protestant thought from Luther, Kant, and Schleiermacher to Karl Barth and Rudolf Bultmann. The primary goal of this part is to address Wobbermin's own understanding of his work's continuity with the great Protestant thinkers of the past, the clash of methodologies represented by his debates with Karl Barth, and the anticipation of some of Bultmann's positions in Wobbermin's work. Implicit in this discussion is a challenge to the prevailing theses of liberal theology as a degeneration of Protestant principles and of the abrupt end of the liberal theological

Introduction

program coincident with the end of the First World War. Wobbermin is especially suited for this purpose because of his consistent occupation with the Protestant theological tradition and because of his prolific production of new work in the "golden age" of dialectical theology in the Weimar era.

In addition to the goals of demonstrating the thesis of interrelation as the key to Wobbermin's theology and of challenging the thesis of liberal theology's demise during the First World War, a further goal of this study is to introduce English readers to Wobbermin's theology. Given the rapid ascendancy of dialectical theology and the immense popularity of Karl Barth after World War I, particularly in light of the "bomb in the playground" that was Barth's *Römerbrief*, the liberal theologians active in the same period have been overlooked by both German-speaking and English-speaking theologians and historians. The bulk of Wobbermin's, Wehrung's, and Stephan's work remains untranslated, and this fact alone means that they will remain largely unknown in the English-speaking world. Furthermore, discussions of these theologians in histories of modern Protestant theology are overwhelmingly critical, many of them produced by theologians and historians sympathetic to Barth and the dialectical theologians. Finally, in the case of Wobbermin politics have perhaps played a particularly important role in his continuing obscurity, unlike the cases of Martin Heidegger, Emanuel Hirsch, or Paul Althaus.[27]

The question remains whether these interwar liberal theologians, Wobbermin in particular, deserve to remain hidden in the shadows of history. Can we learn anything from them now? Do they offer a way forward in the current theological situation? Have we gained enough historical distance to approach Wobbermin on his own terms, acknowledging his support of the Nazis without rejecting for that reason alone all that he proposed as a theologian? Or has history rightly passed Wobbermin and his liberal colleagues by?

Mary Potter Engel and Walter Wyman, Jr., have defined historical theology as "disciplined conversation with the past . . . in order to make one's own decisions about the meaning and truth of Christian faith in and for the present."[28] This study is an invitation to one of the "forgotten

---

27. For a study of Hirsch's and Althaus's (and Gerhard Kittel's) relationship to Nazism, see Ericksen, *Theologians under Hitler*.

28. Engel and Wyman, Introduction to *Revisioning the Past*, 10.

theologians" to join the conversation, to ask whether he, too, has anything to say to us today.

2

Geschichte und Historie

The Problem of Faith and History

THE DISTINCTION BETWEEN *GESCHICHTE* AND *HISTORIE*

The historical consciousness of the nineteenth century created new problems for Protestant theology: how may the new historical science be applied to the Bible? How is faith to maintain its assurance in the midst of historical uncertainty?[1] These questions only intensified when posed with regard to the biblical witness to Jesus Christ and to Christian faith in him. Already in the late nineteenth century, Martin Kähler had attempted to circumscribe a *sturmfreies Gebiet* (literally a "storm-free area") for Christian faith, an area into which the ambiguity and uncertainty of historical criticism could not and should not penetrate. Kähler attempted to secure this area by distinguishing between the historical Jesus and the historic Christ, between the biblical picture of Christ and the portrait provided by historical research. Others (e.g. Wilhelm Herrmann and Wilhelm Bousset) sought to answer these same questions by other means. Their conclusions initiated a spirited discussion of the relationship between faith and history, between the Protestant principle of justification by faith alone and the modern science of historical research.

In a 1911 essay entitled *Geschichte und Historie in der Religionswissenschaft*,[2] Georg Wobbermin revisited some of these ear-

---

1. For some general discussions of the problem of faith and history in the nineteenth-century, see Paulus, *Gott in der Geschichte?* Brachmann, *Glaube und Geschichte*; Rohls, *Protestantische Theologie der Neuzeit*, vol. 1; Welch, *Protestant Thought in the Nineteenth Century*; and Howard, *Religion and the Rise of Historicism*. For a more general study, see Harvey, *The Historian and the Believer*.

2. Wobbermin, *Geschichte und Historie in der Religionswissenschaft*.

lier attempts and argued for the use of a stricter, conceptual distinction between *Geschichte* and *Historie* in order to clarify faith's relationship to Jesus Christ in light of modern historical consciousness. This essay was prompted in part by the recent publication of Arthur Drews's *Die Christusmythe*,[3] in which Drews provocatively suggested that a "historical" Jesus of Nazareth never existed. Drews's radical conclusions sparked intense debate in German theological circles and pointedly raised the question of the relationship between faith and historical knowledge as a question of central significance for Protestant theology.

B. A. Gerrish sketches the contours of the Christ-Myth debate sparked by Drews's book in an article on Ernst Troeltsch's stand in the debate. Gerrish suggests that Drews's thesis was provocative, perhaps even absurd, but nonetheless important because it invited theologians to reflect anew on the question of faith and history, to ask the specific question of the relevance of the historical Jesus for faith.[4]

In his study of *Geschichte* and *Historie*, Wobbermin accuses Drews of ignoring the real and necessary distinction between the active and efficacious picture of Christ within the Christian tradition on the one hand and the results of historical criticism of that same tradition on the other. Drews failed to distinguish, in Wobbermin's terms, between the merely historical [*bloß historisch*] and the immediately historic [*unmittelbar geschichtlich*].[5] By failing to make this important distinction, Drews did not take account of the distinction between the historical Jesus behind the New Testament, of whom very little can be known, and the picture of Christ found in the New Testament and in the Christian tradition through to the present day.

---

3. In the foreword to the first and second editions Drews addresses the aims of this work: "This text seeks to produce evidence that pretty much every trait of the picture of the historical Jesus, at least every important trait of religious significance, has a purely mythical character and there exists no reason at all to seek a historical figure behind the 'Christ Myth.'" Drews, *Die Christusmythe*, xiii-xiv [ET (of the third German edition): *The Christ Myth*, 19]. He reserves specific criticism for the representatives of liberal theology: "It is in fact the fundamental error of liberal theology to think that the development of the Christian church has issued from a historical individual – the man Jesus." Ibid., 225 [ET, 285–86].

4. See Gerrish, "Jesus, Myth, and History."

5. Wobbermin, *Geschichte und Historie*, 2.

Geschichte und Historie

Drews did, in fact, acknowledge such a distinction, but he concluded that the distinction was irrelevant and that it only attempted to ignore the problematical character of Christianity's claim to a historic foundation:

> The reference to history and the so-called "historical continuity of religious development" is obviously only a way out of a difficulty. . . . As if there can still be talk of a "historic basis" where there is no history, but pure myth! As if the "preservation of historical continuity" could consist in maintaining as history what are mythical fictions, just because to this point they have passed for historical truth, when we have seen through their purely fictitious and unreal character![6]

Nevertheless, Wobbermin insists that a conceptual distinction between *Geschichte* and *Historie* will clarify the problem that Drews raised with such force. It is precisely to avoid throwing the historic picture of Christ out with the historically murky bathwater that leads Wobbermin to make a stricter distinction between *Geschichte* and *Historie*.

As with any conceptual distinction, it is important to define the terms as clearly and precisely as possible. In this particular case it is doubly important, because, as Wobbermin candidly admits, such a distinction is an arbitrary one.[7] The terms *Geschichte* and *Historie* (and the corresponding adjectives and adverbs *geschichtlich* and *historisch*) can be used interchangeably in most contexts with little confusion. Such an arbitrary distinction can be justified and even demanded, in Wobbermin's opinion, if it can be shown to provide tangible methodological benefits, such as clarifying conceptual problems.[8] The test of such an arbitrary distinction is finally answered in the application of the distinction itself: will such a distinction prove useful for theological work? If the answer is yes, then such a distinction is justified. If no, then it must be abandoned in favor of a more effective conceptual tool.

---

6. Drews, *Die Christusmythe*, 232 [ET: *The Christ Myth*, 293–94].

7. The arbitrariness of the distinction between *Geschichte* and *Historie* was not lost on many contemporary commentators, most notably Albert Schweitzer, who warned that Wobbermin had ventured onto "dangerous ground" with his insistence on a stricter distinction between the two terms: "He forfeits everything by executing his idea with a play of artful distinctions. Nothing is helped by this. What is essential above all things is that theology employ clear language. Let your speech be yes, yes; no, no. Anything more is of the Evil One." Schweitzer, *Geschichte der Leben-Jesu-Forschung*, 521 [ET: *The Quest of the Historical Jesus*, 408].

8. Wobbermin, *Geschichte und Historie*, 4.

It is important to note here that Wobbermin did not invent the distinction between *Geschichte* and *Historie*; Martin Kähler employed a similar distinction in his critique of the nineteenth-century "Lives of Jesus."[9] Kähler, however, did not attempt to arrive at a systematic or conceptual understanding of the distinction between these terms. The distinction remained for him an auxiliary conceptual aid, but it is Wobbermin who elevates the distinction to the status of a systematic principle, and Wobbermin uses the distinction to clarify the most basic questions addressed in his work.

Despite the arbitrariness of the distinction between *Geschichte* and *Historie*, Wobbermin attempts to provide precise definitions of both terms for the purpose of conceptual clarity. Because he intends to employ the distinction as a systematic principle and not merely as an auxiliary tool, he must be as precise as possible in clarifying the meaning of his terms and their interrelation.

Throughout his essay, Wobbermin continues to refine his definition of *Geschichte*, so that there are finally three distinct yet interrelated definitions, namely, *Geschichte* as what has happened in the past, *Geschichte* as the realm of efficacy or influence, and *Geschichte* as the interrelation of human beings as spiritual-moral beings in their development.

The most basic definition of *Geschichte* is simply "what has happened" [*was ist geschehen* or *was geschah*]. Any event that has happened in the past or any figure who has existed in the past belongs to *Geschichte* and is a *geschichtliche Ereignis* or a *geschichtliche Größe*. *Historie*, by contrast, is a narrower, more precise concept, which Wobbermin defines as "investigated *Geschichte*" [*erforschte Geschichte*],[10] meaning *Geschichte* investigated with the scientific historical method according to the canons of academic historical research. *Geschichte* is simply given; *Historie* must be acquired by scientific investigation.

The *geschichtlich* can potentially confront anyone who stands within history as a historic subject; *Historie* is accessible only to those with the necessary scientific and intellectual tools to discover it. *Geschichte* is prior to *Historie* and is a broader category.[11] Many events and figures of

---

9. See the section on Kähler below.

10. Wobbermin, *Geschichte und Historie*, 5.

11. These terms present significant difficulties when attempting to capture and convey their meaning in English. Unlike German, English has only one noun, "history," and only one adverb, "historically." Like German, however, English does have two adjectives

Geschichte und Historie

Geschichte are lost forever to later generations who must rely on historical research to reconstruct the past. *Historie* depends on sources (texts and various artifacts) by which past events or figures might be reconstructed. Without these sources, *geschichtlich* events or figures threaten to disappear forever. It is the task of the historian to discover and interpret texts or artifacts in order to reconstruct the past. But the absence of sources that would provide evidence for a past event or figure does not constitute final proof that such an event never happened or that such a figure never existed; it only means that such an event or figure cannot be reconstructed by historical research.

Wobbermin further defines *Geschichte*, however, in terms of influence and significance, or what he often calls effect or efficacy [*Wirkung* or *Wirksamkeit*]. Past events or personalities are capable of influencing the future beyond their mere historicity, even if their historicity is questionable on purely historical-scientific grounds. This is especially important in terms of the person of Jesus of Nazareth, who on purely historical grounds is a shadowy figure but who is also clearly a figure of profound historic significance, influence, and efficacy beyond his mere historicity. To put it more precisely, the efficacy of Jesus of Nazareth transcends the mere fact of his historical existence. It is precisely this distinction between mere historicity and profound historic efficacy and significance that a strict distinction between *Geschichte* and *Historie* is meant to clarify.

The realm of *Historie* is the realm of probability. Historians can determine the probability of their research achieving an accurate picture of the past with relative certainty, but the results of scientific historical research always remain relative and hypothetical. Whatever certainty is gained by historical research is never absolute, but approaches only a higher or lower degree of probability. This is not to say, however, that

---

that can be used to indicate the German distinction. But these English terms, like their German counterparts, are usually used interchangeably. Translators of late nineteenth- and twentieth-century theology have generally agreed upon the use of the English adjectives to correspond to the German adjectives. In most cases "historical" corresponds to "historisch" and "historic" corresponds to "geschichtlich," and that is how these terms will be used in this study. See, e.g., Braaten, Introduction to *The So-called Historical Jesus and the Historic Biblical Christ*, by Martin Kähler, 21; Reid, "Translator's Note," in Troeltsch, *The Absoluteness of Christianity*, 21; and Ashcraft, *Rudolf Bultmann*, 35–38. H. Richard Niebuhr attempts to express the same distinction in English with the terms "inner history" and "outer history," or history as lived and history as seen. See Niebuhr, *The Meaning of Revelation*, 31–47.

Geschichte offers absolute certainty, or even necessarily a higher degree of probability than *Historie*. If this were so, Wobbermin suggests, *Historie* would be an unnecessary nuisance and could be safely abandoned. In that case, the goal would be a total separation of *Geschichte* from *Historie*.[12]

But this is not the case. *Historie* serves the vital purpose of removing, as far as possible, the uncertainty of the historic tradition and replacing uncertainty with scientifically ensured results. *Historie*, as Wobbermin defines it, erects well-defined boundaries around *Geschichte* and enables graduated acceptance of probability for the various data of the historic tradition. This leads him to define *Historie* more precisely as "scientifically clarified and refined *Geschichte*."[13] According to this definition, *Historie* serves as a limiting and ordering principle, investigating the historic tradition and presenting the results of its research as the highest possible level of probability. As such, *Historie* is a vital theological tool and plays a necessary role within the Christian religion, precisely because Christianity is a historic religion.

Christianity is a historic religion in at least three important respects. First, Christianity is a historic religion because it is based on the life and teachings of a historic figure, Jesus Christ, in whom it apprehends the revelation of God. Second, Christianity is a historic religion because it refers to a historic document, the New Testament, as the source and norm for its theological reflection. Third, Christianity is a historic religion because it refers to its own history (biblical, liturgical, theological, etc.) for guidance and for resources for its continued development. In order to isolate the truly historic elements within this long tradition, Wobbermin defends a rigorous application of the historical method to the Christian tradition.

---

12. Wobbermin, *Geschichte und Historie*, 6.

13. "*Die historische Forschung dient ja gerade dem Zweck, die Unsicherheit der geschichtlichen Ueberlieferung nach Möglichkeit zu beheben und durch wissenschaftlich gesicherte Resultate zu ersetzen. Wenn es also die historische Forschung doch immer nur zu Wahrscheinlichkeits-Urteilen zu bringen vermag, so kann sich die Geschichte als solche, d.h. nach dem Vorherigen die geschichtliche Ueberlieferung, nicht über das Niveau der historischen Wahrscheinlichkeitsbetrachtung und Wahrscheinlichkeitsgeltung erheben, sondern sie muß noch unter diesem Niveau verbleiben. Erst die Historie erhebt bestimmte Bezirke und Gebiete der Geschichte . . . auf die Höhe wissenschaftlicher Wahrscheinlichkeitsbetrachtung und ermöglicht damit für die einzelnen Daten und Bestandteile der betreffenden Ueberlieferungen eine mannigfach abgestufte Wahrscheinlichkeitsgeltung. Die Historie ist also insoweit die wissenschaftlich geklärte und gereinigte Geschichte – Geschichte nämlich im Sinne der Geschichtsüberlieferung.*" Ibid.

Geschichte und Historie

Here Wobbermin wants to draw a further distinction between the historic tradition of Christianity [*geschichtliche Überlieferung*] and the effects or significance of that history in the present. Wobbermin insists that the entire historic tradition of Christianity must be subjected to the most rigorous historical research both in order to strip away false supports for faith and to uncover or reveal the truly historic elements from that tradition. *Geschichte* in the sense of the historic tradition must be subjected to rigorous historical research in order to uncover or reveal those essential elements. But that research will never provide the *effects* of those historic elements; it will only uncover or reveal the essential elements. The effects of those elements are always prior to historical research of the tradition that carries them and independent of the results of that research.[14] Christian faith, for Wobbermin, requires immediately available historic effects rather than the secondary, provisional results of historical research into the tradition. The historic tradition alone cannot serve as the basis of Christian faith because it always remains past. It is the effects of that history, immediately present and efficacious in the present, that serve as the basis of faith.[15]

Wobbermin also provides a third definition of *Geschichte* based on the philosophy of history of Heinrich Rickert, of which Wobbermin offers only a brief and cursory analysis in his essay. According to Guy Oakes, Rickert's project was largely an attempt to solve the *hiatus irrationalis* be-

---

14. Ibid., 6–7. This is Wobbermin's opinion, but he does not address the possibility that a rigorous historical criticism of these historic elements will perhaps call them into question rather than confirm them. This is one of the major weaknesses of Wobbermin's position, as it also is for Kähler's and for Herrmann's.

15. This further distinction between *Geschichte* and its *Wirkung* or *Wirksamkeit* is a distinction that Wobbermin himself does not make explicit, but he does indicate such a distinction, ever so briefly, when he attempts to distinguish between *Geschichte* as *Überlieferung* and the effect or efficacy of *Geschichte*, its *Wirkung* or *Wirksamkeit*: "The essence of 'history' namely is not exhausted in the fact that it offers the historic tradition – tradition that belongs to the past and that only has value for the present in its recollecting what is past. No, history extends into the present and works itself out in the present – and certainly not merely through individual traditions, but rather through the fact of history itself." ["*Das Wesen der 'Geschichte' ist nämlich nicht damit und darin erschöpft, daß sie geschichtliche Ueberlieferung bietet – Ueberlieferung, die der Vergangenheit angehört und für die Gegenwart nur den Wert der Erinnerung an Vergangenes hat. Nein die Geschichte reicht in die Gegenwart hinein und wirkt sich in der Gegenwart aus – und zwar nicht bloß durch einzelne Ueberlieferungen, sondern durch den Tatbestand der Geschichte selbst.*"] Ibid., 7. This distinction between *Geschichte* as what remains past and the effect or efficacy of *Geschichte* will be discussed in more detail below.

tween concept and reality by means of a chain of reasoning with five links. These five links are a theory of the phenomenology of reality, a critique of epistemological realism, a theory of cognitive interests and a theory of concepts, an analysis of the limits of concept formation in natural science, and a demarcation criterion for distinguishing natural science from historical or cultural science.[16] It is to one part of this final "link" in Rickert's chain of reasoning that Wobbermin appears to turn for support of his final definition of *Geschichte* as the realm of value and as the interrelation of human beings as moral-spiritual beings in their development, and the key to this definition lies in Rickert's understanding of value.

According to Rickert, the theoretical interest of historical science is rooted in the value historians ascribe to the individual as a unique historic entity. The concept of value enables historians to distinguish between important or valuable historic figures and the great mass of all other historic figures. Without such a distinction historical knowledge would be impossible, because of what Rickert called the "extensive and intensive infinity of reality."[17] This is one of the important distinctions between the natural sciences [*Naturwissenschaften*] and the cultural sciences [*Geisteswissenschaften*]. The natural sciences, according to Rickert, are concerned with the general and the universal, while the cultural sciences (including historical science) are concerned with the unique and the individual. Historical science is not ultimately concerned with the past for the sake of the past, but for the sake of the present, namely in terms of a value-relation [*Wertbeziehung*] between the past and the present and in terms of history's essential characteristic of development.[18] Historical

16. Oakes, "Rickert's Theory of Historical Knowledge," xvii.

17. The extensive infinity of reality concerns the endless [*unendlich*] and the unsurveyable [*unübersehbar*] character of reality. Reality is *unendlich* insofar as it cannot be exhaustively incorporated into our experience, and it is *unübersehbar* insofar as it is impossible to survey the whole of reality. The intensive infinity of reality, on the other hand, concerns the individual. The composite elements of each individual event or figure are unlimited in principle, and every event or figure can possess an infinite number of aspects. Rickert summarizes these claims by defining reality as fundamentally irrational, meaning that there is no criterion for deciding what would qualify as complete knowledge of the whole or of the individual aspects. But Rickert claims that this description of reality as irrational is a phenomenological rather than an ontological claim. It concerns our experience of reality rather than reality *in se*. Rickert, *Die Grenzen der naturwissenschaftlichen Begriffsbildung*, 31–45. See also Oakes, "Rickert's Theory of Historical Knowledge," xvii.

18. Rickert describes the concept of development [*Entwicklungsbegriff*] as the concept

science, for Rickert, is about *value* and about reality as it is experienced rather than about reality *in se*. In other words, historical science has a phenomenological rather than an ontological basis.[19]

Rickert does not distinguish between *Geschichte* and *Historie* as Wobbermin uses those terms, but Wobbermin nevertheless believes that his distinction finds support in Rickert's work. While there is a plausible connection between Wobbermin's understanding of *Geschichte* and Rickert's understanding of the uniqueness of historic individuals and of the importance of development and the interrelation of past figures and present individuals in terms of the value of past figures for the present, it is a very slim connection, and Wobbermin does not give an adequate defense of his claim to have found support in Rickert's work.[20]

Wobbermin claims to have arrived at a third definition of *Geschichte* on the basis of his reading of Rickert, but his justification for a Rickertian basis never achieves the clarity necessary to make a judgment on its merits as a faithful interpretation and application of Rickert's philosophy of history. Nevertheless, he claims to have achieved a third definition of *Geschichte* on the basis of Rickert's work, namely *Geschichte* as "the interrelation of human beings as spiritual-moral beings in their development." And again, "the interrelation of spiritual-moral individuals constitutes *Geschichte* – their interrelation, however, in its development. For the element of development also belongs to the essence of *Geschichte*."[21]

---

that "brings to expression the logical essence of historical science" and one that further develops the principle of value-relation. Rickert, *Die Grenzen der naturwissenschaftlichen Begriffsbildung*, 396.

19. Oakes, "Rickert's Theory of Historical Knowledge," xvii.

20. In fact, Wobbermin's treatment barely scratches the surface of Rickert's work, and he appears to draw only one substantial conclusion from his reading of Rickert, namely that cultural value is intimately related to the spiritual-moral life. Unfortunately, Wobbermin fails to provide a sufficient justification for this conclusion, and he does not refer to any of Rickert's own texts to support that specific claim. He does claim that his third and final definition of *Geschichte* is based on Rickert's work, but he fails to give any evidence that this is the case. It is difficult to determine why, then, Wobbermin found it necessary to engage Rickert's work at all. See Wobbermin, *Geschichte und Historie*, 7–14.

21. "Geschichte ist doch letzlich der Zusammenhang der Menschen als geistig-sittlicher Wesen in seiner Entwicklung.... Der Zusammenhang geistig-sittlicher Wesen also stellt die Geschichte dar. Ihr Zusammenhang aber in seiner Entwicklung. Denn auch das Moment der Entwicklung gehört zum Wesen der Geschichte." Ibid., 14. Wobbermin's definition does have a Rickertian basis insofar as it appropriates Rickertian terminology, but beyond this semantic or conceptual similarity there is little substantial engagement with Rickert's philosophy of history.

Geschichte, then, is not merely what is past and static. Rather, it is the realm of interrelation and development, of continuing efficacy and value, which persists and extends into the present. *Geschichte* is not a closed system but a living process and a present relation of individuals to one another and to the past. The embodiment of spiritual-moral relation, Wobbermin suggests, "is the constitutive essential feature of *Geschichte*."[22]

Ultimately it is the concepts of relation and value that serve as the most important aspects of this third definition of *Geschichte*. Value, especially the value of the historic picture of Christ, is an important concept for Wobbermin; however, it is often simply collapsed into the concept of the effects or efficacy of that picture. The concept of relation will become more important in Wobbermin's "religio-psychological circle," which forms the basis of his religio-psychological theological method and which he constructs on the basis of his distinction between *Geschichte* and *Historie*.

Having arrived at three definitions of *Geschichte*, it is now necessary to review these definitions of *Geschichte* and *Historie* and the distinctions and relationships between them. In his opening section Wobbermin begins by offering a basic definition of *Geschichte* as simply what has happened, or what is past. He then refines that definition to emphasize the effects or efficacy of historic events and figures, and finally he expands the definition of *Geschichte* to emphasize the concepts of interrelation, development, and value. All of this, then, is opposed to *Historie*, which is defined as the scientific investigation of *Geschichte* and the results of that investigation. *Historie* serves the purpose of erecting boundaries around *Geschichte*, to separate what is historic from what is not historic.[23] What

---

22. "*Der Inbegriff dieser geistig-sittlichen Beziehungen, die den Zusammenhang der Menschheit als ganzer gewährleisten, ist die konstituierende Wesensmerkmal der Geschichte.*" Ibid., 15. This concept of relation will become much more important in the context of Wobbermin's religio-psychological circle between present individual religious experience and historic facts. The religio-psychological circle will be discussed in more detail in the following chapter.

23. Here it does appear that Wobbermin is granting a more positive role to *Historie* than perhaps he is willing to admit. If *Historie* is capable of separating the truly historic from the broader tradition of Christianity, it is performing a necessary positive function. Wobbermin does grant a positive relationship of *Historie* to *Geschichte* at other points in this essay, but he always qualifies his determination of this role with an insistence that faith in no way depends on the results of historical research. But *Historie* can play a necessary and even positive role in establishing the foundation for faith without thereby *becoming* that foundation. It is, as Wobbermin puts it, second-order reflection on a prior,

is historic, though, is not limited by or confined to *Historie*. The historic will persist beyond and sometimes even in spite of the results of historical research both by virtue of its primacy – *Historie*, Wobbermin maintains, always retains a secondary character to the primacy of *Geschichte* – and by virtue of its significance.

Here it is necessary to introduce a further distinction, one that Wobbermin himself did not consciously or explicitly make. It is necessary to distinguish between *Historie*, *Geschichte*, and the effect or efficacy [*Wirkung* or *Wirksamkeit*] of *Geschichte*.[24] *Geschichte* is subject to historical research, to *Historie*, which produces scientifically ensured results. These results, however, can never serve as the foundation of Christian faith because they always remain secondary *qua* results. What is primary, for Wobbermin, is the *effect* or *efficacy* [*Wirkung* or *Wirksamkeit*] of *Geschichte*, of an historic figure or event that always precedes and transcends historical investigation.[25] That effect or efficacy cannot be provided by historical research and cannot rest on *Historie*, however vigorously prosecuted. It confronts individuals directly in and through *Geschichte* and is immediately available to religious experience. In this sense, then, the historicity or the historical verifiability of a past event or figure is ultimately irrelevant, or at least secondary; the *effect* of that historic event or figure is primary.

One passage in particular provides support for this further distinction. Wobbermin suggests that the "historic fact" of Christ exists apart from and prior to faith, but that it also includes within it a presupposition of faith and therefore can only be *effective* or *efficacious* for faith:

---

primary reality. That prior, primary reality (i.e., *Geschichte*, and more specifically the *effects* or *efficacy* of *Geschichte*) is the foundation of faith.

24. Wobbermin does refer to effect or efficacy in his second definition of *Geschichte*, but in the remainder of his essay effect or efficacy functions as a third category, distinct from both *Historie* and *Geschichte*.

25. It is tempting to label this third element as "Wirkungsgeschichte," or "history of effects" (generally of a text or work of art). Hans-Georg Gadamer, for example, considers the concept of *Wirkungsgeschichte* to be essential for hermeneutics, and it is in the context of *Wirkungsgeschichte* that he develops his concept of a "fusion of horizons" [*Horizontverschmelzung*]. See Gadamer, *Truth and Method*, 300–7 [The original German is available as *Wahrheit und Methode*]. In Wobbermin's understanding of the relationship between *Geschichte* and its effects or efficacy, however, this purely hermeneutical sense is missing. In this case "geschichtliche Wirkung" or "die Wirkung der Geschichte" reflects his intentions more precisely than "Wirkungsgeschichte" in Gadamer's sense, particularly in light of the lack of any attention to hermeneutics as such in Wobbermin's essay.

> The historic fact also exists completely apart from faith. But the historic fact as such also includes within it a reference to a presupposition of faith that is efficacious in it, and it can therefore become efficacious only for faith.[26]

In terms of the relationship between faith and history, it is the immediately available effect or the efficacy of the historic picture of Christ, uncovered or revealed by historical research but not dependent on the results of that research *qua* results or product of that research, that awakens faith in Christ. The person of Christ is a fact of *Geschichte*, and as such is open to the full range of historical research. But it is always *prior to Historie* and in that sense remains independent of it. By distinguishing between *Geschichte* and its effects or efficacy, and by further distinguishing those effects from historical investigation of *Geschichte*, Wobbermin believes it possible to maintain a necessary role for historical research without thereby making faith dependent on its resulting portrait of Jesus Christ. Wobbermin himself did not explicitly draw this distinction between *Geschichte* and its *Wirkung* or *Wirksamkeit*, but if such a distinction proves helpful in clarifying Wobbermin's position it will have proved its usefulness.

Having established his definitions of *Geschichte* and *Historie*, in the second section of his essay Wobbermin turns to earlier efforts to solve the problem of faith and history. Each of these attempts, Wobbermin suggests, shares much in common with his own attempt to solve the problem. But he contends that his distinction between *Geschichte* and *Historie* moves him closer to a solution than these previous attempts by more clearly identifying the problem and by providing a more defensible solution.

WOBBERMIN'S APPRAISAL AND CRITIQUE OF PREVIOUS POSITIONS

Wobbermin did not invent the distinction between *Geschichte* and *Historie*. The explicit distinction had already been made by Martin Kähler in 1892, and others were making similar distinctions between history as what is past and history as modern scientific historical research before

---

26. "*Die geschichtliche Tatsache besteht durchaus auch abgesehen von Glauben. Aber die geschichtliche Tatsache schließt allerdings als solche den Hinweis auf eine in ihr wirksame Glaubensvoraussetzung in sich, und sie kann demgemäß auch nur für den Glauben . . . wirksam werden.*" Wobbermin, *Geschichte und Historie*, 27.

Wobbermin's appeal for a stricter conceptual distinction.[27] In this essay Wobbermin offers appraisals and critiques of four significant attempts to solve the problem of faith and history, those of Gotthold Ephraim Lessing, Martin Kähler, Wilhelm Herrmann, and Wilhelm Bousset. By interpreting what he considers to be the seminal texts on the problem of faith and history as it relates to a distinction between *Geschichte* and *Historie*, Wobbermin hopes to discover where he can build on the strengths and perhaps improve upon some of the weaknesses of these earlier efforts. An analysis of Wobbermin's own critique of these previous positions will show where Wobbermin was able to move the discussion forward and where he became ensnared in similar or unique difficulties.

Gotthold Ephraim Lessing

In his study of Lessing, Gordon Michalson, Jr., describes the impact of Lessing's famous "ditch" on the centuries that followed:

> An image or a metaphor, although introduced almost casually, sometimes takes on a life of its own, insuring a measure of immortality for its inventor. . . . Lessing's "ugly ditch," if not the most frequently cited nonbiblical image within Protestant theology during the past two centuries, is certainly in the running for that dubious title.[28]

Despite the near ubiquity of "Lessing's ditch" in subsequent Protestant theology and the myriad efforts to leap it, Michalson detects a persistent misunderstanding or simplification of Lessing's own presentation in his brief polemical letter, *On the Proof of the Spirit and of Power*. In that text, Michalson argues, Lessing does not present one "ditch," but three.

The first ditch in Lessing's letter is what Michalson calls the "temporal-factual ditch," the great historical distance between, for example, miraculous events occurring in the first century CE and the present.

---

27. See, e.g., Reischle, "Der Streit über die Begründung des Glaubens auf den 'geschichtliche' Jesus Christus." See also Fresenius, "Die Bedeutung der Geschichtlichkeit Jesu für den Glauben" for a use of this distinction by one of Wobbermin's contemporaries. Fresenius, for example, makes explicit what remains merely implicit in Wobbermin's essay, namely the distinction between *Geschichte* and its *Wirkung* or *Wirksamkeit*. Fresenius, "Die Bedeutung der Geschichtlichkeit Jesu," 258. Gordon Rupp briefly sketches the contours of the debate concerning the distinction between *Geschichte* and *Historie* in the 1910s in a chapter entitled "Christ and Cult." See Rupp, *Culture-Protestantism*, 25–32.

28. Michalson, *Lessing's "Ugly Ditch,"* 1.

Lessing makes a distinction between first-hand experience of an event and second-hand knowledge of that event based on testimony: "Miracles that I see with my own eyes, and have an opportunity to test, are one thing; miracles of which I know only historically [*historisch*] that others claim to have seen and tested them are another."[29] The historical distance between the past event and the present invariably weakens that event's power to convince because it is now being mediated through any number of persons or institutions. Lessing asks, "Is what I read in credible historians invariably just as certain for me as what I experience myself? I am not aware that anyone has ever made such a claim."[30]

However, as Michalson suggests, Lessing's first, "temporal-factual ditch" is in fact a "red herring," because the issue for Lessing is not primarily factual but logical. Historical reports are unreliable, not for any factual reason, but because they cannot be demonstrated logically. As Lessing puts it, "If no historical truth [*historische Wahrheit*] can be demonstrated, then nothing can be demonstrated *by means of* historical truths. That is, *accidental truths of history [Geschichtswahrheiten] can never become the proof of necessary truths of reason*."[31] This Leibnizian[32] distinction between contingency and necessity (what Lessing actually calls the "broad, ugly ditch"[33]) is what Michalson calls the "metaphysical ditch," the problem of two classes of truth (i.e., historical truth and religious or metaphysical truth). And it is this shift from the temporal-factual to the metaphysical that marks the transition to the heart of Lessing's argument. In this section, Lessing asks how he is to accept as true the claim that Christ is the Son of God on the basis of his resurrection from the dead. Lessing is willing to accept as true the fact that Jesus *proclaimed* himself to be the

---

29. Lessing, "Ueber den Beweis des Geistes und der Kraft," 3 [ET: "On the Proof of the Spirit and of Power," 84].

30. Ibid., 5 [ET, 85].

31. Ibid. Emphasis in original.

32. Toshimasa Yasukata notes that Lessing borrowed this distinction between truths of history and truths of reason from a similar distinction drawn by Gottfried Wilhelm Leibniz between truths of reason [*vérités de raisonnement* or *Vernunftswahrheiten*] and factual truths [*vérités de fait* or *Tatsachenwahrheiten*]. The distinction, for Leibniz, rested on the distinction between impossibility and possibility: "Truths of reason are necessary and their opposite is impossible; factual truths are contingent and their opposite is possible." Leibniz, cited in Yasukata, *Lessing's Philosophy of Religion*, 60.

33. Lessing, "Ueber den Beweis des Geistes und der Kraft," 7 [ET: "On the Proof of the Spirit and of Power," 87].

Son of God and that his disciples also *claimed* this on the basis of the resurrection of Jesus from the dead, because, Lessing admits, he has no serious historical objections to the resurrection. These claims concern the same, historical class of truth.

The "metaphysical ditch" is encountered when these historical, *contingent* truths are made the basis of religious or rational *necessary* truth. Lessing continues:

> But to make the leap from this historical truth [*historischen Wahrheit*] into a quite different class of truths, and to require me to revise all my metaphysical and moral concepts accordingly; to expect me to change all my basic ideas on the nature of the deity because I cannot offer any credible evidence against the resurrection of Christ – if this is not a μετάβασις εἰς ἄλλο γένος [transition into another category], I do not know what Aristotle meant by that phrase.[34]

This distance between two classes of truths is the "broad, ugly ditch" that Lessing claims to be unable to leap. By surveying this ditch and by mapping its terrain, its breadth and its depth, Lessing introduced something novel into Western religious thought. According to Henry Allison, "Lessing was the first thinker to separate the question of the truth of the Christian religion from the question of its historical foundation."[35] Or, to put it even more boldly, Lessing's argument constitutes "the complete elimination of the historical from religion."[36]

As Michalson suggests, however, Lessing is perfectly comfortable making his home on the "necessary" side of this ditch, because for Lessing the truth of Christianity is rational and, if not antihistorical, at least unhistorical in nature.[37] The first ditch, the temporal-factual ditch, becomes irrelevant for Lessing precisely because the truth of Christianity finally has nothing to do with history at all. Or, as Michalson notes, for Lessing Christianity is true because of its rational, "inner" truth and not because of its historical facticity.[38] For Lessing then, only the *meaning* of Christianity can be conveyed by history, never its *truth*. Its truth is

---

34. Ibid., 7 [ET, 87].

35. Allison, *Lessing and the Enlightenment*, viii.

36. This is the judgment of Gottfried Fittbogen, cited in Allison, *Lessing and the Enlightenment*, 103.

37. Michalson, *Lessing's "Ugly Ditch,"* 12.

38. Ibid., 32.

necessary and rational rather than contingent and historical. Michalson summarizes Lessing's position in terms of the illustrative power of history and the rational essence of Christian faith:

> Ultimately, then, Lessing's position on faith and historical knowledge is derived from more fundamental commitments concerning faith and reason on the one hand, and reason and revelation on the other: authentic faith is rational and potentially universalizable, meaning that it does not hang on the acceptance of any historical facts; and historical revelations do not introduce new and indispensable religious information but simply illustrate, or bring into our field of vision, what we are capable of knowing all along.[39]

There is, however, yet another "ditch" in Lessing's letter. This third and final ditch is what Michalson calls the "existential ditch" or the problem of religious appropriation, and he suggests that this ditch is the common theme running through the entire letter. It is the problem of a modern person appropriating and believing a message that is strange, incredible, and perhaps even scandalous. In this context Lessing is particularly concerned with the autonomy of the rational human being, and he is unwilling to sacrifice that autonomy in order to believe a message solely on the basis of the authority of Scripture, church, or tradition. For Lessing it is ultimately a matter of distinguishing between the "outer" (e.g., historical events) and the "inner" (the autonomous, moral-religious self).[40] Lessing's preference for the "inner truth" of Christianity over against its external, historical foundations or "proofs" marks the first time in the West that "the question of the facticity of the Christian revelation was held to be irrelevant for the truth of the Christian religion."[41] As Lessing claims in response to Hermann Samuel Reimarus,

> The letter is not the spirit, and the Bible is not religion. . . . The religion is not true because the evangelists and the apostles taught it, but they taught it because it is true. The written traditions must be explained according to their inner truth, and no written tradition can give it any inner truth if it has none.[42]

---

39. Ibid., 39. Lessing's references to the illustrative power of history will be adopted by Kant and later reworked by Wobbermin, who, surprisingly, does not refer to this element of Lessing's thought.

40. Ibid., 48–49.

41. Allison, *Lessing and the Enlightenment*, 96.

42. Lessing, cited in Allison, *Lessing and the Enlightenment*, 95–96.

The Christian religion is true, then, insofar as it expresses this inner, rational truth that is immediately available to rational human beings. It is not true on the basis of historical demonstrations, or on the basis of the testimony of the apostles or the evangelists, or on the basis of the Christian tradition or the authority of the church. This is so because, as Lessing puts it in his famous "metaphysical" ditch, "accidental truths of history can never become the proof of necessary truths of reason."[43]

Wobbermin's Appraisal and Critique of Lessing's Position

In introducing the section in which he appraises previous positions on the problem of faith and history, Wobbermin notes that he is purposely selecting positions with which he finds some level of agreement.[44] He also admits that Lessing does not belong directly to the group that follows, primarily because Lessing is not, strictly speaking, a Protestant theologian. Wobbermin's critique of Lessing will therefore be of a more general character than those that follow.

Lessing's famous "ditch" plays an important role in subsequent discussions of the relationship between Christian faith and history, and Wobbermin restricts his comments to this one sentence of Lessing's letter *On the Proof of the Spirit and of Power*. There is nothing in Wobbermin's analysis to indicate that he appreciated any of the nuances in Lessing's presentation, or that he was aware of the possibility that more than one "ditch" is being discussed. Everything hangs on Lessing's one sentence: "Accidental truths of history can never become the proof of necessary truths of reason."[45]

Wobbermin suggests that Lessing's "ditch" suffers from certain conceptual ambiguities, most importantly in terms of the relationship between truth and history. Such conceptual ambiguity can be eliminated, Wobbermin offers, by reframing Lessing's statement with specific reference to the distinction between *Geschichte* and *Historie*. Thus Wobbermin would restate the proposition to read: "Individual historical cognitions can never become proof of eternal truths of *Geschichte*."[46]

---

43. Lessing, "Ueber den Beweis des Geistes und der Kraft," 5 [ET: "On the Proof of the Spirit and of Power," 85].

44. Wobbermin, *Geschichte und Historie*, 16.

45. "*Zufällige Geschichtswahrheiten können der Beweis von nothwendigen Vernunftswahrheiten nie werden.*" Lessing, "Ueber den Beweis des Geistes und der Kraft," 5 [ET: "On the Proof of the Spirit and of Power," 85].

46. "*Historische Einzelerkenntnisse können der Beweis von ewigen Geschichtswahrheiten*

Toshimasa Yasukata notes that Lessing uses the terms *historische Wahrheiten* (historical truths) and *Geschichtswahrheiten* (truths of history or historic truths) interchangeably, and he argues, similarly to Wobbermin (but without mention of Wobbermin's criticisms of Lessing), that Lessing's position would be strengthened by a distinction between the two terms. Lessing proposes that "if no historical truth [*historische Wahrheit*] can be demonstrated, then nothing can be demonstrated by means of historical truths. That is, accidental truths of history [*Geschichtswahrheiten*] can never become the proof of necessary truths of reason."[47] Yasukata suggests that Lessing's argument lacks conceptual clarity precisely at this point.[48] Wobbermin shares this concern, and he reworks Lessing's "ditch" to distinguish between *Geschichte* and *Historie*, thereby attempting to redirect attention to what he considers to be the more difficult problem of faith and history.

According to Wobbermin, Lessing's ditch suffers from a metaphysical deficit, which is especially ironic given Michalson's conclusion that this particular statement concerns precisely the "metaphysical" problem of relating two different classes of truth. But Wobbermin does not share Michalson's definition of the problem. The problem, as Wobbermin sees it, is not between two classes of truth; the problem is the assumption that there *can be* two classes of truth at all. For Wobbermin, unlike Lessing, there is only one class of truth: eternal truths of *Geschichte*. There is no such thing, therefore, as "accidental" or "contingent" truths. What Lessing calls accidental truths of history, Wobbermin calls individual historical cognitions. All truths are truths of *Geschichte* because only in and through *Geschichte* can truth be represented to thinking subjects who themselves stand within *Geschichte*.[49]

---

nie werden." Wobbermin, *Geschichte und Historie*, 17.

47. Lessing, "Ueber den Beweis des Geistes und der Kraft," 5 [ET: "On the Proof of the Spirit and of Power," 85].

48. Yasukata does admit that there was no such distinction between *Geschichte* and *Historie* in the late eighteenth century. But he also suggests that Lessing was aware of a historicity [*Geschichtlichkeit*] that cannot be approached by historical science, and he asks, "But if he knows this, why, then, is he so careless in his use of these terms?" The answer, Yasukata suggests, is to be found in Lessing's relation of revelation to reason, or in what Michalson calls the "existential ditch." Yasukata, *Lessing's Philosophy of Religion*, 68; 165, nn. 57 and 58.

49. Wobbermin, *Geschichte und Historie*, 18.

Geschichte und Historie

Here Wobbermin parts company with Lessing on the nature of truth. While Lessing wants to define truth in purely rational terms, Wobbermin prefers to speak of truths operative in and through *Geschichte*. Wobbermin hopes to avoid Lessing's rejection of historical demonstrations of truth by distinguishing between *Historie* and *Geschichte*. Historical research (or, to use Wobbermin's term here, "individual historical cognitions") will never provide eternal, historic truths precisely because historical research yields results that are always provisional, relative, and probable. But *Geschichte*, being the realm of value and of efficacy, withstands historical inquiry and serves as the vehicle of absolute, eternal truths.

Wobbermin's reasoning is not clear at this point, as he does not take the further step of defining precisely *how* eternal truth is present within and through *Geschichte*.[50] Only later does he address the role of Scripture (as divine revelation and the early church's testimony) as the vehicle of eternal truth, but that further step is missing in this early essay.

Wobbermin is content to define eternal truths specifically as *religious* truths: "The label 'eternal' should be understood in the specific sense of religious faith – truths belonging to the world of eternity, established in it, and originating in it."[51] Because, according to Wobbermin, "eternal truths" are supramundane, they cannot be proved by historical research. Such truths defy proof and confront historic subjects only in and through *Geschichte*. As such they are accessible only to faith.

To put it in Michalson's terms, here Wobbermin is attempting to solve the problem of religious appropriation, to leap across what Michalson calls Lessing's "existential ditch." But whereas Lessing turns to the "inner self" to discover a truth already present in reason, Wobbermin turns to *Geschichte* as the vehicle of eternal truth. Lessing has no need at all of *Historie or Geschichte* in any but an illustrative capacity; Wobbermin, on the other hand, bases everything here on a distinction between truth provided by historical science and religious truth becoming immediately present to believers in and through *Geschichte*, independent of any historical inquiry into past facts, figures, or events. It is enough for Wobbermin

---

50. There are indications, discussed below, of such a step in Wobbermin's critique of Bousset's position, in which Bousset subordinates *Geschichte* to reason. Wobbermin prefers to subordinate reason to *Geschichte*, which puts him at odds with Lessing as well.

51. "Das Beiwort 'ewig' soll also im spezifischen Sinne des religiösen Glaubens verstanden werden: Wahrheiten, die der Welt der Ewigkeit angehören, in ihr begründet sind, aus ihr stammen." Wobbermin, *Geschichte und Historie*, 19.

that these eternal truths of *Geschichte* cannot be proved or disproved by historical research:

> Eternal truths of this type, as our statement says, cannot be proved through individual historical cognitions. Because all historical research continues in the form of individual historical cognitions, these eternal truths cannot be proved through historical research. And therefore truths of this type belong to *Geschichte*; they are to be described as truths of *Geschichte*. Indeed, in no other way than in *Geschichte* and through *Geschichte* do such truths come to human beings.[52]

Wobbermin does not offer an analysis of Lessing's entire argument in *On the Proof of the Spirit and of Power*. Had he done so, he might have realized how close his position finally is to Lessing's in many important respects. Most significantly for the purposes of this study, Wobbermin, perhaps without realizing it, wants to avoid the same dangers as Lessing. Lessing's primary concern is to make the religious message available to modern men and women without requiring them first to make an intellectual sacrifice by believing secondary historical accounts of dubious events occurring in the distant past. This is Wobbermin's concern as well. The differences between their positions finally appear in their respective solutions to the problem of religious appropriation rather than in their identification of the problem itself.[53]

Martin Kähler

Paul Tillich, one of Kähler's last surviving students, reflected on Kähler's theological legacy in his foreword to the English translation of Kähler's *The So-called Historical Jesus and the Historic Biblical Christ*. Tillich remembers Kähler as a "strictly systematic thinker who developed his ideas

---

52. "*Ewige Wahrheiten dieser Art, sagt dann also unser Satz, können durch historische Einzelerkenntnisse nicht bewiesen werden. Sie können folglich, da alle historische Forschung in der Form historischer Einzelerkenntnis verläuft, überhaupt nicht durch historische Forschung bewiesen werden. Und doch gehören Wahrheiten dieser Art der Geschichte an; als Geschichtswahrheiten sind sie zu bezeichnen. Ja gar nicht anders als in der Geschichte und aus der Geschichte kommen solche Wahrheiten an den Menschen heran.*" Ibid., 19–20.

53. Perhaps the later Wobbermin would have found even more support in Lessing's proposals, specifically as Wobbermin developed the religio-psychological circle precisely (yet unconsciously with regard to Lessing) to bridge all three of Lessing's ditches, the "temporal-factual," the "metaphysical," and the "existential."

Geschichte und Historie

under the principle of the Reformers – 'justification through faith by grace,'" and as a scholar with a "profound insight into the problem of the historical Jesus in the light of the scholarly research into the sources."[54] Bearing in mind the intention to think systematically under the guidance of the doctrine of justification through faith by grace, Kähler's primary concern in these essays on the historical Jesus and the historic, biblical Christ is to win an "invulnerable area" [*sturmfreies Gebiet*][55] for faith, kicking away the false supports for faith in order to give faith its proper object: Christ the Lord.

According to Carl Braaten, Kähler's quest for an invulnerable area for faith is defined by two interrelated questions: How can the Bible remain a trustworthy and normative document of revelation when historical criticism has shattered confidence in its historical reliability? And second, how can Jesus Christ be the basis and content of Christian faith when historical science can never provide indisputable, certain knowledge of the historical Jesus?[56]

Kähler sets out to answer these questions by means of a two-fold argument. First, he attempts to secure Jesus Christ as the basis and content of Christian faith in face of historical doubt by drawing a distinction between the historical Jesus [*der historische Jesus*] and the historic Christ [*der geschichtliche Christus*]. Second, on the basis of this distinction between the historical Jesus and the historic Christ, he attempts to maintain confidence in the authority of Scripture by equating this historic Christ with the biblical Christ rather than with the historical Jesus lying somewhere "behind" the texts of the New Testament.

At work behind these arguments is a profound pastoral sensitivity to the situation of lay Christians, the great mass of those who do not possess the capacity or the training to engage in complex historical-critical investigations of the New Testament in order to discover the "real" Jesus in whom they should believe.[57] Were this erudition necessary for Christian

---

54. Tillich, foreword to *The So-called Historical Jesus and the Historic Biblical Christ*, by Martin Kähler, vii.

55. This catchword, "invulnerable area," has become synonymous with Kähler's entire theological project, especially in terms of the problem of faith and history. See, e.g., Brachmann, whose chapter on Kähler is entitled "Das 'sturmfreie' Gebiet des Glaubens bei Martin Kähler." Brachmann, *Glaube und Geschichte*, 22–26.

56. Braaten, introduction to *The So-called Historical Jesus*, 10.

57. This pastoral sensitivity is often more formally expressed in the desire for certain-

faith, Kähler notes, there would have been no true Christians for almost seventeen centuries, and there would be very few true Christians even in his own day:

> If [Christians living before the advent of historical-critical scholarship] contemplated and worshipped the Jesus of the Gospels in just this obscurity which [historians] profess to find in these texts and feel bound to remove, then indeed they would not have known their Savior. And so it would be for all Christians after them, right up to us.[58]

The situation is not as dire as this, of course, as Kähler insists that the Jesus of the historians is not the "real Christ" at all, but a figment of the historians' imaginations.[59] The entire Life of Jesus movement,[60] Kähler contends, "conceals from us the living Christ."[61] It is a real and present danger to the faith of Christians and must be rejected. It is, Kähler argues, a "blind alley."[62] But a blind alley very often appears to be the correct route; otherwise no one would travel it at all. There is something legitimate about the "quest for the historical Jesus," and Kähler finds its legitimacy in the critique of an abstract dogmatism that threatens to conceal or obliterate the humanity of Jesus. The quest becomes illegitimate as soon as it falls into the error of regarding Jesus as nothing *more* than a mere

---

ty [*Gewißheit*] that permeates Kähler's work. For an analysis of the problem of certainty in Kähler's work, see Mencke, *Erfahrung und Gewißheit des Glaubens*.

58. Kähler, *Der sogenannte historische Jesus*, 61 [ET: *The So-called Historical Jesus*, 61].

59. Ibid., 55 [ET, 55].

60. These attempts at a historical biography of Jesus are chronicled in Schweitzer's *Geschichte der Leben-Jesu-Forschung* [ET: *The Quest of the Historical Jesus*]. The Quest for the Historical Jesus reemerged in the middle of the twentieth century in the so-called "Second Quest" inaugurated by Ernst Käsemann and others. See Robinson, *A New Quest of the Historical Jesus*, and Harvey and Ogden, "Wie neu ist die 'Neue Frage nach dem historischen Jesus'?" [ET: "How New is the 'New Quest for the Historical Jesus'?"].

61. Kähler, *Der sogenannte historische Jesus*, 44 [ET: *The So-called Historical Jesus*, 43].

62. Ibid., 47 [ET, 46]. The term Kähler uses here is "Holzweg," which is literally a "logging road" or "logger's path," a rough path in the forest that is difficult to travel and often simply ends, leading nowhere. In German it can refer to anything that leads to confusion or to anything that is misleading. It can be expressed in a variety of English idioms, including "barking up the wrong tree," "being on the wrong track," or "leading someone up the garden path." Braaten translates it as "blind alley," which is a meaning closer to the original, literal meaning of the German.

Geschichte und Historie

man.⁶³ In other words, in reacting against the perceived Docetism of an abstract dogmatism, the Life of Jesus movement falls prey to a subtle (or, in some cases, not so subtle) Ebionitism.

The fatal flaw of the Life of Jesus movement, according to Kähler, is its failure to recognize the unique character of the biblical texts. The modern biographers of Jesus approach the gospels as historical documents of an equal value as all other historical documents and expect to find objective, unbiased sources for reconstructing the personality and life of Jesus of Nazareth. Kähler rejects this presupposition and argues that no such objective, unbiased sources are available in the New Testament, and that there are therefore no sources in the New Testament adequate to the task of constructing a reliable historical biography of Jesus. Or as Kähler puts it:

> We have no sources for a "Life of Jesus" that a historian can accept as authentic and sufficient. I stress: for a biography of Jesus of Nazareth according to the currently accepted standards of historical scholarship. A credible picture of the Savior for believers is a completely different thing.⁶⁴

It is the method of historical research itself that leads Kähler to this conclusion. The gospels exist in almost total isolation, so that nothing else is known of Jesus of Nazareth except what is contained in them. The gospels cannot with any certainty be traced to eyewitnesses. The gospels themselves only tell us about select periods of Jesus' life. Finally, even within the New Testament itself there are two radically different types of gospels (synoptic and Johannine), and these often contradict one another (to say nothing of the contradictions within the synoptic tradition itself).⁶⁵ Any hope of producing a comprehensive and accurate historical biography of Jesus of Nazareth from these sources alone is a slim hope indeed. What one finds, instead, is a "vast expanse of the ruins [*Trümmerfeld*] of individual traditions."⁶⁶

Alongside the problem of adequate sources, another problem faces historians who wish to compose a reliable, accurate biography of Jesus of Nazareth. One of the hallmarks of the historical method is the use of

63. Ibid., 47–48 [ET, 46–47].
64. Ibid., 49 [ET, 48].
65. Ibid. [ET, 48–49].
66. Ibid., 49–50 [ET, 49].

the principle of analogy. The historian must find an analogy in current human events or experience in order to explain what is difficult or obscure in the past, and here the biographical task breaks down. Faced with so many gaps in the supposedly historical record of the life of Jesus, the modern historian is forced to find an analogy in his own life or in human life in general, so that "it is mostly Jesus being refracted through the spirit of these gentlemen themselves."[67] What is typically produced is a Jesus in the image of the historian, the Jesus he has hoped to find from the outset of his research. This Jesus, then, is supposed to be the object of Christian faith. Braaten suggests that this use of the historical-critical method to secure the object of faith is finally a subtle form of works righteousness:

> In terms of the reformation [sic] doctrine of justification by grace alone, through faith *alone*, in the Word *alone*, the actuality of salvation is not dependent upon the preparatory works of man, whether moral, religious, or intellectual, whether philosophical or historical.[68]

There is a further flaw inherent in the application of the principle of analogy to the biblical sources concerning Jesus. According to Kähler, modern historians (whether they are conscious of it or not) are looking for a Jesus who resembles them, their moral and religious sensibilities, and their *Zeitgeist*. This bias requires them to search for a Jesus who is fundamentally *like* all other human beings. While Jesus is like all other human beings by virtue of the humanity he shares with them, he is, more importantly, utterly unique in human history: he is the sinless Son of God, unlike all other human beings in kind and not only in degree.[69] Those who seek Jesus in order to see the Father through him (John 14:9) do not seek him because he is like them, but because he is radically *unlike* them. Or as Kähler puts it, "I am not seeking someone like myself, but rather my counterpart [*Gegenstück*], my completion [*Ergänzung*], my Savior."[70]

---

67. Ibid., 57 [ET, 57]. Kähler's criticism of the use of the principle of analogy in historical-critical analysis of the New Testament is quite similar to the position later taken by Wolfhart Pannenberg. See Pannenberg, "Heilsgeschehen und Geschichte" [ET: "Redemptive Event and History"].

68. Braaten, "Christ, Faith, and History," 47. Emphasis in original.

69. Kähler, *Der sogenannte historische Jesus*, 53 [ET: *The So-called Historical Jesus*, 53].

70. Ibid., 59 [ET, 59].

This Jesus is not the historical Jesus of modern biography, but the historic Christ, the revelation of God.

Historical science, no matter how faithfully and thoroughly employed, cannot provide this historic Christ for faith. The historic Christ, the Christ of the Bible, comes to people not through the "midwifery [*Hebammenkünste*] of historical research,"[71] but through the preaching of the church. The real Christ is the Christ who is preached, and this Christ is the Christ of faith.[72]

Here the distinction between the historical [*historisch*] and the historic [*geschichtlich*] is crucial. For Kähler, the historical Jesus is Jesus as he is known by historical research. The historic Christ, however, is the earthly Jesus in his significance, as he is the object of faith.[73] Kähler is so unwilling to "go behind" the texts of the New Testament that he is unwilling to make any distinction at all between the historic and the biblical Christ; the historic Christ *is* the Christ of the Bible.[74] This Christ is the Christ of apostolic preaching, the Christ who awakened faith in the disciples and who is therefore confessed as Lord. He is, according to Kähler, the originator of the biblical picture of Christ, the basis and the content of faith.

The identification of the historic Christ with the biblical Christ raises serious difficulties for Kähler's position. Most importantly, Kähler seems ultimately to be unwilling to grant historical criticism any significant role, even though he repeatedly denies this charge.[75] If the historic Christ *is* the Christ of the whole Bible, then it is difficult to determine how and where historical criticism might gain a foothold for its work. New Testament scholar Georg Strecker makes a similar observation in an essay on the historical and theological problem of the "Jesus question":

71. Ibid., 18 [ET, 121].

72. Ibid., 66 [ET, 66].

73. Given the importance of this distinction for his argument, it is surprising that Kähler nowhere offers a clear definition of these terms beyond their immediate relevance to the topic at hand. It is especially interesting to note, too, that Kähler rarely distinguishes between the nominal forms *Historie* and *Geschichte*. The distinction exists for him almost solely in the adjectival forms *historisch* and *geschichtlich*, and only with reference to Jesus Christ.

74. Ibid., 86 [ET, 86].

75. Kähler claims to have accepted historical inquiry into the New Testament texts "for certain purposes," and accuses those who deny that he has any positive use for historical criticism to have misunderstood him. Ibid., 20 [ET, 124].

> An uncritical adoption of Kähler's position should be impossible since his attempt to liberate theology from the probability judgments of the historical-critical method did not face up to the question of the theological right, and the theological necessity of historical criticism. . . . As a literary entity, the biblical witness of the historic Christ cannot be excluded from further historical-critical inquiry. Above all, however, a decision to ignore the historical-critical framing of the question would be, theologically, a problematical failure. It would not take into account the understanding of reality which underlies the historical-critical method, nor the self-understanding of the modern world generally.[76]

Nevertheless, Kähler is more concerned to allow the historic, biblical Christ to confront readers and hearers of Scripture directly than he is to maintain any independence or validity for historical criticism.

The historical Jesus is of no interest to faith; this much Kähler makes absolutely clear. The historic Christ, the Christ of the Bible, is the object of Christian faith, available to every person in every time and place through the church's proclamation of Christ as Lord. But there is a third category operative in Kähler's treatment, namely, the suprahistoric [*übergeschichtlich*].[77] The suprahistoric, according to Kähler, designates that which would not exist apart from history but whose significance is not exhausted within the confines of the historical nexus. In the suprahistoric, then, "what is universally valid is joined to the historic to become an effective presence [*Wirksam-Gegenwärtigen*]."[78] The suprahistoric Christ is Christ in his immediate significance and presence for humanity, who is always related to the historic Christ but never limited to his historicity. Kähler contends that historical research is incapable of producing this suprahis-

---

76. Strecker, "The Historical and Theological Problem of the Jesus Question," 202.

77. Braaten translates "übergeschichtlich" as "suprahistorical" rather than "suprahistoric," which fails to convey the meaning Kähler intended. The suprahistoric, for Kähler, is related to the historic and *not* to the historical at all. To translate "übergeschichtlich" as "suprahistorical" simply adds unnecessary confusion to the issue.

78. Kähler, *Der sogenannte historische Jesus*, 48, n. 1 [ET: *The So-called Historical Jesus*, 47, n. 2]. For more on the suprahistoric in Kähler, see Hägglund, "Martin Kählers teori om det överhistoriska i kristendomen" and Leipold, *Offenbarung und Geschichte als Problem des Verstehens*, especially Chapter 4, "Der Begriff des Übergeschichtlichen." For a slightly different approach than Kähler's, see Dibelius, *Geschichtliche und übergeschichtliche Religion* and Bultmann's review, "Geschichtliche und übergeschichtliche Religion" [ET: "Historical and Supra-historical Religion in Christianity"], the English translation of which also adds to the confusion by translating *geschichtlich* as "historical."

toric Christ because the suprahistoric Christ transcends history and is not limited to the chain of cause and effect determinative of normal historical development. Christ's "historic-suprahistoric effect" is present and effective within the church, in its confession of faith, and in the living faith of Christians themselves.[79] In other words, the suprahistoric Christ is *only* present to faith and therefore cannot be provided by historical research.[80] Braaten also notes the impossibility of direct historical knowledge of the suprahistoric:

> Faith which lives only in history can be related to the suprahistorical revelational reality because this reality has entered into history and is now knowable exclusively through history. . . . General science can deal with the suprahistorical only indirectly, namely, by analyzing the words and statements that have been transmitted in the documents of redemptive history, and by taking account of the historical effects of these statements in history.[81]

Despite the wide-ranging implications of a further distinction between the historic and the suprahistoric, Kähler does not explore those implications in his essays on the distinction between the historical Jesus and the historic Christ. Had he done so, he might have avoided or at least more successfully defended his position against the charge of failure to grant historical criticism access to the biblical picture of Jesus Christ. He clearly moves in this direction by defining the biblical texts variously as sermons, confessions, or testimonies rather than mere historical documents, as such ultimately remaining unaffected by historical inquiry, but his failure to make a stricter distinction between the historic Christ of the Bible and the suprahistoric Christ as the immediately present and efficacious Lord keeps his position open to charges of biblicism, however unfair those charges ultimately may be.

---

79. Kähler, *Der sogenannte historische Jesus*, 94 [ET: *The So-called Historical Jesus*, 95].

80. This is so, Leipold suggests, because for Kähler the suprahistoric originates in and is available through revelation alone. Christ, in his significance for faith (i.e., as the revelation of God in history), represents the actual content of the concept of the suprahistoric. It is utterly unique as Christ is utterly unique, and its use, especially in Kähler's dogmatics, is limited to descriptions of the content of salvation, the reconciliation of the world to God and the justification of sinners. Leipold, *Offenbarung und Geschichte*, 98–107. Kähler refers readers to his dogmatics for more on the concept of the suprahistoric. See Kähler, *Die Wissenschaft der christlichen Lehre*, §13, 13–15. Kähler gives the same definition there as he does above.

81. Braaten, "Christ, Faith, and History," 89–90.

Faith at the Intersection of History and Experience

As it stands, Kähler is content to equate the historic Christ with the biblical picture of him and to locate the efficacy and the presence of Christ in the church's proclamation of him as its Lord. By removing the biblical picture of the historic Christ from the realm of critical historical investigation, and by laying bare the revelatory character of this picture and its continuing presence in the proclamation of the church, Kähler hopes to have secured an invulnerable area for faith in Christ.

But has he succeeded in establishing and protecting this invulnerable area for faith? Is his position finally impervious to a thoroughgoing historical criticism of the sources? Wilhelm Brachmann, for example, concludes that Kähler was unsuccessful in his attempt to establish this invulnerable area. Brachmann suggests that the weakness of Kähler's position is his reliance on the Easter experience of the disciples as the origin of testimony about the risen Christ, an experience that Kähler suggests is finally of a suprahistoric reality. Despite Kähler's insistence that this event is suprahistoric rather than historic, the experience itself nevertheless occurs within history. According to Brachmann, then, one must reckon with the *possibility* that a historical explanation will be found for what Kähler insists is a suprahistoric reality. Or as Brachmann puts it, "a mortal danger threatens Kähler's thesis of an invulnerable area for faith from the side of history."[82]

Perhaps Kähler's shortcomings can be attributed, at least in part, to two related characteristic features of his theological work: his suspicion of historical criticism as it is applied to theological work and his flirtation with an uncritical biblicism. His suspicion of historical criticism and its role in theological work hinders its important negative function in a theological analysis of the New Testament. Kähler fears stumbling onto a slippery slope if historical criticism is permitted free and unrestrained access to the biblical tradition, and he constructs his invulnerable area for faith in order to protect both faith and the Bible from any unnecessary incursions by historical criticism.[83]

---

82. Brachmann, *Glaube und Geschichte*, 26.

83. Braaten addresses Kähler's attitude toward historical criticism in the introduction to his translation of part of Kähler's *Der sogenannte historische Jesus*, but he does not reach the same conclusion regarding Kähler's suspicions of unrestricted historical criticism. See Braaten, "Introduction," 26ff.

Geschichte und Historie

Wobbermin's Appraisal and Critique of Kähler's Position

Wobbermin's position would appear to be quite close to Kähler's, especially in terms of the importance of a distinction between *Geschichte* and *Historie*. Wobbermin praises Kähler for so effectively exposing the "blind alley" of the Life of Jesus movement, both in terms of the limits of historical knowledge in general and of historical inquiry into the gospels in particular. Wobbermin agrees that the entire Life of Jesus movement is a blind alley, insofar as it attempts to provide an enduring foundation for Christian faith in the results of its research.[84]

On the surface, even Kähler's and Wobbermin's distinctions between *Geschichte* and *Historie* appear to be identical. For both, the historical Jesus is the Jesus of modern historical biography, the product of historical investigation of the biblical texts. The historic Christ, on the other hand, is the Savior who confronts readers and hearers of the New Testament directly, without what Kähler called "the midwifery of historical research." To base faith on a product of historical scholarship is to require a false foundation for faith, to make faith dependent on the relative and probable results of historical scholarship and on the authority of historians rather than the living Christ.

Wobbermin parts company with Kähler, however, on the definition of the historic Christ. Kähler insists that there is no distinction at all between the historic Christ and the Christ of the Bible; he is *der geschichtliche, biblische Christus*. Wobbermin is unwilling to equate the historic Christ with the biblical Christ, instead insisting that the historic Christ is a narrower figure than the biblical picture of him. Wobbermin does not object to the fact "'that' Kähler identifies the historic with the biblical Christ, but to 'how' he does this."[85] The historic Christ is the biblical Christ for Wobbermin as well as for Kähler. But the biblical Christ, Wobbermin argues, cannot simply be *equated* with the historic Christ as if there were no distinction between the two.

A thoroughgoing historical criticism will clarify the picture of the historic, biblical Christ so that only those elements that are "truly" historic will remain. Kähler, Wobbermin argues, was unable or unwilling to carry his distinction between *Geschichte* and *Historie* to its logical conclu-

---

84. Wobbermin, *Geschichte und Historie*, 21.

85. "*Nicht 'daß' Kähler, sondern 'die Art, wie' er den geschichtlichen und den biblischen Christus identifiziert, beanstande ich.*" Ibid., 22.

sion, which, at least in Wobbermin's estimation, would require a further distinction between the biblical Christ and the historic Christ. In other words, it is not Kähler's definition of *Geschichte,* but rather his limitation of historical inquiry into the biblical texts (and by extension his definition of *Historie*) that constitutes his failure to carry his own distinction to a fruitful end.[86]

According to Wobbermin, free and unrestrained historical investigation of the biblical picture of Christ would make any wholesale identification of this picture with the historic Christ impossible. Whereas Kähler concludes that the two cannot be distinguished in any meaningful way, Wobbermin contends that historical research finally limits the historic Christ to three essential elements: his ethical disposition toward love, his unity of will with his heavenly Father, and his elevation to the Father following his suffering and death.[87] These three elements alone constitute the essential picture of the historic Christ that confronts Christians in the New Testament.

The decisive question here is a question of method: how have these three elements of the New Testament picture of Christ been isolated and presented as the essential picture of the historic Christ? Wobbermin intends to isolate these three elements by applying his distinction between *Geschichte* and *Historie* to the texts of the New Testament. By applying this distinction to the biblical picture of Christ, Wobbermin intends to separate every element of that picture that is merely historical [*historisch*] from those elements that are considered historically [*geschichtlich*] active and efficacious [*wirksam*] in the Christian tradition and into the present. Only these active and efficacious elements are to be considered decisive for the historic picture of Christ. They are not considered decisive on the basis of historical judgment alone, because this would fail to free faith from a dependence on the judgments of historians. They are considered decisive because these three elements confront readers of the New Testament directly and because they continue to represent the decisive picture of Christ throughout the history of the Christian tradition and into the present.

---

86. Ibid., 20-21.

87. "*Seine ethische Liebesgesinnung in ihrer Reinheit und Kraft, seine Willenseinheit mit dem himmlischen Vater und – mit dieser letzteren aufs genaueste zusammenhängend – seine Erhebung zum Vater nach erlittenem Kreuzestode: das sind die Momente, die im letzten Grunde das Bild des geschichtlichen Christus ausmachen.*" Ibid., 23.

Geschichte und Historie

The isolation of these three essential elements of the picture of Jesus Christ places Wobbermin on rather shaky ground in strictly historical terms. He fails to account for the limited historical perspective of the reader of the New Testament and appears to affirm the possibility of what Rudolf Bultmann would later call a "presuppositionless exegesis" (or what might also be called "purely objective exegesis").[88] This limitation of perspective – or, to put it another way, the dependence on the reader's own historical, philosophical, and cultural context – is especially clear in terms of Wobbermin's first essential element. In emphasizing Jesus' ethical disposition toward love, Wobbermin is dependent on the moral and ethical emphasis of nineteenth-century liberal Protestantism, which was later critiqued by Karl Barth and others as being rooted in bourgeois sentiments or a so-called *Kulturprotestantismus* rather than a purely historical reading of the "strange world" of the New Testament.

But the selection of these three "essential elements" also raises the question of both the freedom of historical-critical inquiry and the transparency of its use. Wobbermin consistently affirms his openness to a free and unrestrained historical investigation of the New Testament, both in order to strip away any false supports for faith and to allow the truly efficacious historic elements to remain, independent of historical research. Here Wobbermin's method breaks down, precisely because he insists *both* that he has granted historical criticism free and unrestrained access to the biblical picture of Christ *and* that these three essential elements of the biblical picture of Christ remain unaffected by historical criticism. These three elements, he suggests, are historic because they have remained active and efficacious throughout the history of the Christian tradition.[89] To his credit, he does briefly engage in a historical-critical investigation of some pertinent texts to illustrate and support his claim.[90] But he does not account for the possibility that continued historical investigation of the New Testament might one day cast doubt on the historical reliability

---

88. See Bultmann, "Ist voraussetzungslose Exegese möglich?" [ET: "Is Exegesis without Presuppositions Possible?"]. As Bultmann would argue a few decades later, presuppositionless exegesis is impossible because the exegete is always also a historic subject who stands within the history being investigated and continues to be influenced by it. The goal in that case is not to pretend one is capable of freeing oneself from any and all presuppositions, but to acknowledge these presuppositions and to do one's exegetical work with them constantly in mind.

89. This claim on its own is rather difficult to support in strictly historical terms.

90. Wobbermin, *Geschichte und Historie*, 24–25.

of one or more of these three essential elements of the historic picture of Christ, a possibility that is inherent in the nature of historical investigation itself. Wobbermin is confident that these three elements will remain unaffected by historical investigation, but in this case such confidence is almost certainly unwarranted.

Furthermore, it is ironic that Wobbermin insists that these three elements are unaffected by historical criticism while also suggesting that they are provided by historical investigation.[91] Here Wobbermin fails to abide by his own requirement that the historic picture of Christ not be provided by historical research. Also, it might be true that these three essential elements of the biblical picture of the historic Christ have remained active and efficacious throughout the history of Christianity, but it might also be true that they will cease to be so at some point in the future, and that new "essential elements" will emerge on the basis of the continuing development of the church as a historic institution and its continuing use and proclamation of Scripture. This alone is not sufficient reason to abandon these elements, but it is perhaps grounds for a more restrained confidence in their permanent and enduring value and their imperviousness to free historical inquiry.

Wobbermin insists that what is historic is ultimately what is active and efficacious in history, beyond mere historicity. The key to this insistence is the concept of efficacy or effect [*Wirksamkeit* or *Wirkung*]. What is historical is of interest primarily to historians and is the product of their research, while what is historic is efficacious beyond its mere historicity and continues to affect and influence the present from the past.[92] In this case, his selection of these three essential elements can be justified. Wobbermin moves beyond Kähler by attempting to distinguish between the biblical Christ and the historic Christ both by means of historical investigation of the New Testament and by means of a preference for the historic over the historical, the presently efficacious [*wirksam*] over what

---

91. Ibid., 24.

92. This definition of the effect or efficacy of the historic is remarkably similar to Kähler's occasional use of the term "übergeschichtlich." It is quite curious, then, that Wobbermin never mentions Kähler's use of this term. In his study of faith and history, Wilhelm Brachmann entitles his chapter on Wobbermin "Die übergeschichtliche Wahrheit," even though Wobbermin himself never, to my knowledge, actually uses this term. But there are clear similarities between Wobbermin's understanding of the *effects* of history, or the efficacy of the historic picture of Christ, and Kähler's infrequent use of the term "suprahistoric." See Brachmann, *Glaube und Geschichte*, 57–61.

remains in the past. His position remains open to critique on purely historical grounds, however, which in this case might be inevitable given the nature of the matter itself, namely, basing the historic effects of Christ in some sense on a figure of history, Jesus of Nazareth.

Wilhelm Herrmann

Herrmann did not make a consistent distinction between *Geschichte* and *Historie*, yet his work is permeated with the question of faith and historical knowledge.[93] Like Kähler and Wobbermin, Herrmann operates with a strong suspicion of the ability of historical research to provide certainty for faith:

> The decision reached [by historical criticism] makes a claim at the outset to nothing more than probability. We are always prepared for the possibility that our results can be modified by a more precise consideration or through the discovery of new accounts. It is obvious that such a decision cannot provide us with facts on which religious faith could be based.[94]

Historical judgments are always judgments of probability, and even the highest possible probability is insufficient as a foundation for faith. He asks, "What kind of a religion would that be which would want to accept the basis for its conviction with the consciousness that it was only probably safe?"[95] According to Herrmann, then, the value of historical research in the theological task is its shattering of false supports for faith and its continuing comparison of faith's picture of Jesus Christ with the results of historical investigation of the New Testament:

> Historical work on the New Testament is not without value for faith. In the first place, it shows us how little the New Testament texts provide for a historical account undertaking to set forth, as a result of scientific evidence, what the person of Jesus means for the Christian. As earnest historical work on the New Testament

---

93. See, e.g., Herrmann, "Der geschichtliche Christus der Grund unseres Glaubens"; "Soll es eine besondere theologische Geschichtsforschung geben?"; "Warum bedarf unser Glaube geschichtlicher Tatsachen?"; and "Grund und Inhalt des Glaubens." For more on Herrmann's Christology, see Sockness, "The Ideal and the Historical in the Christology of Wilhelm Herrmann" and Greive, *Der Grund des Glaubens*.

94. Herrmann, *Der Verkehr des Christen mit Gott*, 57 [ET: *The Communion of the Christian with God*, 69].

95. Ibid., 59 [ET, 72].

destroys such claims, it shatters false supports for faith, and that is a great gain. The Christian who imagines that the reliability of the tradition as historical documents gives certainty to faith should be startled from rest by historical work. This ought to make it clear that Christianity cannot be had as cheaply as one thinks. Secondly, historical work is constantly yielding new and modified results obtained from the tradition. By this means the Christian faith is constantly called upon to compare the picture of Jesus that it holds as absolute truth with the relative truth of historical knowledge [*historische Erkenntnis*]. And this helps us not to forget that the most important fact of our life cannot be given to us once for all, but must be continually grasped with all our soul.[96]

When the false supports are eliminated, presumably faith has clear and immediate access to its proper object. According to Herrmann, the basis of Christian faith is the fact of Jesus Christ's appearance in history,[97] God's revelation, through whom and through which Christians are assured that they commune with God. Historical research is incapable of providing this "indubitable fact" [*zweifellose Tatsache*] of Jesus Christ because historical research can only attain higher or lower degrees of probability. If historical research cannot provide the fact of Jesus Christ *as the basis of faith* to modern men and women, this fact must be appropriated by other means:

> If . . . the person of Jesus is so certain to us Christians that we see in him the basis of our faith and the present revelation of God to us, this conviction is not established by a historical judgment [*historisches Urteil*]. . . . It is something else entirely that banishes all doubt from the picture of Jesus. If we have that picture at all, we have it as the result, not of our own efforts, but as an effect of the power of Jesus himself.[98]

---

96. Ibid., 63–64 [ET, 76–77].

97. "When we speak of the historic Christ we mean a unitary personal life that speaks to us from the New Testament as the disciples' testimony of faith, but that, when we hear it, always strikes us as a miraculous revelation. That historical research cannot give us this we *know*. But neither will it ever take this from us by any of its discoveries; this we *believe*, the more we experience what this picture of the glory of Jesus works in us." Ibid., 64 [ET, 77–78].

98. Ibid., 59 [ET, 72]. Herrmann names the church – the fellowship of Christians – as the locus of this picture's effectiveness. It is through the testimony of Christians that the inner life of Jesus is mediated to others. But, Herrmann suggests, once one has been impressed by the power of the inner life of Jesus, mediation is no longer necessary. Ibid., 59–60 [ET, 72–73].

Geschichte und Historie

Herrmann, like Wobbermin and unlike Kähler, is not willing simply to equate this indubatable fact of the historic Christ with the biblical picture of him. For Herrmann there is a necessary distinction between what he calls the inner life of Jesus [*das innere Leben Jesu*] and the New Testament picture of him. It is possible that many features of the life of Jesus presented in the gospels are the product of the evangelists' ability to create powerful moral and religious symbols, but for the Christian who has been touched by the inner life of Jesus, all doubt vanishes.[99] For the Christian who has experienced the power of the inner life of Jesus, historical criticism no longer presents any danger because it is the power of the inner life of Jesus, not the results of historical criticism of the gospels or even the New Testament picture of Christ that is preserved in the preaching of the church, that is the basis of faith.

Herrmann suggests that the personality of Jesus cannot be obscured or muted by any imperfections or inconsistencies that might appear in the evangelists' accounts of his life. The power of this personality shines through those inconsistencies and "give[s] us courage to believe in God."[100] It does this at first by the mediation of Scripture, of testimony, or of preaching, but once one has been touched by the power of this inner life, all need for mediation vanishes and the believer is left with a direct experience of the power of Jesus' inner life.

Brent Sockness argues that Herrmann interweaves two distinct strands of argumentation in his discussions of the relationship between faith and history. First, Herrmann insists on what Sockness calls a "therapeutic function of historical critical research," whereby false security is destroyed by emphasizing the fact that faith lives from what is given in the present rather than from what in the past is reconstructed on the basis of historical scholarship. Second, Herrmann appeals not to historical

---

99. "Whenever we are actually able to see the person of Jesus, then, under the impression of this inner life that breaks through all the veils of the tradition, we ask no more questions about the credibility of the narrators. The question of whether the person of Jesus belongs to history or fiction is silenced in everyone who learns to see it at all, because through it one first experiences what the true reality of personal life is." Ibid., 62 [ET, 75]. For a study of Herrmann's theology with an emphasis on the experience of God and the inner life of Jesus, see de Boor's article, published in two parts as "Der letzte Grund unseres Glaubens an Gott."

100. Herrmann, *Der Verkehr*, 63 [ET: *Communion*, 76].

reconstruction of the past, but to the certainty of this presently given faith itself.[101]

In order to bolster this appeal to the certainty of presently given faith, Herrmann makes a distinction between Jesus Christ as the *basis* of faith (faith's *Grund*) and Jesus Christ as the *content* of faith (faith's *Inhalt*). He understands this distinction to be a crucial one, because any confusion in this matter can have profoundly negative implications for the doctrine of justification by faith alone. In his essay "Grund und Inhalt des Glaubens," he defines the basis of faith as "the man Jesus Christ."[102] The content of faith, on the other hand, is the New Testament picture of the historic Christ, which is kept alive and transmitted through the preaching of the church. The content of faith is, to use another term, composed of *Glaubensgedanken* (ideas or thoughts of faith) *about* Christ. The basis is always prior to the content, and the content always presupposes and re-presents the basis. The basis itself is the sole fact of the appearance of Christ in history and the continuing effect of the power of his inner life. All else is secondary and is ultimately unnecessary for the faith of one who has already been touched by this power. If one were to be brought to faith by the content of faith, by the *Glaubensgedanken about* Christ rather than the power *of* Christ himself, then faith would essentially be thrown back upon itself and would become a human work rather than a free gift of the gracious God. Herrmann argues that his distinction between the basis of faith and the content of faith places him firmly within the Reformation tradition and protects his position from charges of works righteousness.[103]

This distinction marks a significant departure from Kähler's position, for example.[104] Kähler, who was unwilling to distinguish at all between the

---

101. Sockness, *Against False Apologetics*, 84–85. Sockness draws this conclusion based on his analysis of Herrmann's review of Ernst Troeltsch's essay, "Die Bedeutung der Geschichtlichkeit Jesu für den Glauben," but these two strands run throughout Herrmann's work as a whole.

102. Herrmann, "Grund und Inhalt des Glaubens," 282.

103. "With these three sentences I actually stay by the original Reformation doctrine of justification. It is hence possible for me to take seriously that faith is experienced by us not as our own work, but as God's free gift, and that faith itself is the new life, the *nova et spiritualis vita*, in which we are redeemed persons." Ibid., 292.

104. Kähler was certainly aware of Herrmann's critique of his position, having published a rejoinder to Herrmann in an essay entitled "Grund und Inhalt des Christenglaubens: Deckt sich der geschichtliche Christus mit dem biblischen?" included

Geschichte und Historie

historic Christ and the biblical picture of Christ, was even less willing to make a further distinction between Christ as the basis of faith and Christ as the content of faith. For him, Christ is both the basis and the content of faith in exactly the same way: as the total historic, biblical Christ.

Herrmann, on the other hand, introduces a further distinction between the inner life of Jesus, which serves as the basis of faith, and the biblical picture of the historic Christ, which serves as the content of that faith.[105] One of the keys to Herrmann's position is the concept of the power of the inner life of Jesus and how this power is rooted in a historic figure while simultaneously transcending its historicity (thus making it, according to Herrmann, impervious to historical skepticism). For Herrmann, the question of the reliability or the accuracy of the historical records about Jesus Christ is rendered moot once an individual has been gripped by the power of the inner life of Jesus. As Claude Welch puts it, "The question, then, is not what we make of the story (by historisch study), but what the contents of the story make of us."[106] Herrmann discusses this at length in *Der Verkehr des Christen mit Gott*, and one passage in particular places his position in a clearer light:

> It is precisely the most difficult thing to comprehend in the historic reality of Jesus that sets us free from the tradition, because it finally imposes itself on us as something presently effective on us. Those who have found the inner life of Jesus through the mediation of others, insofar as that has happened, have become free even of that mediation. They are set free by the significance that the inner life of Jesus has obtained for those who have seen it. If we have experienced his power over us, we need no longer look to the testimony of others to hold fast to his life as something real. We start, indeed, from the tradition; but we first grasp the fact that the tradition presents us when we have become aware of the enrichment of our

---

in Kähler, *Der sogenannte historische Jesus*, 149–206. This essay provides much material for a comparison of Kähler and Herrmann, but that particular line of inquiry lies beyond the scope of this study.

105. There is some indication in *Der Verkehr* that Herrmann also attempts to differentiate between the basis and the content of faith on the basis of the classical distinction between the *fides quae creditur* and the *fides qua creditur*: "The subjective experience of the Christian religion cannot be severed from the thoughts that in Christian doctrine one seeks to formulate as the contents of faith. That experience does not end in mere feeling, but comes to its perfection in those thoughts." Herrmann, *Der Verkehr*, 38 [ET: *Communion*, 47].

106. Welch, *Protestant Theology in the Nineteenth Century*, 2:52.

own inner life by contact with the Living One.... The appearance of a personality that becomes visible to us in this way absolutely cannot be handed over to us through the communication of others. It arises in us as the free revelation of the living to the living. Thus also the inner life of Jesus becomes part of our own reality. Those who have experienced this will certainly no longer say that, strictly speaking, they can comprehend only the tradition of Jesus as something real. Jesus himself becomes a real power to us when he discloses his inner life to us, a power that we perceive as the best thing our life contains.[107]

The fact of the appearance of Jesus in history is, according to Herrmann, nothing other than the revelation of God.[108] The fact of the historic Jesus Christ, impressing himself upon men and women and becoming part of their own reality, is the basis of Christian faith and, according to Herrmann, is impervious to historical criticism. It is based in the historic tradition of the New Testament, but it finally transcends the mediation of history by means of a direct, indeed miraculous effect of Christ on the individual.[109] The certainty of faith is thus found in the experience of this effect within the individual rather than in any external "prop."

With this distinction between the basis of faith and the content of faith and with this emphasis on the immediate effect of the historic Christ on the individual, Herrmann hopes to have described a faith that is ultimately untroubled by any historical inquiry into its basis. The question still remains, however, of how successful Herrmann was in his attempt to remove faith from the vicissitudes of history.

Unlike Kähler, Herrmann is willing to grant historical criticism free access to the biblical texts. He is free to do this because he does not ultimately base faith on the reliability of the biblical accounts of Jesus Christ, but rather on the power of the inner life of Jesus that lies behind those narratives. Or as Herrmann puts it, "It is thus perfectly clear that we are in a very good position to detach the content of a narrative both from the

---

107. Herrmann, *Der Verkehr*, 60-61 [ET: *Communion*, 73-74].

108. Ibid., 48-49 [ET, 59].

109. Elsewhere, in an article entitled "Der geschichtliche Christus der Grund unseres Glaubens," Herrmann explicitly identifies this direct effect of the inner life of Jesus on the individual as a miracle: "I have emphasized that Christ as the basis of faith bears within himself a claim that exceeds every human dimension and is simply miraculous." Herrmann, "Der geschichtliche Christus," 164.

narrative itself and from its author and to regard it as an element of that reality with which we have to come to terms."[110] To confuse the power of the inner life of Jesus with the narratives *about* that life and that power is to confuse the content of faith for the basis of faith.

By detaching the content of the narratives from the narratives themselves, Herrmann does make great strides toward removing the basis of faith from the fluctuations of historical research into those narratives. But how is that content gained if not by means of the narrative? Herrmann admits that this must be the case because one first learns of Jesus and the power of his life through Scripture, testimony, or preaching. One finds in and through that testimony the basis of faith, the inner life of Jesus and its power as the revelation of God in history. Christians can rest assured that the picture of Christ meditated by the church faithfully reflects the essence of Jesus of Nazareth, even if Herrmann is unwilling to base that assurance on any historical judgment. He is convinced that the picture of Jesus Christ possessed and handed down by the church is historically accurate in its essentials, but he claims that this is a judgment of faith rather than a result of historical research.

If, as Herrmann argues, the narratives are necessary only at an intermediate stage to provide the original mediation for the power of the inner life of Jesus to shine through, after which time they are no longer necessary for the one who has been touched by the power of Jesus' inner life, the narratives still have an important role to play. These narratives might provide an accurate, reliable picture of Jesus Christ and the power of his inner life, or they might, in the end, prove to be unreliable. It is difficult to determine how Herrmann hopes to have made the narratives (and historical criticism of them) irrelevant for providing the basis of faith simply by declaring them to be unnecessary once one has been touched by the power of the inner life of Jesus through the mediation of those narratives themselves, while at the same time insisting that faith nevertheless has an accurate picture of the historic Jesus Christ.

Herrmann's position rests on what Sockness has called a "pseudo-historical approach," in which Herrmann "blocks the path from historical judgments to faith, [but] leaves movement in the opposite direction

---

110. Herrmann, *Der Verkehr*, 58 [ET: *Communion*, 71].

open."¹¹¹ Sockness concludes that Herrmann finally suffers from a lack of both "historical nerve and theological imagination":

> Theologically speaking, the insistence that the portrait of Jesus must faithfully reflect the actual man Jesus of Nazareth or else it is *merely* a fiction or a product of the poetical imagination, and therefore untrue, betrays Herrmann's lack of appreciation for the poetical and representational character and function of the biblical texts.¹¹²

Wobbermin's Appraisal and Critique of Herrmann's Position

Wobbermin's critique of Herrmann's position is the most subtle of his treatments of the four theologians he has chosen to engage in his essay. Wobbermin's position is actually quite close to Herrmann's in many significant respects, including the rejection of the capability of historical research to provide the basis of faith, the positive evaluation of historical research as a necessary means of destroying false supports for faith, and the insistence that there must be some distinction between the historic and the biblical Christ (*contra* Kähler).

These similarities correspond to some shared weaknesses as well. Both are ultimately unclear on the precise nature of the relationship between the positive and negative roles of historical-critical research, especially vis-à-vis the "inner life" of Jesus or the "essential elements" of the picture of Christ. Both intend to free faith from the vicissitudes of history by establishing the certainty of faith in the religious experience of the efficacy (Wobbermin) or power of the inner life (Herrmann) of the historic Christ, yet both maintain that this certainty will withstand rigorous historical scrutiny without any justification for that claim beyond the continuing existence of the Christian faith. Both succumb to what Sockness called in Herrmann's case a "pseudo-historical approach" that fails to take seriously the possibility that rigorous historical criticism will undermine the essential elements of their respective pictures of Christ.

Wobbermin's critique of Herrmann and the differences between their respective positions can be distilled into one main point with two lines of argument. It concerns the picture of the historic Christ, subdivided into a

---

111. Sockness, "The Ideal and the Historical," 386.
112. Ibid., 387.

concern about the relationship between the basis of faith and the content of faith, and a concern about the place of the resurrection in that picture.

Unlike Kähler, Herrmann is not willing to equate the historic Christ with the total biblical picture of him. To do so, Herrmann suggests, is to conflate Christ as the basis of faith (the power of his inner life) with Christ as the content of faith (the *Glaubensgedanken* about Christ). The inner life of Jesus shines through these ideas of faith and is expressed in them, but it must be kept distinct. Otherwise the resulting picture of Jesus would be vulnerable to historical criticism and would depend on the results of historical research, only ever attaining probable reliability rather than the certainty of the direct experience of the power of Jesus' inner life itself.

Wobbermin rejects this separation of Christ as the basis of faith and Christ as the content of faith because, in his estimation, it divorces the historic Christ from the total historic context by which he becomes present to faith. He fears that this separation of the basis and the content threatens to throw the picture of Christ back into the realm of historical research and historical judgments, requiring historical verification of the accuracy of that picture before it can become the object of faith. He recognizes Herrmann's intention to bypass historical judgments by emphasizing the immediate effects of the power of the inner life of Jesus, but he questions whether Herrmann succeeds in doing so:

> To the extent that the person of Jesus Christ is taken out of the total historic context in which he stands, he now becomes, so to speak, a historical figure in a narrower sense, i.e., such a figure who is not already ensured by means of the total historic context in which he stands and to which he is included as an indispensable link, but rather one who invites historical research and first could be ensured by it.[113]

For Wobbermin, the continuing efficacy of the picture of Christ within the Christian tradition (the "total historic context"), not historical research, is what ultimately authenticates the picture of Christ. Herrmann

---

113. "*In dem Maße, als die Person Jesu Christi aus dem geschichtlichen Gesamtzusammenhange, in dem sie steht, herausgenommen wird, wird sie eben zu einer im engeren Sinne so zu nennenden historischen Größe, d.h. zu einer solchen, die nicht schon durch den geschichtlichen Gesamtzusammenhang, in dem sie steht und dem sie als unveräußerliches Glied eingefügt ist, hinreichend sichergestellt ist, sondern die zu einer historischen Detailuntersuchung auffordert und erst durch eine solche sichergestellt werden könnte.*" Wobbermin, *Geschichte und Historie*, 45. Here again is the concern to differentiate between the primary character of *Geschichte* and the secondary character of *Historie*.

claims that the inner life of Jesus accomplishes this same objective by the effect of its power, but Wobbermin claims that this is not possible if the inner life of Jesus is not understood within the larger historic context in which that picture continues to be present and effective. To separate the inner life of Jesus from the larger historic context of its efficacy or effects is, in Wobbermin's estimation, a sacrifice of the historic character of that inner life.

Wobbermin contends that this danger is only latent in Herrmann's treatment because Herrmann does not completely separate the basis from the content of faith.[114] The inner life of Jesus as the basis of faith is still handed down through the Christian tradition and is therefore not completely distinct from it. The "total historic context" is still a part of that picture, even if it is secondary to it and derived from it.

However, Wobbermin argues that Herrmann's position succumbs to difficulties because he has not carefully distinguished between *Geschichte* and *Historie*. Such a distinction would require Herrmann to rethink the distinction between Christ as the basis of faith and Christ as the content of faith. Wobbermin argues that Herrmann, by distinguishing between the basis of faith and the content of faith, requires a historical judgment to determine that basis. Because Herrmann claims that this basis is the inner life of Jesus as it lies *behind* the texts of the New Testament and as it is distinct from what Wobbermin calls the "total historic context" in which it continues to be present and efficacious, Wobbermin contends that Herrmann is forced to rely on historical judgments to determine the character of this inner life of Jesus:

> Such an attempt, according to the nature of the matter at hand, can only be carried out by means of historical research; where it is undertaken, it thus leads to a historical approach in a narrower sense, so to speak. Herrmann's position will not be able to elude the force of this fact. In fact, at this point a "historically" oriented series of thoughts crosses his position and destroys it. For along with the "historical" series of thoughts, their relativity, their hypothetical character, and their probability also enter into Herrmann's picture of Christ.[115]

---

114. Ibid., 44. This is obviously contrary to what Herrmann himself insisted.

115. "*Ein solcher Versuch kann aber der Natur der Sache zufolge nur mit den Mitteln historischer Forschung ausgeführt werden; wo er unternommen wird, führt er also zu einer im engeren Sinn so zu nennenden historischen Betrachtungsweise. Dem Zwange dieses Sachverhalts wird sich auch Herrmanns Position nicht entziehen können. Tatsächlich wird*

Geschichte und Historie

Nowhere does this difference between Herrmann and Wobbermin come into clearer relief than it does in the question of the resurrection of Jesus. The decisive question in terms of the resurrection is whether the element that came to expression in resurrection faith can be separated from the New Testament picture of Christ as a historic fact. While Herrmann wants to make such a distinction, at least provisionally, Wobbermin argues that such a distinction must unconditionally be rejected. For Wobbermin, "as soon as such a separation is made, the historic picture of Christ ceases to be, in our judgment, what it always has been according to its historic existence and also what it is and means in the present."[116]

In the case of the resurrection the question is not one of *Historie* (it has been dismissed by the nature of the matter at hand) but is rather a question of how *Geschichte* is defined and understood. Because Herrmann wants to distinguish between the inner life of Jesus lying *behind* the texts of the New Testament and the narratives and tradition *about* the power of his inner life, Wobbermin accuses Herrmann of failing to account for the essential significance of the resurrection for the total historic picture of Christ. The resurrection is significant precisely because it is presupposed by the entire Christian tradition, from the New Testament itself through to the present day. Any attempt to "go behind" the tradition to the historicity of the resurrection event itself necessarily requires an inappropriate dependence on historical research and historical judgments, which cannot provide any foundation for Christian faith. But whereas Herrmann understands this to mean that the resurrection itself should not and cannot constitute an essential element of the basis of faith, Wobbermin insists that it must constitute an essential element of the historic picture of Christ precisely because the resurrection is presupposed by the entire Christian tradition as an event of decisive and enduring (i.e. historic) significance and efficacy.

Again, the crux of this debate on the place of the resurrection within the picture of Christ is the difference between Herrmann's and

---

sie an diesem Punkt durch eine 'historisch' orientierte Gedankenreihe gekreuzt und um ihre Geschlossenheit gebracht. Denn mit der 'historischen' Gedankenreihe kommt unvermeidlich auch deren Relativität, ihr hypothetischer oder Wahrscheinlichkeits-Charakter in das Herrmannsche Christusbild hinein." Ibid., 42.

116. "*Sobald eine solche Trennung ernstlich vollzogen wird, hört jenes Bild u.E. auf, das zu sein, was es seinem geschichtlichen Bestande nach immer gewesen ist, was es seinem geschichtlichen Bestande nach auch gegenwärtig für uns ist und bedeutet.*" Ibid., 36.

Wobbermin's definition of the picture of Christ as the basis of faith. Herrmann limits the essential elements to the "inner life" of Jesus, while Wobbermin places these elements within a wider context, namely the picture of Christ present within the "total historic context" of the New Testament and the Christian tradition. For Herrmann, including the elements of the tradition in the picture of Christ moves away from the inner life of Jesus as the basis of faith and toward the *Glaubensgedanken* that are the content of faith, and therefore such a move must be rejected. For Wobbermin, limiting the picture of Christ to the inner life of Jesus in (and behind) the New Testament picture requires historical and psychological judgments that are difficult if not impossible to make.

Herrmann does not argue for a wholesale rejection of the Christian tradition in its significance for the picture of Christ, and Wobbermin rightly acknowledges this. Tradition plays an important role in Herrmann's discussion, for the picture of Christ is present and handed down in the tradition through the proclamation of the gospel.[117] But tradition always serves as the means by which the picture of Christ is represented and is never part of that picture itself; it is, once again, a matter of distinguishing between the basis of faith and the content of faith. Where Herrmann sees a clear distinction between the person of Jesus Christ and the tradition concerning him, Wobbermin sees a unity.[118] Wobbermin prefers to speak of the picture of Christ as standing within a much broader historic context, and he accuses Herrmann of removing the person of Christ from this context. Wobbermin believes it is necessary to include the resurrection in the historic picture of Christ as the object of faith precisely because the

---

117. "In Christianity there is nothing else consistently as necessary as the preaching of Christ." Herrmann, *Der Verkehr*, 65 [ET: *Communion*, 80]. Herrmann also notes the importance of tradition when he suggests a relationship between the person of Jesus and apostolic preaching: "We have the person of Jesus only in the preaching of the disciples who believed in him." Ibid., 93 [ET, 113].

118. Herrmann's and Wobbermin's conflicting positions on the relation of the person of Christ to the tradition concerning him anticipates a similar debate in the middle of the twentieth century concerning the relation of the early Christian kerygma to the proclamation of Jesus, addressed in the work of Rudolf Bultmann, Eberhard Jüngel, and others. See, e.g., Bultmann, *Das Verhältnis der urchristlichen Christusbotschaft zum historischen Jesus* [ET: "The Primitive Christian Kerygma and the Historical Jesus"] and Jüngel, *Paulus und Jesus*. Wobbermin's position is influenced by Schleiermacher's, particularly Schleiermacher's discussion of the unbroken unity of the influence of the Redeemer on the disciples and the testimony of his influence through the proclamation of the church.

resurrection has always been included in the picture of Christ, from the New Testament to the present:

> For us it is only a question of whether the element that found its expression in resurrection faith is to be separated from the picture of Christ that is given to us from the New Testament as a historic fact, of whether it is to be separated from it at least provisionally, as Herrmann wants to do. And this question, it appears to us, must be answered with an unconditional no. As soon as such a separation is seriously made, that picture, in our opinion, ceases to be what it always was according to its continued historic existence and also what it presently is and means for us according to its continued historic existence.[119]

According to Wobbermin, Herrmann's position finally succumbs to a dependence on the *historisch* thinking it seeks to avoid. By refusing to include the resurrection in the essential traits of the life of Jesus, Herrmann isolates the picture of the historic Christ from the wider historic context of that picture, which, Wobbermin argues, must include the resurrection. By excluding the resurrection from the picture of the historic Christ, there is then the temptation of considering the person of Jesus as a historical rather than historic figure, insofar as that picture is then limited to the earthly life of Jesus.

Wobbermin's criticisms of Herrmann remain subtle and limited essentially to the two points described above. Their respective positions are finally quite close.[120] Both agree on the necessary negative role of historical criticism, both question the benefits and even the possibility of

---

119. "*Es fragt sich für uns nur, ob von dem Christusbilde, das uns vom Neuen Testament her als geschichtlicher Tatbestand gegeben ist, das Moment, das im Auferstehungsglauben seinen Ausdruck gefunden hat, überhaupt zu trennen ist; ob es von ihm wenigstens vorläufig, wie Herrmann will, zu trennen ist. Und diese Frage scheint uns bedingungslos verneint werden zu müssen. Sobald eine solche Trennung ernstlich vollzogen wird, hört jenes Bild u. E. auf, das zu sein, was es seinem geschichtlichen Bestande nach immer gewesen ist, was es seinem geschichtlichen Bestande nach auch gegenwärtig für uns ist und bedeutet.*" Wobbermin, *Geschichte und Historie*, 36.

120. Wobbermin concludes that his position represents something of a "middle line" between Kähler's and Herrmann's, although he also claims that this was not his intention. He acknowledges both Kähler's and Herrmann's influence, along with Adolf Harnack's and Julius Kaftan's, in developing his thoughts on the distinction between *Geschichte* and *Historie* and on the problem of faith and history. Although Wobbermin implies that his position falls roughly equidistant from Kähler's and Herrmann's, after closer analysis it appears that his position falls closer to Herrmann's than to Kähler's. Ibid., 46–47.

equating the historic Christ with the total biblical picture of him, and both attempt to find some certainty for faith independent of the fluctuating results of historical-critical research. They claim to have found this certainty in different places, but in the end their positions suffer from the same weaknesses. Both Herrmann and Wobbermin claim to have avoided making faith dependent on historical judgments, but both positions are more open to criticism than either is willing to admit. In Herrmann's case, by limiting the basis of faith to the earthly life of Jesus it is difficult to determine how he manages to claim that he has removed faith from the vicissitudes of historical research. And Wobbermin, by claiming to have guaranteed the picture of Christ by tracing its effects through the history of the Christian tradition, is ultimately making a historical judgment without admitting that it is, in fact, a historical judgment. How else but by historical inquiry could one hope to isolate the essential features of the picture of Christ as it is effective and efficacious throughout the history of the Christian tradition? Here again it is helpful to recognize the implicit distinction in Wobbermin's essay between *Geschichte* and its effects or efficacy, but this is a distinction Wobbermin never made explicit.

Similarly, both Herrmann and Wobbermin contend that faith can confidently assume that it has an accurate picture of the historic Jesus Christ, a confidence that is based either in the power of the inner life of Jesus (Herrmann) or the efficacy of the historic Christ within the Christian tradition (Wobbermin). This is anything but a foregone conclusion. The possibility will exist, in both cases, that faith's confidence in the historical reliability of its object is mistaken. But, as B. A. Gerrish notes, "Neither Herrmann nor Wobbermin, any more than Kähler before them, could resist the temptation to move back from the confidence of faith to confidence in the historicity of the Synoptic Jesus."[121]

In fact, it is difficult to see how Wobbermin has made any significant advances beyond Herrmann's position.[122] There are differences, but ultimately their positions are open to the same criticisms, especially in terms of the role of historical criticism and the extent to which both have or have not avoided throwing faith back into the vicissitudes of history. Both

---

121. Gerrish, "Jesus, Myth, and History," 34.

122. One advance, which only becomes clear as an advance with some historical distance, is Wobbermin's insistence that the resurrection must belong to the basis of faith. The resurrection and its significance for faith will become a central theme in the theology of the mid-twentieth century, especially that of Herrmann's student, Rudolf Bultmann.

Geschichte und Historie

attempt to locate the certainty of faith outside the realm of historical research by emphasizing the immediate presence and efficacy of the picture of Christ as mediated by the Christian tradition. But this in itself does not remove the picture of Christ from the realm of historical judgments. Charles Carlston's criticism of Kähler actually applies to Herrmann and Wobbermin as well:

> The principle [that genuinely historical figures are known in their effects] must not be extended so broadly as to justify all subsequent interpretation of all historical figures; it must leave room for a negative critical function, judging the concinnity between the historical personage and later interpretation. Neither the Protestant Principle nor serious historical study can survive otherwise.
>
> The effects of a historical figure are, at least in theory, knowable by the same methods as the figure himself; a decision of faith is not called for in winnowing the Napoleon tradition in post-Napoleonic times. The apostolic understanding of Jesus in *this* sense is available through historical inquiry.[123]

It is only later, with the development of the religio-psychological circle between personal religious experience and the historic efficacy of the picture of Christ, and with it the attempt to build on the distinction between *Geschichte* and *Historie* in a broader and more systematic context, that Wobbermin begins to distance himself from Herrmann's position.

Wilhelm Bousset

The fourth and final figure Wobbermin considers in his section of appraisals and critiques of previous positions is Wilhelm Bousset. Likely the least familiar of the four figures, Bousset taught at Göttingen and Gießen and was one of the founders of the *religionsgeschichtliche Schule*.[124] His

---

123. Carlston, "Biblicism or Historicism?" 35.

124. There is surprisingly little literature on Bousset, considering his role in founding the *religionsgeschichtliche Schule*. The only comprehensive study of Bousset is a dissertation by Anthonie Frans Verheule entitled *Wilhelm Bousset, Leben und Werk*. Verheule also sketches the contours of the debate concerning the distinction between *Geschichte* and *Historie* from Kähler to Pannenberg in an article entitled "'Historie' en 'Geschichte.'" He briefly discusses Wobbermin's distinction as a precursor of Bultmann's and wonders why Wobbermin's work on the distinction has not played a larger role in the work of later generations of theologians.

most significant works are historical studies of the origins of Christianity, of which *Kyrios Christos* is perhaps the best known.[125]

At the fifth World Congress for Free Christianity and Religious Progress, held in Berlin in 1910, Bousset delivered a paper entitled "Die Bedeutung der Person Jesu für den Glauben."[126] In his paper Bousset attempts to maintain the significance of the person of Jesus for faith without throwing faith back into a dependence on the fluctuating results of historical research. He moves from a discussion of earlier attempts to solve this problem (from the "older rationalism" to Schleiermacher to Ritschl) to an analysis of the conflicting assumptions of science and religion, and finally to a constructive proposal for securing a faith that is not subject to the uncertainties of historical knowledge.

The problem, as Bousset understands it, is the problem of faith and history and their relationship to one another. As long as theologians attempt to base faith on historical particularities (e.g., the atoning death of Christ, his inner life, or his messianic self-consciousness), faith will continue to depend to a greater or lesser degree on the results of historical research into his person and work. Bousset is not willing seriously to entertain Drews's thesis that Jesus of Nazareth never existed, but, assuming that he did in fact exist, what can be known with any historical certainty about his person and his work? Not very much, finally:

> What we know of the pragmatic context of his life would fit on a single sheet of paper. The preaching or the gospel of Jesus is an often insoluble web of community tradition and possibly authentic words of the master. What our gospels hand down concerning the unique self-consciousness of Jesus and its forms, and therefore of the inner life of his personality, is overshadowed by the dogma of the community.[127]

---

125. Bousset, *Kyrios Christos* [ET: *Kyrios Christos*].

126. Bousset, "Die Bedeutung der Person Jesu für den Glauben." Wobbermin also delivered a paper at this congress, entitled "Aufgabe und Bedeutung der Religionspsychologie." Other presenters included Adolf Harnack, Hermann Gunkel, and Ernst Troeltsch. Wobbermin was in attendance and heard Bousset deliver his paper, and he recalls that he immediately took Bousset aside and remarked that their positions are ultimately quite close in many important respects, except for their respective judgments of the relationship between *Geschichte* and *Historie*. Wobbermin, *Geschichte und Historie*, 48.

127. Bousset, "Die Bedeutung der Person Jesu," 292.

The dubious character of the New Testament witness raises the question of how willing Christians should be to entrust the certainty of their faith to the fluctuating results of historical research into that witness. Bousset suggests that this question is most pressing for the liberal theology of his day, because, in his estimation, modern liberal theology is characterized by a "historically [*geschichtlich*] conditioned anti-rationalism" that contradicts both Lessing's insistence that accidental historical truths cannot serve as proof of necessary truths of reason and Kant's principle of the illustrative rather than the demonstrative character of history.[128]

By attempting to base faith in the historical person of Jesus, whether from the side of the teaching or gospel of Jesus or from the side of his person and the impulse that proceeds from him, liberal theology is forced to consider the question of historical accuracy and reliability. And this, Bousset suggests, means that "the looming possibility that perhaps we know very little about the personal life of Jesus, so little that it does not present an impressive, vivid picture, must seriously threaten that view."[129]

All of the attempts to base the certainty and content of faith in history are, as Bousset puts it, "oppressed by singular difficulties." In order to move beyond and perhaps overcome these difficulties, faith must seek another foundation, one that is outside of history. That foundation, Bousset proposes, is available in reason:

> History [*Historie*], earnestly and vigorously prosecuted, points beyond itself and compels us to seek another foundation outside of history, and that foundation would be reason [*Ratio*].... Religion is something innate in human beings, understood on the basis of the necessity of its rational capacity; religion is not borne to human beings from outside them, thrust upon them from above by revelation, and it does not rest on supernatural revelation in the specific sense of the word.[130]

Religion, then, is not based in history or in historic events at all. It is an "original capacity [*ursprüngliches Vermögen*] of the human being" that unfolds within history but is not based in history.[131] By basing religion

---

128. Ibid., 293.
129. Ibid., 296.
130. Ibid., 298.
131. Ibid., 298–99.

in reason rather than in history, Bousset has moved religion to the realm of ideas. Ideas, he suggests, do not need the authority of history; rather, ideas are the norm by which individual historic personalities and events are measured. This applies to all historic personalities and events, including the person of Jesus Christ.

Here, however, is where the "old" rationalism erred, according to Bousset.[132] The old rationalism concludes from this series of arguments that history has no meaning for religion, that it is merely a crutch that is used to raise oneself up to the world of ideas and is then discarded. This would be true, Bousset suggests, in the realm of science and mathematics. But religious ideas are not propositions like those of science and mathematics, which are logically demonstrable. Religion, according to Bousset, concerns the idea of the meaning and value of existence [*Sinn und Wert des Daseins*], categories that are completely foreign to science.[133]

Truths of science and truths of religion, then, are two fundamentally different classes of truth. Science is concerned with the tangible, meaning that the material, that which persists in space and time, is ultimate truth for science. Religion, on the other hand, is concerned with ideas. But religious faith does not live immediately from ideas, because, according to Bousset, ideas always remain incomprehensible and ungraspable on their own. They require symbolization to be grasped and comprehended: "the world of eternity can only become conceivable and objective [*gegenständlich*] when [these ideas] shimmer transparently through the world of finitude. The poet's words contain the deepest truth: 'All that is past is only a parable.'"[134]

It is in this sense that history must be understood as significant for faith. In history, naked ideas are clothed in symbols that convey their truth to human beings. In terms of history, too, there is a fundamental difference between science and religion. For science, the past always recedes further and further into the distance. It is, to use Bousset's colorful image, merely "fertilizer for the future [*Dünger für die Zukunft*]."[135] But in religion (as in art) the past remains alive for the present; the realm of the

---

132. Bousset never names any representatives of the "old rationalism."

133. Ibid., 300.

134. Ibid., 302. The poet is Goethe, and the line "Alles Vergängliche ist nur ein Gleichnis" is from the final chorus of the last act of *Faust*. It is also the epitaph on the tombstone of the poet Kurt Tucholsky.

135. Bousset, "Die Bedeutung der Person Jesu," 303.

symbolic knows no linear progress: "here presides the unpredictability of the individual, of the genius and the hero."[136]

In this sense it is possible to speak of a relationship between faith and history. The great religious personalities (of which Jesus is certainly one) continue to exert a powerful influence in the history of the communities that emerged and developed around them. But the significance of these personalities is not primarily historic. Their significance is rooted in their value as symbols. Bousset suggests that the great religious personalities not only create the symbols of faith; they themselves *become* that symbol for the community of faith. So in the case of Jesus, he not only created the symbolism of the gospel; he himself became the symbol of the gospel.[137]

With this move to consider the symbolic character of religious personalities, Bousset hopes to have removed the person of Jesus from the vicissitudes of history and the fluctuations of historical research. When Jesus Christ is understood as a symbol rather than as a historical person, the question of history ceases to be the dominant and dominating question it has been in the history of modern liberal theology. There is no longer any need to delineate what might be historically accurate and demonstrable from the later additions of the early Christian community, and there is no longer any need to protect faith from the results of historical research:

> It comes down to the symbol and the picture itself, not, at this point, to ultimate truth and reality. That lies behind the symbols, in the immovable, God-given depths of human reason and in the eternal value of ideas. The symbol serves for illustration, not for demonstration. Therefore we also make the remarkable observation that the picture of Jesus, as his immediate community presented it in the gospels, remains and will remain more effective as poetry and truth than as any historical attempts at reconstruction, precise as they might be.[138] This faith does not inquire into the historic reality in a narrow sense, but into the religious and the morally practical; it stops, consciously or unconsciously, at the

---

136. Ibid. Bousset's *Kyrios Christos* is partly devoted to analyzing the cultic status of Christ, in which elements of the genius and the hero are certainly present.

137. Bousset, "Die Bedeutung der Person Jesu," 304.

138. "Poetry and Truth" [*Dichtung und Wahrheit*] is the title of Goethe's autobiography. Bousset was almost certainly aware of this connection, as he had already quoted Goethe (without naming him) earlier in his paper. See Goethe, *Goethes Werke*, vol. 5, *Dichtung und Wahrheit* [ET: *Goethe's Collected Works*, vols. 4–5, *From My Life*].

picture. . . . And if science were to pronounce the most extreme verdict that Jesus did not exist, faith will not be lost, because it rests on its own internal foundation and, moreover, the picture of Jesus in the gospels would nevertheless remain, and even if only as great poetry, still as poetry of eternal symbolic significance.[139]

The value of the gospels does not rest in their historical veracity but in their capacity poetically and symbolically to convey the "eternal truths of faith." And if the gospels are understood in this way, as the product of "poetic fantasy" rather than as historical documents, then, Bousset believes, it is still possible to confess that "the Logos became flesh and we beheld his glory."[140]

Bousset hopes to have removed faith from the vicissitudes of historical research by completely removing the basis of faith from history, establishing it in reason instead. There might be a historic basis of faith or there might not; the question of historicity is irrelevant. What matters most is the power of the symbol of Jesus Christ to convey what Bousset calls the "eternal truths of faith." The symbol of Jesus Christ exerts a powerful influence in the Christian tradition, and it is this symbol that serves as the basis of faith. There is an underlying truth, but by itself it is incomprehensible. It requires poetic, symbolic representation in order to be understood.

For Bousset, then, faith is not dependent on history at all. It is, as he candidly admits, a matter of faith resting on its own internal, rational foundation. Bousset has removed faith from the vicissitudes of history, but he has made faith its own product, a move that is difficult to defend as somehow remaining true to the Protestant tradition.[141] He seeks to avoid the problem of faith and history altogether by turning to a rational foundation for faith, in the tradition of, for example, Lessing, Kant, and Jakob Friedrich Fries.[142] And while his solution does make faith completely independent of the results of historical research, it will not be a satisfactory solution to the problem of faith and history for those who still want to have some historic basis for faith.

139. Bousset, "Die Bedeutung der Person Jesu," 305.

140. Ibid.

141. To be fair, Bousset never claims that he is attempting to defend a specifically Protestant understanding of faith.

142. These are the three figures whom Bousset acknowledges as influencing his own thought on the rational foundation of religion. Ibid., 299–300.

Geschichte und Historie

Wobbermin's Appraisal and Critique of Bousset's Position

Like Bousset, Wobbermin is concerned to remove the basis of faith from the vicissitudes of historical research. Unlike Bousset, he is not willing to divorce faith completely from any historic foundation. All of Wobbermin's criticisms of Bousset's position are based on one fundamental concern, namely the lack of terminological precision when discussing history and historical research. Bousset uses the terms *geschichtlich* and *historisch* interchangeably, and Wobbermin attributes many of his own misgivings to this lack of terminological precision in Bousset's paper. The question of whether Bousset himself might admit the possibility of greater clarity by means of such a distinction is left unasked. For Wobbermin, Bousset's position would be much improved were such a distinction consistently employed.

Wobbermin agrees with Bousset that the results of historical research cannot serve as the basis of faith. To claim to do so is to give up the security of faith from the outset.[143] Wobbermin further agrees that the historical [*historisch*] can never serve as a foundation because it is by nature always secondary, never primary.[144] But Bousset also claims that faith cannot be based on the historic [*geschichtlich*] appearance of Jesus of Nazareth.[145] Where Bousset wants to deny the possibility of basing faith on *either* the results of historical research *or* the historic appearance of Jesus of Nazareth, Wobbermin wants to make a distinction between these two possibilities. As Wobbermin puts it:

> To want to entrust the security of our faith to historical research is for me an absolutely senseless undertaking. For that means nothing other than to give up the security of this faith at the outset. But on the "historic appearance of Jesus of Nazareth" – more precisely put: on the historic picture of the person of Jesus Christ, on the picture of the person of Jesus Christ as history presents it to us in order to establish faith, that appears to me, then, absolutely to be warranted, if one does not understand this picture of the person of Jesus Christ as separate and unrelated to our own spiritual life, but

---

143. Wobbermin, *Geschichte und Historie*, 50.

144. "*Das Historische kann unmöglich als etwas Fundamentales gelten, denn es ist nichts Primäres, sondern etwas durchaus Sekundäres.*" Ibid., 51.

145. Bousset, "Die Bedeutung der Person Jesu," 291–92.

rather precisely in its relation to this our own spiritual life and in its significance for it.[146]

Again, Wobbermin is concerned to establish the continuity of the historic picture of Christ with its efficacy persisting in and through history. The efficacy of this picture will persist regardless of historical inquiry into its origins, and its value [*Wert*] is based precisely on the fact that it *will* persist, regardless of the results of historical inquiry into its origins. The value of the picture of Christ lies in its dependence on *Geschichte*, specifically that it proves itself to be historically [*geschichtlich*] efficacious. And this historic efficacy also proves that the picture is not merely the product of what Bousset called "poetic fantasy."[147]

Both Bousset and Wobbermin agree that historical research cannot provide the foundation for faith, but they disagree on what should provide that foundation. Bousset suggests that faith finds its foundation in reason, whereas Wobbermin suggests that the foundation is furnished by *Geschichte* (as distinct from *Historie*) "in its significance for the personal life of faith."[148] Wobbermin is unwilling to follow Bousset in securing

---

146. "*Der historischen Forschung die Sicherheit unseres Glaubens anvertrauen wollen, das ist für mich ein schlechthin sinnloses Unternehmen. Denn das heißt gar nichts Anderes, als die Sicherheit dieses Glaubens von vornherein preisgeben. Auf die 'geschichtliche Erscheinung Jesu von Nazareth' – genauer gesprochen: auf das geschichtliche Personbild Jesu Christi, auf das Personbild von Jesus Christus, wie es uns die Geschichte zeigt, den Glauben zu gründen, das scheint mir dann durchaus berechtigt, wenn man dies Personbild von Jesus Christus nicht abgesondert für sich und beziehungslos faßt, ohne Beziehung auf unser eigenes Geistesleben, sondern gerade in seiner Beziehung auf dieses unser eigenes Geistesleben und in seiner Bedeutung für dasselbe.*" Wobbermin, *Geschichte und Historie*, 50.

147. At this point it must be said that perhaps Wobbermin has missed Bousset's point. Bousset claims that the symbol of Christ as the product of poetic fantasy remains the means by which the eternal truths of faith are conveyed to human beings. Wobbermin does not put the efficacy of the picture of Christ in terms of eternal truths immediately available to reason, but refers to the efficacy of the picture of Christ within history as the enduring value of the picture. Both Wobbermin and Bousset arrive at the same goal from different starting points. Yet Wobbermin insists that his goal cannot be reached through a product of poetic fantasy, that historic efficacy is proof that the picture is *not* the product of poetic fantasy but of a historic figure. It is difficult to see how this is a valid argument against Bousset, or how historic efficacy *must* have its origin in a historic figure rather than in poetry or symbol.

148. "*Das andere Fundament liefert die Geschichte. Die Geschichte nämlich, wie dieser Begriff durch die bewußte Unterscheidung vom Begriff der Historie näher bestimmt wird. Diese Geschichte in ihrer Bedeutung für das persönliche Glaubensleben ist oder liefert das nötige Fundament.*" Ibid., 55–56. Wobbermin also suggests that this is the beginning of

the foundation of faith in reason because, in his estimation, Bousset has inverted the proper relationship between reason and *Geschichte*. While Bousset subordinates *Geschichte* to reason, Wobbermin insists that reason must be subordinated to *Geschichte*.

According to Wobbermin, reason must be subordinated to *Geschichte* because human reason is only exercised and developed within *Geschichte* and is therefore necessarily dependent on it. Reason exists and functions only within the realm of *Geschichte* precisely because human beings are historic subjects standing within *Geschichte*. To rationalize religion – to remove it from the realm of *Geschichte* and to place it above and beyond *Geschichte* – is to give it up, because religion is irreducibly historic.[149]

Geschichte, not reason, is the realm of religious truth. For Wobbermin, the historic character of the Christian religion is rooted in the *historic picture* of Jesus Christ as its creative source. Bousset prefers to speak of the *symbol* of Christ as the creative source of the Christian religion. The person of Christ, he suggests, transcends mere historicity and creates a living symbol that is "more effective as poetry and truth" than as a historic figure. The symbol of Christ, according to Bousset, illustrates the ultimate truth and reality lying behind the symbol. He paraphrases Kant to make precisely this point: "the symbol serves for illustration, not for demonstration."[150]

Wobbermin also appeals to Kant's proposition to make his case against Bousset's rationalization of religion, but he makes one important addition. Kant suggested that the "*Historische*" does not serve for the demonstration, but for the illustration of truth.[151] Wobbermin revises Kant's dictum to read, "*Geschichte* does not serve for a demonstration of religious truth, nor merely for its illustration; *Geschichte* serves for the

---

his religio-psychological method, which he will develop more fully in his three-volume systematics (see Chapter 3, "Systematic Theology according to the Religio-Psychological Method").

149. Wobbermin, *Geschichte und Historie*, 64

150. Bousset, "Die Bedeutung der Person Jesu," 305.

151. Kant's original proposition refers to the role of the historical in relating truth: "The historical [*das Historische*] serves only for illustration, not for demonstration." For the original proposition, see Kant, *Lose Blätter aus Kants Nachlaß*, 3:66 [ET: *Notes and Fragments*]. In the third volume of his systematics, Wobbermin suggests that, for Kant, *das Historische* signifies *Geschichte* itself and not merely historical research. Wobbermin, *Systematische Theologie nach religionspsychologischer Methode*, vol. 3, *Wesen und Wahrheit des Christentums*, 308, n. 1.

invention of religious truth."[152] For Wobbermin it is *Geschichte*, not reason, that is the essential and permanent condition for the acquisition of religious truth, both because all truth is essentially historic and because human beings and religion itself are irreducibly historic:

> This picture of Jesus Christ as a historic figure is the norm and not merely the symbol of the Christian religion. It does not serve merely for the illustration of Christian faith in God. It serves for its invention and indeed in a double respect: it serves faith for its practical religious life of faith as the way to the living God, and it serves theology for its theological work as the methodological means of a more precise definition of the Christian idea of God.
>
> Indeed not as a *dogmatic* confession, but also not only as a product of poetic fantasy, but rather as a confession of faith that seeks and finds the revelation of God in history do we adopt the words: The Logos became flesh and we beheld his glory. Yes, we may adopt it even more wholeheartedly and say: The Logos became flesh and we *behold* his glory.[153]

On the basis of his conclusion, it is clear that Wobbermin is not willing to give up the importance of divine revelation in history in favor of a purely rational or symbolic foundation for faith. And this is the primary difference between his position and Bousset's, despite many important similarities. Bousset is willing to give up revelation as a historic event, while Wobbermin insists that to give up historic revelation is to give up the Christian religion. So in spite of many similarities, which Wobbermin

---

152. "*Die Geschichte dient zwar nicht zur Demonstration der religiösen Wahrheit, aber sie dient auch nicht bloß zu ihrer Illustration; die Geschichte dient zur **Invention** der religiösen Wahrheit.*" Wobbermin, *Geschichte und Historie*, 70. Emphasis mine. It is interesting that Wobbermin chooses to use the English word "Invention" here rather than the German "Erfindung."

153. "*So ist dies Bild Jesu Christi als geschichtliche Größe die Norm und nicht bloß das Symbol der christlichen Religion. Es dient nicht bloß zur Illustration des christlichen Gottesglaubens. Es dient zur Invention desselben und zwar dies in doppelter Hinsicht: dem Glauben für sein praktisch-religiöses Glaubensleben als Weg zum lebendigen Gott selbst, der Theologie für ihre theologische Arbeit als methodisches Mittel der Näherbestimmung des christlichen Gottesgedankens. Zwar nicht als **dogmatisches** Bekenntnis, aber auch nicht nur als Erzeugnis dichterischer Phantasie, sondern als Bekenntnis des die Offenbarung Gottes in der Geschichte suchenden und findenen Glaubens, eignen wir uns das Wort an: Der Logos ward Fleisch und wir sahen seine Herrlichkeit. Ja wir dürfen es uns noch rückhaltloser aneignen und sagen: Der Logos ward Fleisch und wir **sehen** seine Herrlichkeit.*" Ibid., 72. Emphasis in original.

Geschichte und Historie

himself acknowledges, he is unwilling to follow Bousset's rational approach to secure a faith above the shifting results of historical research.

After an extensive engagement with these four figures – Lessing, Kähler, Herrmann, and Bousset – Wobbermin hopes that his own position has become clearer with respect to the problem of faith and history. He indicates that his own position fits somewhere between Kähler's and Herrmann's. This is consistent with his intention to maintain a historic foundation for Christian faith, as opposed to the rationalist and antihistorical tendencies of Lessing's and Bousset's positions. Now that he has determined where he stands vis-à-vis similar positions from the past, he next turns his attention to a constructive sketch of his own position on the problem of faith and history.

THE HISTORIC PICTURE OF JESUS CHRIST

In a 1911 essay entitled "Psychologie und Erkenntniskritik der religiösen Erfahrung," Wobbermin emphasizes the historic character of the Christian religion and seeks to define Christianity in its relation to *Geschichte* and in opposition to *Historie*:

> Certainly genuine religion must be completely and unconditionally free vis-à-vis every merely historical tradition (i.e., tradition comprehensible only by means of historical research), and it must therefore grant such research unconditional and complete freedom. But this is not to say that the link that immediately connects religion with *Geschichte* itself must be severed. Rather, this link may not be severed if religion itself is not to be harmed in its most proper essence.
>
> For a relation to *Geschichte* belongs to the continued existence of every genuine and healthy religion. . . . And in Christianity the relation to *Geschichte* is concentrated in the picture of Jesus Christ as it radiates outward toward us from the New Testament, as it is available and comprehensible to every religious experience independent of all historical criticism of the tradition.[154]

---

154. "*Gewiß muß echte Religion gegenüber aller bloß historischen d.h. nur mit den Mitteln historischer Forschung faßbaren Überlieferung ganz und unbedingt frei sein und sie muß also solcher Forschung unbedingte und völlige Freiheit zugestehen. Aber damit ist doch nicht gesagt, daß auch das die Religion mit der Geschichte selbst unmittelbar verknüpfende Band zerschnitten werden muß. Vielmehr darf dies Band nicht zerschnitten werden, wenn nicht die Religion selbst in ihrem eigensten Wesen verletzt werden soll. Denn eine Beziehung zur Geschichte gehört eben zum Bestande aller echten und gesunden Religion hinzu. . . . Und im Christentum konzentriert sich die Beziehung zur Geschichte in dem*

Wobbermin admits that this position is often misunderstood, especially in terms of the role of historical criticism. He argues for the unrestricted access of historical criticism to the Christian tradition, including the picture of Jesus Christ found in the New Testament. However, if this picture is to be available and comprehensible to religious experience, it must be in some sense also immediately available, without first being provided by historical research. The New Testament picture of Christ must be subjected to rigorous historical criticism, both in order to strip away any false supports for faith and to allow the effects or efficacy of that picture to shine through the tradition and become immediately available to religious experience. It is specifically the *effect* or *efficacy* of this picture for religious experience that is independent of historical research and remains unaffected by it.

Here Wobbermin's implicit distinction between effect or efficacy and *Historie* becomes vitally important. Historical research can uncover or reveal the effects or efficacy of the New Testament picture of Christ, but Wobbermin insists that these effects are not thereby made the *product* of historical research. The effects or efficacy of the picture remain prior and superior to *Historie*, which serves only the purpose of uncovering or revealing the effects so that they are immediately available to religious experience.

Wobbermin's three "essential elements" of the historic picture of Christ can serve as a test case for this theory. Each of the three essential elements – Christ's ethical disposition toward love, his unity of will with his heavenly Father, and his elevation to the Father following his suffering and death, along with the effects or efficacy of these elements in the present – exist prior to historical criticism of the New Testament texts, but it is only by means of historical research that these three elements are isolated from the remainder of the biblical picture of Christ.[155]

Bilde von Jesus Christus, wie es uns aus dem Neuen Testament entgegenleuchtet und wie es unabhängig von aller historischen Kritik der Überlieferung jeder religiösen Erfahrung zugänglich und faßbar ist." Wobbermin, "Psychologie und Erkenntniskritik der religiöse Erfahrung," 349.

155. This, then, is why Wobbermin cannot agree with Kähler that the historic Christ cannot be separated from the biblical picture of him. The results of historical investigation of the New Testament texts finally demand such a distinction, in Wobbermin's opinion.

The significance of the picture of Christ for religious experience is determined by religious experience itself.[156] Historical research cannot detract from the value of this picture because the relationship between the historic figure of Christ and individual religious experience is primarily a historic, not historical, relationship. This relationship exists prior to historical inquiry into that picture and does not depend on the results of that inquiry for its value. It does not have to do with a historically [*historisch*] questionable figure from the past, but with a historic figure that is active and efficacious in the present: "For religious experience, the New Testament picture of Christ is an immediately given historic figure; it maintains its value and its reality through its *effect* on the moral-religious life."[157]

Again, the decisive question in this context is how this historic picture of Christ is defined in order for it to remain independent of historical criticism. Wobbermin suggests that individual events and statements in the life of Jesus must be subjected to historical criticism, but that the overall impression, the main and decisive traits of the picture (and therefore its effect or efficacy), are those stressed by the entire New Testament and which therefore are a result of the power of the historic figure of Christ himself. These main and decisive traits are the three "essential elements" uncovered or revealed by historical research of the New Testament texts.

The third trait is the most significant for Wobbermin, and it is this trait that most clearly distinguishes his position from Herrmann's, for example. The resurrection belongs to the essential picture of Christ both because Christian faith is always Easter faith in the risen Christ and because the resurrection is the basic presupposition of the entire New Testament. There are many important historical considerations to be taken into account, most importantly whether the resurrection can be considered a historical event at all. Wobbermin does not answer this question in his early work and only discusses this aspect of the question much later, in

---

156. This is the beginning of the so-called "religio-psychological circle" [*religionspsychologischer Zirkel*], which will be discussed in more detail in the next chapter.

157. "*Für die religiöse Erfahrung ist das neutestamentliche Christusbild eine unmittelbar gegebene geschichtliche Größe; sie bewährt ihren Wert und ihre Wirklichkeit durch ihre Wirkung auf das sittlich-religiöse Leben.*" Emphasis mine. Wobbermin further argues that this effect on the moral-religious life is the first and most important criterion for evaluating the New Testament picture of Christ from a religious perspective. Wobbermin, *Geschichte und Historie*, 75–76.

his systematic theology.[158] In *Geschichte und Historie* his primary concern is to clarify the essential traits of the historic picture of Christ found in the New Testament.

But there is a more basic question that must be raised in relation to the historic picture of Christ, namely, is it true? Wobbermin treats this problem in three parts: first, in terms of the actual question of truth; second, in terms of the question of the historic reality of the person of Jesus Christ; and third, in terms of the question of historicity or of historical comprehensibility.[159]

Is the New Testament picture of Jesus Christ actually true? The religious interest in the picture of Christ is concerned only with truth in the strictest, ultimate sense, i.e., as eternal truth. It is not primarily a question of truth as posed in the realm of scientific knowledge, which understands truth in terms of the highest possible probability. Rather, truth in this case is an expression of the conviction of faith that the picture of Christ is God's self-revelation. That the picture of Christ represents and embodies the self-revelation of God is always a conviction of faith, never of historical knowledge.[160]

The decisive question for Wobbermin is the question of value, specifically the value of this conviction of faith for the moral-religious life.[161] The Christian worldview is essentially and characteristically an ethical worldview because it finds its ground and basis in a personal, ethical God who is revealed in the person of Jesus Christ. This conviction raises the second, equally decisive question of the historic reality of the picture of Christ. For Christian faith the question of the reality of the picture of Christ is not simply collapsed into the question of its historicity or its historical comprehensibility. The key to this question is the central role of religious experience in Christian faith:

> For faith, the decisive criterion for the unique historic reality of Jesus Christ is the fact that the corresponding conviction of faith,

---

158. Wobbermin, *Wesen und Wahrheit*, 280ff.

159. Wobbermin, *Geschichte und Historie*, 77–78.

160. This recalls Wobbermin's criticism of Lessing's distinction between contingent and necessary truths, particularly Wobbermin's insistence that truth has an irreducibly eternal character. Unfortunately neither there nor here does he offer an adequate definition of eternal truth.

161. Ibid., 78ff. It is a question related to his third definition of *Geschichte*, as the interrelation of human beings as spiritual-moral beings in their development.

as it finds expression in communion with the exalted Lord, is the surest and most effective guarantee for the truth of the picture of Christ as the revelation of God. However, this is independent of the question of the historical comprehensibility of the person of Jesus Christ.[162]

Finally, for Wobbermin the question of historicity is ultimately irrelevant. It can be answered affirmatively or negatively on the basis of historical research, but it cannot serve as the basis for faith. Faith would cease to be faith were it based solely on the results of historical research. Although Wobbermin does not put it in such terms, there is here a distinction between the man Jesus of Nazareth *behind* the texts of the New Testament and the New Testament picture of him. The man Jesus of Nazareth *behind* the New Testament texts is a shadowy figure and can be known only by historical research (and even then very little can be known with any certainty). He becomes the historical Jesus of modern biography and historical research. The historic picture of Christ, as it confronts Christians in and from the New Testament, is the Christ of faith. That picture ultimately transcends the historical existence of Jesus of Nazareth. Faith is not primarily interested in the man Jesus of Nazareth; faith is primarily interested in the three "essential elements" of the picture of the historic Christ (particularly their effects and efficacy) handed down in the New Testament and the Christian tradition.

According to Wobbermin, Christian faith could withstand a negative answer to the question of the historical existence of Jesus of Nazareth because faith is not ultimately concerned with *Historie*, but with *Geschichte*. As he puts it, "the historicity – the historical comprehensibility – of Jesus is not an essential presupposition for the truth of the New Testament picture of Christ at all."[163] A faith that is based on the results of historical research into the question of the historicity of Jesus – whether that historicity is affirmed *or* denied – ceases to be faith:

162. "*Dem Glauben ist das entscheidende Kriterium für die geschichtliche Einzelwirklichkeit Jesu Christi der Umstand, daß die entsprechende Glaubensüberzeugung, wie sie sich im Verkehr mit dem erhöhten Herrn Ausdruck verschafft, die sicherste und wirkungskräftigste Bürgschaft für die Wahrheit des Christusbildes als der Offenbarung Gottes ist. Das ist aber unabhängig von der Frage nach der historischen Faßbarkeit der Person Jesu Christi.*" Ibid., 80.

163. "*Denn unumgängliche Voraussetzung für die Wahrheit des neutestamentlichen Christusbildes ist die Historizität – die historische Faßbarkeit – Jesu überhaupt nicht.*" Ibid., 84.

> To doubt the historicity of Jesus signifies historical arbitrariness. The question of the historicity of Jesus may and must be affirmed with the best historical conscience.
>
> But I may not and will not base my faith on the affirmative answer to this question. For then it rests on my historical understanding. And faith would cease to be faith if it were based on historical understanding.
>
> Thus, if necessary, faith would also be able calmly to accept a negative answer to the question of the historicity of Jesus Christ. *It does not stand or fall on the affirmative or negative answer to this question.*[164]

The only legitimate historical question in this matter, as Wobbermin sees it, is the question of the Christian tradition itself. Christian faith can trace itself back to the first Christians and throughout its history consistently refers to a historic personality. Because the historicity of Jesus of Nazareth is neither historically comprehensible nor theologically relevant, according to Wobbermin, the question of the unbroken succession of Christian self-consciousness leading back to the first Christians, in which the New Testament picture of Christ remains immediately present and available to religious experience, becomes the decisive question. But it is the question of *Geschichte*, not of *Historie*, that is finally decisive for Christian faith:

---

164. "*Die Historizität Jesu zu bezweifeln, bedeutet historische Willkür. Die Frage nach der Historizität Jesu darf und muß mit bestem historischem Gewissen bejaht werden. Aber meinen Glauben darf und will ich auf die Bejahung dieser Frage nicht gründen. Denn sie beruht auf meiner historischen Einsicht. Und der Glaube würde aufhören, Glaube zu sein, wenn er auf historische Einsicht gegründet würde. Also würde der Glaube auch die Verneinung der Frage nach der Historizität Jesu Christi gegebenenfalls ruhig hinnehmen können.* **Er steht und fällt nicht mit der Bejahung oder Verneinung dieser Frage.**" Ibid., 82. Emphasis in original. In light of this affirmation of the ultimate irrelevance of the historical comprehensibility of the existence of Jesus of Nazareth and what that means or does not mean for Christian faith, Wobbermin's criticisms of Drews come into sharper focus. While Drews concluded from the historical incomprehensibility of Jesus that he did not exist at all, Wobbermin concludes from the perspective and the presuppositions of Christian faith that the historicity of Jesus is not the primary question. The primary question is the efficacy of the New Testament picture of Christ, and that question must not be collapsed into the question of historical comprehensibility. Drews and Wobbermin both agree that the existence of Jesus of Nazareth cannot be demonstrated with absolute certainty by historical research, but they disagree on what that means for Christian faith. And that is the important question, at least for Wobbermin.

Geschichte und Historie

For the Christian religion is that religion, that form or highest phase of religious life, which came into existence under the impression of the picture of the person of Jesus Christ and which has its permanent norm in just this picture of the personal and salvific life of Jesus Christ, the norm namely for its individual forms of embodiment as well as the norm for its historic development.[165]

It is this question of the relationship between the historic picture of Christ and personal religious experience that will occupy Wobbermin for the better part of his career. The distinction between *Geschichte*, *Historie*, and *Wirkung* or *Wirksamkeit* serves as the foundation of the religio-psychological method that he developed in his three-volume systematic theology and defended in a series of *Streitschriften* directed against Karl Barth and dialectical theology. It is to this method, and more specifically to what Wobbermin called the "religio-psychological circle," that we now turn.

---

165. "*Denn die christliche Religion ist diejenige Religion, diejenige Form oder Stufenhöhe religiösen Lebens, die unter dem Eindruck des Personbildes Jesu Christi entstanden ist und an eben diesem Bilde des Person- und Heilandslebens Jesu Christi ihre bleibende Norm hat, die Norm nämlich für ihre individuellen Ausgestaltungsformen sowie die Norm für ihre geschichtliche Entwicklung.*" Ibid., 86.

3

Erfahrung und Glaube

Wobbermin's Religio-Psychological Circle and the Doctrine of Faith

SYSTEMATIC THEOLOGY ACCORDING TO THE RELIGIO-PSYCHOLOGICAL METHOD

The Religio-Psychological Method

WOBBERMIN APPROACHES SYSTEMATIC THEOLOGY from the perspective of the psychology of religion;[1] his *magnum opus*, published between 1913 and 1925, is entitled *Systematische Theologie nach religionspsychologischer Methode*. In the first volume he begins with a detailed presentation of the religio-psychological method from its origins in the work of Friedrich Schleiermacher and William James,[2] continues in

---

1. For a detailed study of Wobbermin's religio-psychological method, see Klünker, *Psychologische Analyse und theologische Wahrheit*. Klünker pays special attention to the psychological and logical structure of religious consciousness and the methodological significance of *Geschichte* and of the religio-psychological circle (Chapter 2) as well as Wobbermin's Schleiermacher research (Chapter 4).

2. Wobbermin, *Systematische Theologie nach religionspsychologischer Methode*, vol. 1, *Die religionspsychologische Methode in Religionswissenschaft und Theologie*. Wobbermin was particularly interested in the unique approaches to the psychology of religion in Germany, where the subject was typically approached from the perspective of systematic theology (examples of which are Friedrich Schleiermacher and Julius Kaftan) and the United States, where the subject was typically approached from the perspective of empirical psychology, exemplified by William James's 1901–1902 Gifford Lectures, published as *Varieties of Religious Experience*. Wobbermin published the first German translation of *Varieties* as *Die religiöse Erfahrung in ihrer Mannigfaltigkeit*. Also see Wobbermin's entry under "Religionspsychologie" in *RGG*[2] 4. For a study of James's influence on Wobbermin, see Newhall, "The Influence of William James on Georg Wobbermin's Psychology and

the second volume with a definition of the essence of religion,[3] and concludes with a study of the essence and truth of Christianity in the third volume.[4] Wobbermin's systematic theology is thoroughly indebted to Schleiermacher, whose influence is freely and constantly acknowledged.[5]

For Wobbermin, the religio-psychological method stands in opposition to three contemporary methodologies: dogmatic traditionalism, constructive rationalism, and historicism. In Schleiermacher Wobbermin discerns a conscious attempt to overcome both dogmatic traditionalism and constructive rationalism, while there is a less explicit opposition to historicism. Both a conscious orientation toward epistemological issues and a clear sense of the centrality of *Geschichte* are necessary to combat what Wobbermin considers to be the fatal flaws of these theological methods.[6]

It is important for Wobbermin to emphasize the inadequacy of a purely empirical psychological position (with which he is concerned his own method will be identified)[7] because empirical psychology, in his es-

---

Philosophy of Religion."

3. Wobbermin, *Systematische Theologie nach religionspsychologischer Methode*, vol. 2, *Das Wesen der Religion* [ET: *The Nature of Religion*].

4. Wobbermin, *Systematische Theologie nach religionspsychologischer Methode*, vol. 3, *Wesen und Wahrheit des Christentums*.

5. Wobbermin's intention in the first volume is to define the boundaries and procedures of the religio-psychological method in systematic theology. Referring primarily to the work of Schleiermacher and James, he intends to take up what he calls the "Schleiermacher-Jamesschen Problemstellung" by combining an interest in religious experience with the task of systematic theology. Wobbermin is ultimately dependent on Schleiermacher alone; it is Schleiermacher, not James, who was always a theologian first. Schleiermacher provides the foundation for Wobbermin's work in the psychology of religion and with the religio-psychological circle: see, for example, Chapter 18 of the first volume, which is entitled "Die Grundtendenz der Methode Schleiermachers als Leitmotiv des religionspsychologischen Verfahrens." Wobbermin, *Die religionspsychologische Methode*, 328ff.

6. Wobbermin, *Die religionspsychologische Methode*, 331.

7. In his *RGG*[2] entry on the psychology of religion, Wobbermin provides a brief overview of empirical psychology and its chief representatives. He credits G. Stanley Hall as the founder of this movement. Hall was a student of William James and spent time in Wilhelm Wundt's laboratory in Leipzig before serving as the first president of the American Psychological Association. Wobbermin also names Edwin D. Starbuck and James H. Leuba as important representatives of this school. Starbuck's *The Psychology of Religion* is, in Wobbermin's opinion, the seminal study produced by this movement. See Wobbermin, "Religionspsychologie."

timation, can provide neither an epistemological orientation nor a sense of history:

> Empirical psychology cannot prepare questions of value and worth (wherein the epistemological orientation must come to the surface), nor can it teach us to understand historic contexts and developments (wherein historical reflection must prove itself).[8]

Empirical psychology, insofar as it has to do with religious phenomena, can only be of preliminary significance for systematic theology and can never serve as the sole foundation for a properly theological method.

In opposition to such a one-sided empirical method, Wobbermin prefers Schleiermacher's use of psychology in the *Glaubenslehre* (which Wobbermin defines as "transcendental psychology"), especially insofar as this definition indicates a psychological analysis of the forms of experience on the basis of a transcendental question of the presuppositions of true religion.[9] It is this "transcendental psychology" that serves as the basis of Wobbermin's psychology of religion.[10]

---

8. "*Empirische Psychologie kann weder die Fragen nach Wert und Geltung vorbereiten – worin die erkenntniskritische Orientierung zutage treten muß, noch kann sie geschichtliche Zusammenhänge und Entwicklungen verstehen lehren – worin sich die geschichtliche Besinnung bewähren muß.*" Wobbermin, *Die religionspsychologische Methode*, 331. The importance of value and worth in history recalls Wobbermin's very brief appeal to Rickert's philosophy of history in *Geschichte und Historie*; however, there is no such appeal to Rickert in this context.

9. Wobbermin, *Die religionspsychologische Methode*, 351. On Schleiermacher's psychology and its significance for his *Glaubenslehre*, see Siegmund-Schultze, *Schleiermachers Psychologie in ihrer Bedeutung für die Glaubenslehre*.

10. Wobbermin briefly discusses the distinction between empirical and transcendental psychology in his *RGG*[2] entry on the psychology of religion. Empirical psychology, as Wobbermin defines it, is what is now commonly called experimental psychology, and it is an understanding of psychology that shares many methods and theoretical foundations with the "hard sciences." Wobbermin notes that this was the dominant psychological method in the United States in the late nineteenth and early twentieth century. Transcendental psychology, on the other hand, is more closely aligned with philosophy and the humanities, and Wobbermin notes that this was the common understanding of psychology in Germany (with some exceptions, notably Wilhelm Wundt, who is generally considered to be the father of modern experimental psychology). Wobbermin, "Religionspsychologie." Emil Brunner, in *Erlebnis, Erkenntnis und Glaube*, also treats both types of psychology at length, although he focuses on the American work on empirical psychology more than the German work on transcendental psychology, ultimately rejecting both approaches as irredeemably subjective. See Brunner, *Erlebnis, Erkenntnis und Glaube*, Chapter 2.

Erfahrung und Glaube

The emphasis on the transcendental character of the psychology of religion raises the related question of the logical structure of religious consciousness. Wobbermin suggests that the interest in truth is the most important element of the structure of religious consciousness. When he speaks of truth, he is referring specifically to faith's interest in "ultimate" (i.e. eternal or religious) truth rather than a purely rational or cognitive interest in truth.[11] It is the claim to ultimate truth that is constitutive for religious consciousness, and Wobbermin contends that this truth claim includes within it a reference to revelation. The idea of revelation is an expression of the claim of religious experience to truth.[12] In a material sense, the idea of revelation is the basis of religious consciousness; in a formal sense, it is the criterion of religious consciousness.[13] Ultimate truth is related to religious consciousness in general, but this relation is observed only in the individual:

> If the religious consciousness brings truth to expression, then this truth must communicate itself through the driving fundamental motives of religious consciousness, through its specifically religious motives.[14]

The Religio-Psychological Circle

According to Wobbermin, any comprehension of religious consciousness in general must be mediated through individual religious experience, or, more precisely, through the historic forms of expression of the religious consciousness. This claim forms the basis of the religio-psychological circle:

> We want to attain the criteria of pure religiosity for the purposes of evaluating and norming our own individual religious life on the basis of historic facts. By means of these historic facts, namely the forms of expression of religious life in the history of humanity, we can understand and interpret in no other way than according

---

11. This is consistent with Wobbermin's critique of Lessing's division of truth into different "classes." See the section on Lessing in Chapter 2.

12. Wobbermin, *Die religionspsychologische Methode*, 390.

13. Ibid., 389–390.

14. "*Denn wenn überhaupt – der religiösen Überzeugung zufolge – das religiöse Bewußtsein Wahrheit zum Ausdruck bringt, dann muß sich diese Wahrheit durch die treibenden Grundmotive des religiösen Bewußtseins, also durch seine spezifisch religiösen Motive, vermitteln.*" Ibid., 404.

to the requirement of our individual religious experience, of our individual religious consciousness.[15]

This circle – between historic fact and individual religious experience – is the foundation of Wobbermin's religio-psychological method, and he traces the methodological significance of the religio-psychological circle back to Schleiermacher's emphasis on religious self-consciousness and particularly his definition of Christian doctrines as accounts of the Christian religious affections brought to speech.[16] In this sense, then, one can speak of Wobbermin's theology as a *Bewußtseinstheologie* (a theology of consciousness). Here Wobbermin's religio-psychological method shows some similarities to Ernst Troeltsch's approach in his lectures on *Glaubenslehre*, in which Troeltsch contrasts his (and Schleiermacher's) theology of consciousness with a theology of facts [*Theologie der Tatsachen*]:

> We have a theology of consciousness instead of a theology of facts.... For the theology of consciousness that traces its roots to Schleiermacher, contact with these [facts] is never possible without subjective experience. They can be seen only through the veil [*Schleier*] of our inner life, never directly or concretely apart from the subject, but rather always only indirectly. But they are nevertheless really had, just because they are matters of subjective experience. "Subjective" here obviously does not mean that it depends on arbitrary taste; rather, here "subjective" means being saturated with God.[17]

Wobbermin certainly shares this concern to maintain the role of subjective experience in the apprehension of *Heilstatsachen*, and he attempts to do so by means of the religio-psychological circle between objective historic facts and personal religious experience. The religio-psychological circle thus lies at the heart of Wobbermin's theology, particularly in terms of his effort to maintain the interrelation of objectivity and subjectivity

---

15. "*Wir wollen zur Beurteilung und Normierung des eigenen religiösen Lebens auf Grund der geschichtlichen Tatbestände die Kriterien reiner Religiosität gewinnen, und wir können doch diese geschichtlichen Tatbestände, nämlich die Ausdrucksformen des religiösen Lebens in der Geschichte der Menschheit, nicht anders als nach Maßgabe unserer eigenen religiösen Erfahrung, also unseres eigenen religiösen Bewußtseins, verstehen und auslegen.*" Ibid., 405–6.

16. Schleiermacher, *Der christliche Glaube*, §15, 1:105 [ET: *The Christian Faith*, 76].

17. Troeltsch, *Glaubenslehre*, 132 [ET: *The Christian Faith*, 115]. See also Gerrish, "Ernst Troeltsch and the Possibility of a Historical Theology," 104, n. 14.

Erfahrung und Glaube

in his work.[18] The successful use of the religio-psychological circle to achieve this interrelation depends on precise definitions of theology as a discipline and of the Protestant understanding of faith.[19]

Wobbermin defines theology as "the science of the Christian religion in its significance for the religious life"[20] whose "uniting and unambiguous method" is that of the psychology of religion.[21] He draws deeply from Schleiermacher's work for his definition of theology. Schleiermacher rejected the method of the old Protestant *Loci*,[22] preferring instead to emphasize the religious affections in relation to God, on whom all existence is absolutely dependent.[23] Wobbermin explicitly applies Schleiermacher's

---

18. Edmond Grin, reviewing Wobbermin's systematic theology for the Swiss journal, *Revue de Théologie et de Philosophie*, puts this effort in terms of the union of several strands of thought reaching back to Schleiermacher: "Wobbermin's method is, in short, the union of history, psychology, and speculation [i.e., the philosophy of history and the philosophy of religion] with a distinctly religious accent. Here Wobbermin clearly possesses the spirit of Schleiermacher. But, better than the author of the *Reden*, he affirms the rights of history and the constant relationship between the subjective and the objective. Thus, again better than Schleiermacher, he keeps his theology safe from the reproach of subjectivism." Grin, "Une Théologie de la Synthèse," 283. It is interesting that Grin echoes Wobbermin's own misgivings about the extent of Schleiermacher's conscious attention to a historical interest in the *Glaubenslehre*. Whether that historical interest is enough to safeguard Wobbermin from "the reproach of subjectivism" is another matter, however, as it became a major line of attack against Wobbermin in Barth's critiques of his work. See Chapter 4 for more on Wobbermin's and Barth's debates on theological method and the legacy of Schleiermacher.

19. For more on Wobbermin's theological method, see Günter Irle's dissertation, "Theologie als Wissenschaft bei Georg Wobbermin."

20. "*Die (christliche) Theologie ist also die Wissenschaft von der christlichen Religion in ihrer Bedeutung für das religiöse Leben überhaupt.*" Wobbermin, *Die religionspsychologische Methode*, 107.

21. "*So kommt hier alles auf die Gewinnung einer einheitlichen und eindeutigen, der Natur der Sache entsprechenden Methode an.*" Ibid., vii.

22. See, e.g., the various editions of Philipp Melanchthon's *Loci*; Chemnitz, *Loci theologici* [ET: *Loci theologici*]; Gerhard, *Locorum theologicorum*; and Quenstedt, *Theologia didactico-polemica sive systema theologicum* [ET of the first three chapters: *The Nature and Character of Theology*]. For a dogmatics of this type written by a contemporary of Schleiermacher's, see Schmid, *Die Dogmatik der evangelisch-lutherischen Kirche* [ET: *The Dogmatics of the Evangelical Lutheran Church*].

23. Schleiermacher, *Der christliche Glaube*, §4, 1:23ff. [ET: *The Christian Faith*, 12ff.]. There are striking similarities between Schleiermacher's notion of "absolute dependence" and Paul Tillich's definition of the object of theology and faith as that which "concerns us ultimately." Tillich, *Systematic Theology*, 1:12. In *Dynamics of Faith*, Tillich also suggests that "ultimate concern" encompasses both the content of faith [*fides quae creditur*]

definition to the life of faith, arguing that Christian doctrines must be developed on the basis of the Christian life of faith, that is, out of the Christian relationship to God.[24] It is this emphasis on the human-divine relationship that underlies Wobbermin's religio-psychological method, and the contours of this method are best understood in its application to the doctrines of faith, revelation, Scripture, and Christ.

THE DOCTRINE OF FAITH IN LIGHT OF THE RELIGIO-PSYCHOLOGICAL METHOD

The Reciprocal Relationship between the fides quae creditur and the fides qua creditur

The relationship between the individual and God is the fundamental Christian relationship, and the Protestant understanding of faith expresses this fundamental relationship by assuming a specifically relational character. Wobbermin is particularly fond of Luther's exposition of the First Commandment, where Luther suggests that God and faith belong together.[25] Based on his reading of Luther, Wobbermin locates Christian faith between what he calls the twin "poles" of subjectivity and objectivity. Any movement away from one in favor of the other threatens to undermine the Protestant doctrine of faith. Movement toward God and away from individual religious experience threatens to become a pure objectivism divorced from any personal experience of God. Similarly, movement toward the individual and away from God threatens to become a pure subjectivism divorced from any reference to God outside the individual and his or her personal religious experience.

Wobbermin often expresses the relationship between the objective and subjective poles in terms of what he considers to be the twin dangers threatening the Protestant theology of his time. He warns of a

---

and the act of faith [*fides qua creditur*], meaning that being ultimately concerned can never be divorced from the object of ultimate concern. In other words, faith overcomes the split between subject and object: "The ultimate of the act of faith and the ultimate that is meant in the act of faith are one and the same." Tillich, *Dynamics of Faith*, 11. Wobbermin's position clearly fits within this tradition as well.

24. Wobbermin, *Die religionspsychologische Methode*, 401.

25. Luther, "Der große Katechismus," 560 [ET: "The Large Catechism," 386]. Wobbermin wrote two essays on this theme in Luther: "Die Frage nach Gott in Luthers großem Katechismus" and "Wie gehören für Luther Gott und Glaube zuhaufe?"

Erfahrung und Glaube

temptation toward what he calls a "one-sided historicism" [*einseitiger Historismus*][26] on the objectivizing side and a "one-sided psychologism" [*einseitiger Psychologismus*] [27] on the subjectivizing side.[28] Historicism, as Wobbermin defines it, represents a purely objective understanding of faith, particularly as it attempts to base faith solely on "objective" historic or historical facts;[29] psychologism represents a purely subjective understanding of faith, particularly as it attempts to base faith solely on the content of individual religious experience. Both historicism and psychologism, in Wobbermin's estimation, threaten the Protestant doctrine of faith by attempting to provide some foundation for Christian faith in addition to God in Christ. To put it in more classical terms, both historicism and psychologism violate the Reformation *sola fide*, the doctrine of justification by faith alone.

Wobbermin traces the roots of "one-sided historicism" to the nineteenth-century "Life of Jesus" movement,[30] but he refers specifically to the

---

26. For more on the broad intellectual movement of historicism, see, e.g., Rust, "Historismus"; Davaney, *Historicism*; Howard, *Religion and the Rise of Historicism*; Wittkau-Horgby, *Historismus*; Blanke and Rüsen, eds., *Von der Aufklärung zum Historismus*; and Fülling, *Geschichte als Offenbarung*.

27. For more on psychologism, see, e.g., Wobbermin, *Richtlinien evangelischer Theologie zur Überwindung der gegenwärtigen Krisis*, 3ff.; Wobbermin, "Im Kampf gegen Historismus und Psychologismus" [The original Swedish is available as *Den evangeliska teologins kris och dess övervinnande*]; and Wobbermin, "Psychologismus."

28. Emil Brunner reaches the same conclusion concerning the twin dangers of psychologism and historicism in his 1921 study, *Erlebnis, Erkenntnis und Glaube* (citations are to the second and third editions, published in 1923): "The religious and theological thought of the last decades stands under the signs of historicism and psychologism. These are the last remnants of that movement, begun in the Renaissance and openly pursued by the Enlightenment, which we may name in one word as *subjective-anthropological*. It is a series of variations of world-historic dimensions over the theme, 'The human being is the measure of all things.'" Brunner, *Erlebnis, Erkenntnis und Glaube*, 1. Despite similar appraisals of their contemporary theological situation, Brunner and Wobbermin propose radically different strategies for addressing the dangers of historicism and psychologism, Wobbermin by means of a religio-psychological approach that builds on the best of the nineteenth century and Brunner by means of a clean break with the liberal tradition in favor of the new dialectical theology.

29. The pure objectivity of historical facts is an illusion, according to the nature of historical research. The results of historical research remain relative and hypothetical and are always based, in part, on the interpretation of the historian, who is also a historic subject.

30. See Schweitzer, *Geschichte der Leben-Jesu-Forschung*, on the major works of the 19th-century "Life of Jesus" movement.

Ritschlians as representatives of the danger of such a one-sided historicism.[31] Ritschl himself escapes accusation, but his followers, most notably Adolf Harnack, are accused of moving beyond Ritschl's appropriate interest in history to a full-fledged historicism. Wobbermin refers to the Ritschlian attempt to base all theological work on historical research and the attempt to answer any and all theological questions with the results of that research as the first step on the path toward a one-sided historicism. The most important example of this type of theology, as Wobbermin sees it, are Harnack's lectures on the essence of Christianity.[32] In these lectures Harnack claims, *as a historian*, to have answered sufficiently and exhaustively the final questions of the essence and truth of Christianity. Such confidence in the scientific historical method ignores the inherent probability and contingency of the results of historical research and finally bases faith on the judgments of historians and not on the immediate presence of the historic Christ, resulting in what Kähler had called an *Autoritätsglauben*.

Wobbermin's own relationship to historicism is rather ambiguous. In many respects he clearly belongs to the movement generally called "historicism," by which is meant a methodological attention to historical questions and an acknowledgement of the historicity of existence in general and of human culture, institutions, and knowledge in particular. When Wobbermin refers to a "one-sided historicism," however, he is confining his criticism to those theologians who attempt to answer the fundamental questions of the Christian faith – even to the point of providing the basis for Christian faith itself – by means of scientific historical research.[33]

---

31. Wobbermin, *Richtlinien*, 2–3.

32. Harnack, *Das Wesen des Christentums* [ET: *What is Christianity?*].

33. Some of this ambiguity may be related to the origins of the term "historicism." According to Calvin Rand, while the movement known as Historicism originated in the nineteenth century, the term itself was not commonly known until the 1920s through the writings of Ernst Troeltsch, specifically his essay, "Die Krisis des Historismus" and the collection of essays comprising the third volume of his collected works: *Gesammelte Schriften*, vol. 3, *Der Historismus und seine Probleme*. Rand suggests that there are two closely related but distinct meanings of the term *Historismus*. It is a specific way of historical thinking that can refer either to a methodology or to a *Weltanschauung*, and Rand suggests that this ambiguity has been present with the term since its origin. See Rand, "Two Meanings of Historicism." Wobbermin used the term pejoratively at the same time it was being popularized by Troeltsch, and it is unclear whether Wobbermin intended his use of the term to correspond to Troeltsch's and, by extension, to what has become the

Erfahrung und Glaube

While a one-sided historicism is an attempt to base faith on historical facts as provided by scientific historical research (emphasizing the objective side of faith), a one-sided psychologism is an attempt to base faith on the results of an empirical-psychological analysis of religious phenomena and especially of religious experience.[34] Wobbermin traces the roots of this one-sided psychologism to misunderstandings of Schleiermacher's psychology of religion, specifically his emphasis on intuition, feeling, and religious consciousness.[35] He refers to Schleiermacher's *Glaubenslehre* as a particularly successful example of a systematic theology that makes good use of the perspective of psychology while remaining faithful to the Protestant understanding of faith. The key to this faithfulness, as Wobbermin understands it, is Schleiermacher's insight that the object of faith and the act of faith stand in an interdependent relationship.[36]

---

common understanding of the term.

34. Wobbermin, *Richtlinien*, 3.

35. See Schleiermacher, *Der christliche Glaube*, §4 for his discussion of feeling and self-consciousness, and the *Speeches* (especially the first (1799) and second (1806) editions) for a sustained discussion of feeling and intuition within his philosophy of religion. For the 1799 edition, see Schleiermacher, "Über die Religion," in *Friedrich Daniel Ernst Schleiermacher Kritische Gesamtausgabe*, vol. 1, pt. 2, 185–326. For the 1806/1831 edition, see Schleiermacher, "Über die Religion," in *Friedrich Daniel Ernst Schleiermacher Kritische Gesamtausgabe*, vol. 1, pt. 12, 1–321.

36. Schleiermacher, *Der christliche Glaube*, §14. Here Schleiermacher defines faith in Christ as well as the role of experience and testimony: "In the same sense we spoke above of faith in God, which was nothing other than the certainty of absolute dependence as such, i.e., as conditioned by a being outside us and expressing our relationship to the same being. The faith of which we are now speaking is a purely factual certainty [*rein tatsächliche Gewißheit*], but a certainty of a completely internal fact [*einer vollkommen innerlichen Tatsache*]. It cannot exist in an individual until there is in him or her, through an impression he or she receives from Christ, a beginning, even if only infinitesimal, a real premonition [*Ahnung*] of the abolishment of the state of being in need of redemption. Here the expression 'faith in Christ,' however, as faith in God before, relates this state as effect to Christ as cause. . . . So from the beginning only those have attached themselves to Christ and to his new community whose religious self-consciousness had taken the form of being in need of redemption and who have now become certain in themselves of the redemptive power of Christ. So that the more strongly both appeared in anyone, the more one could also help elicit the same inner experience in others through the representation of the fact, which includes the description of Christ and his activity. Those in whom this now happened became believers, the others did not. Herein has consisted the essence of all direct Christian proclamation ever since, which can always only take the form of testimony, namely testimony of one's own experience, which shall stimulate in the others the desire to have the same experience." Ibid., §14.1, 1:95–96 [ET: *The Christian Faith*, 68–69].

Wobbermin prefers to express this relationship in classical terms: the understanding of the *fides quae creditur* (the content of faith) is conditioned by the understanding of the *fides qua creditur* (the act of faith) and *vice versa*.[37]

This insight of Schleiermacher's, Wobbermin suggests, can be traced back to Luther, specifically to his exposition of the First Commandment in the Large Catechism.[38] For Luther, God and faith belong together. Luther asks, "What does it mean to have a god, or, what is God?" His answer emphasizes the interdependence of the objective and subjective elements of faith:

> To have a god is nothing other than to trust and believe in that one from the heart . . . the trust and faith of the heart alone make both God and idol. If your faith and trust are right, then your God is the true one, and in turn where your trust is false and wrong, there you do not have the true God. For the two belong together [*gehören zuhaufe*], faith and God. Anything on which your heart relies and depends, I say, that is really your god.[39]

Wobbermin considers Luther's answer to the question of God to be decisive for the Protestant doctrine of faith, particularly in terms of its

---

37. Wobbermin, *Richtlinien*, 22.

38. B. A. Gerrish defines Wobbermin's theological project as an attempt to steer the Protestant theology of the 1930s back to Luther by way of Schleiermacher. Gerrish, "Doctor Martin Luther," 53. Gerrish's definition is consistent with Wobbermin's own self-understanding of his place within the Protestant tradition, which will be the theme of Chapter 4. Wobbermin is convinced that Schleiermacher is the theological successor to Luther, so much so that Calvin (to whom Schleiermacher is equally indebted, if not more so) never appears in Wobbermin's discussions of Schleiermacher. By ignoring Calvin, Wobbermin misses the opportunity to retrieve an important element of Calvin's thought that could support his intention to overcome the radical division between objectivity and subjectivity, namely Calvin's emphasis in the *Institutes* on two-fold knowledge (knowledge of self and knowledge of God). Wobbermin's ignorance of Calvin can perhaps be attributed to the fact that Wobbermin very self-consciously stood within the Lutheran theological tradition and read Schleiermacher solely through Lutheran eyes. Nevertheless, the question of the extent of Schleiermacher's indebtedness to Luther is not the primary question in this instance. The primary question is how *Wobbermin* understood Schleiermacher to stand in a line leading back to Luther, and how Wobbermin based his own work on what he consistently called the "Luther-Kant-Schleiermacher line."

39. Luther, "Der große Katechismus," 560 [ET: "The Large Catechism," 386]. The word "zuhaufe" in modern German is typically spelled "zuhause" or "zu Hause," which literally means "at home."

relational quality. To have the true God is not merely to know that such a being exists, nor is it merely to "feel" or experience an Other within oneself. To have the true God is, as Luther puts it, to place one's whole heart and confidence in God alone, to grasp and cling to God with the whole heart.[40]

Wobbermin anticipates misunderstandings of this claim to interdependence and rejects any attempt to understand it in ontological terms:

> This is not interdependence in an ontological sense, not that the existence of God depends on human faith – it is interdependence only for us: God gives himself to us in his revelation to be grasped only through the mediation of faith – and accordingly we approach God only on the way of faith.[41]

Put another way, faith as subjective attitude (*fides qua creditur*) is rightly understood only in terms of its relation to its objective content (*fides quae creditur*). The objective content is the necessary basis of faith, its *conditio sine qua non*.[42] The objective is primary and the subjective is secondary in their interdependent relationship. Nevertheless, the transcendent God is comprehensible only by subjective faith.

To avoid any sense of ontological dependence, Luther includes the objective emphasis when he claims that there is no way to God other than that which God provides. Any attempt to reach God solely from the human side inevitably leads to idolatry and works-righteousness. For Luther, faith and the divine promise are always interrelated: *promissio et fides sunt relativa*.[43] There can be no faith without the divine promise, and, likewise, where there is no faith the divine promise is meaningless.

---

40. Ibid., 560 [ET, 386–87].

41. "*Die Wechselbeziehung freilich nicht im ontologischen Sinne, nicht so, daß die Existenz Gottes vom Glauben der Menschen abhinge. Wohl aber die Wechselbeziehung für uns: Gott gibt sich uns in seiner Offenbarung nur zu fassen durch Vermittlung des Glaubens – und demgemäß kommen wir an Gott nur heran auf dem Wege des Glaubens.*" Wobbermin, *Richtlinien*, 21–22.

42. Ibid., 120.

43. Luther, "Diui Pauli apostoli ad Romanos Epistola," 45 [ET: "Lectures on Romans," 39]. As Karl Barth notes (see p. 145, n. 95), Wobbermin consistently misquotes Luther at this point. Wobbermin quotes Luther as saying "fides et promissio sunt correlativa," when Luther actually has "relativa." The English translation available in *LW* 25, however, translates "relativa" as "interrelated," a meaning closer to Wobbermin's misquotation. Wobbermin suggests that this sentence could also read, "Verbum dei et fides sunt correlativa." Wobbermin, *Wort Gottes und evangelischer Glaube*, 6.

Wobbermin refers to the role of personal experience in Luther's thought as an important foundation for his own psychology of religion. As Luther claims in *Temporal Authority*:

> Just as little as one can go to hell or heaven for me can one believe or not believe for me, and just as little as one can open or close heaven or hell to me can one lead me to belief or unbelief.[44]

Personal religious experience, therefore, is an essential element of faith. This personal religious experience, Wobbermin suggests, is to be understood specifically as experience that presupposes faith as a gracious gift of God.[45] Such faith is characterized by obedience: the Protestant doctrine of faith includes within it both the experience of faith and the obedience of faith. Faith, in the Protestant sense, is not merely assent to an external authority, nor is it merely internal experience without an external point of reference. The object of faith is God alone, accessible by means of God's revelation in history. To put it in more classical terms, the point of contact between obedient faith and the one true God is the divine revelation in history: the Word of God.

Wobbermin's discussion of the doctrine of faith is based almost entirely on Luther, who emphasized both the subjective, experiential and the objective, external elements of faith. Like Luther, Wobbermin refers to the divine revelation, the Word of God, as the mediating element between the believer and God. Recalling Luther's condemnation of the so-called "Enthusiasts" [*Schwärmer*], Wobbermin rejects any attempt to isolate revelation solely within personal experience without any external point of reference. Likewise, again recalling Luther, he also rejects any attempt so to objectivize revelation that faith becomes nothing more than cognitive assent to certain facts. Revelation, he argues, is an objective event that occurs within history and is directed toward the individual subject standing within history, and for this reason a clear and strict distinction between *Geschichte* and *Historie* is essential for a proper understanding of the Protestant doctrine of faith.[46]

---

44. Luther, "Von weltlicher Oberkeit," 264 [ET: "Temporal Authority," 108].
45. Wobbermin, *Richtlinien*, 26.
46. Ibid., 128–29.

Erfahrung und Glaube
Fides historica and fides iustificans
in Light of the Distinction between Geschichte and Historie

The distinction between *Geschichte* and *Historie* first appeared in the work of Martin Kähler. Its roots, however, can be traced back to the Reformation, most notably to Article XX (*De bonis operibus*) of the Augsburg Confession:

> People are also reminded that this term "faith" here does not signify only historical knowledge [*significet tantum historiae notitiam*], such as the ungodly and the devils have, but it signifies faith that believes not only the history but also the effect of the history [*non tantum historiam, sed effectum historiae*], namely, this article of the forgiveness of sins, that is, that we have grace, righteousness, and forgiveness of sins through Christ.[47]

There is a clear correspondence between *fides historica* and *Historie* on the one hand and *fides iustificans* and *Geschichte* on the other, as

---

47. "Confessio Augustana," 79 [ET: "The Augsburg Confession," 56]. Melanchthon later refers to Augustine's distinction between faith and knowledge: "Augustine also reminds his readers in this way about the word 'faith' and teaches that in the Scriptures the word 'faith' is to be understood not as knowledge [*non pro notitia*], such as the ungodly have, but as trust [*fiducia*] that consoles and encourages terrified minds." Ibid., 79–80 [ET, 56]. The German text is similar: "We must also explain that we are not talking here about the faith possessed by the devils and the ungodly, who also believe the historical facts [*Historien glauben*] that Christ suffered and was raised from the dead. But we are talking about true faith, which believes that we obtain grace and forgiveness of sin through Christ. All who know that through Christ they have a gracious God thus know God, call upon him, and are not without God, like the heathen. For the devil and the ungodly do not believe this article about the forgiveness of sin. Therefore they are enemies of God, cannot call upon him, and do not hope for anything good from him. And as has now been indicated, Scripture talks about faith but does not mean by faith knowledge such as the devils and the ungodly have. For Hebrews 11 teaches that faith is not only a matter of historical knowledge [*Historien wissen*], but a matter of having confidence in God, to receive his promise. Augustine also reminds us that we should understand the word 'faith' in Scripture to mean confidence in God, that God is gracious to us; it does not mean such historical knowledge [*Historien wissen*] as the devils also have." "Die augsburgische Konfession," 79–80. In the most recent English edition of *The Book of Concord*, the translators of the Augsburg Confession choose to translate "Historien wissen" alternately as "know the stories" or "knowledge of the stories" and "historical knowledge." See "The Augsburg Confession," 56. The previous edition of the Augsburg Confession is more consistent, where "Historien glauben" is translated as "believe the history" and "Historien wissen" as "knowledge of historical events." See "The Augsburg Confession," in Tappert, ed., *The Book of Concord*, 44–45. See Appendix 1 for more texts from the Lutheran Reformation on the distinction between *fides historica* and *fides iustificans*.

Wobbermin uses these terms. Neither pair is synonymous,[48] but there are important similarities between each pair of concepts. *Fides historica* is little more than assent to historical facts – that Jesus was born, crucified, buried, etc. There is nothing in this type of assent to historical facts to indicate that such belief constitutes saving faith. It is, to use Kähler's term again, mere *Autoritätsglauben*.[49] Such belief does not include obedience or the personal experience of divine grace characteristic of the Protestant doctrine of faith. Such belief, as Melanchthon suggests, can be held by disinterested historians, the ungodly, and even "the devils."

Fides iustificans, on the other hand, requires the correlative relationship between the divine promise and human faith, between the objective content of faith and the subjective act of faith. This faith is not acquired (neither by historical research nor by any other human work), but is a free gift of the gracious God. That Melanchthon treats this topic in the article on good works is especially significant, particularly when read alongside Wobbermin's essay on the distinction between *Geschichte* and *Historie*. In that essay, Wobbermin distinguishes between the acquisition of relative historical truth [*Historie*] on the one hand and *Geschichte*, which is simply given [*gegeben*], simply there, on the other.[50] In the context of Article

---

48. The impossibility of a simple equation of the two sets of terms is further supported by the fact that "historical consciousness" is a product of the eighteenth century. Joachim Knape argues that the category "*Geschichte*" is unknown to Melanchthon. Melanchthon only knows the category "*historia*." Knape, "Melanchthon und die Historien," 112–113.

49. Wobbermin uses the term *Autoritätsglauben* in his entry on Schleiermacher in the *RGG²* to define *fides historica* or *fides implicita* in a comparison of Schleiermacher's dogmatics with Catholic or "catholicizing" dogmatics: "It is the insight already gained by Schleiermacher that in evangelical circles every statement of so-called dogmatics is really in the strictest sense a proposition *of faith* and thus brings the Christian conviction of faith to expression and itself bears the character of a conviction of faith. Other types of statements have no place at all in evangelical dogmatics, and thus no statements of purely theoretical knowledge, be they of a historical or rational or speculative type. Schleiermacher thereby brings Luther's evangelical concept of faith to bear on theological work. Also the expression 'Christian religious affections' primarily emphasizes precisely that insight and claim. Just these Christian convictions of faith are meant which have an objective content, which refer to God and the revelation of God, which have God and the revelation of God as their object. The antithesis that Schleiermacher has in mind is always one of dogmas in the Catholic or catholicizing sense, of dogmas that have mere *faith in authority* (*fides historica* or *fides implicita*) as their correlate." Wobbermin, "Schleiermacher," *RGG²* 5:175. Emphasis in original.

50. Here again, Wobbermin's implicit but unarticulated distinction between *Geschichte* and its *Wirkung* or *Wirksamkeit* comes into play, and a more explicit articulation of this distinction would help Wobbermin clarify both his understanding of history

XX of the Augsburg Confession, *fides historica* is likewise something that is acquired or achieved solely by human work and therefore cannot be saving faith. *Fides iustificans*, however, is a gift [*Gabe* or *Geschenk*] of God to the human being, undeserved and unearned. It is given solely in and through *Geschichte* to historic individuals by means of divine revelation.

Wobbermin suggests that an emphasis on salvation history underlies Melanchthon's distinction between *fides historica* and *fides iustificans*:

> This radical rejection of *fides historica* has for a presupposition and a condition the acknowledgment of the salvation history of God with humanity, which culminated in Jesus Christ. . . .
>
> True faith refers to salvation history, faith which – to speak once again with the Augsburg Confession – believes that "we attain grace and forgiveness of sins through Christ, and which now knows that it has a gracious God through Christ, and thus knows God, calls on him, and, unlike the heathen, is not without God."[51]

Melanchthon relates *fides iustificans* to *Heilsgeschichte*, the history of God's saving activity culminating in Jesus Christ. The saving effects of *Heilsgeschichte* are not provided by historical research, and mere *Historien wissen* or *notitia historiae* is insufficient for obtaining "grace and forgiveness." Saving faith is related to *Heilsgeschichte* because in that history (recorded in Scripture and handed down by the church) the revelation of God is present, effective, and accessible to men and women of every time and place.[52]

---

and his appropriation of Melanchthon's distinction between *fides historica* and *fides iustificans*. Melanchthon's definition of *fides iustificans* as faith that believes the effects of the history [*effectum historiae*] is precisely the point Wobbermin tries to make in *Geschichte und Historie*, a point that would be much clearer had he made a further explicit distinction between *Geschichte* and its *Wirkung* or *Wirksamkeit*. That distinction, however, never comes fully to expression in that essay, and therefore Wobbermin's appeals to Melanchthon never come as sharply into focus as they might otherwise have done.

51. "*Diese radikale Verwerfung der* fides historica *hat aber zum Komplement, ja zur Voraussetzung und Bedingung, die Anerkenntnis der in Jesus Christus gipfelnden Heilsgeschichte Gottes mit den Menschen. . . . Auf diese Heilsgeschichte bezieht sich der wahre Glaube, der – um nochmals mit der Augustana zu reden – glaubt, daß 'wir durch Christum Gnade und Vergebung der Sünden erlangen, und der nun weiß, daß er einen gnädigen Gott durch Christum hat, kennet also Gott, rufet ihn an, und ist nicht ohne Gott wie die Heiden.*'" Wobbermin, *Richtlinien*, 131.

52. On revelation, history and faith in Melanchthon's work, see Haendler, "Offenbarung – Geschichte – Glaube." Haendler treats Melanchthon's distinction between *fides historica* and *fides iustificans*, or what Haendler prefers to call *notitia* and *fiducia*, respectively, with particular reference to the Augsburg Confession and the various editions

FAITH AT THE INTERSECTION OF HISTORY AND EXPERIENCE

*Word and Faith: Scripture, Revelation,
and Experience in the Doctrine of Faith*

For Wobbermin faith and history meet precisely at the point of divine revelation. *Heilsgeschichte* must be defined in such a way, therefore, as to allow the fullest possible freedom for the divine revelation. Protestant scholastic orthodoxy failed to allow this freedom by limiting salvation history to what Wobbermin calls "dogmatically and historically narrowed scholastic doctrine."[53] In order to eliminate any temptation to equate sal-

---

of Melanchthon's *Loci* (see Appendix 1). He argues that the key to Melanchthon's concept of faith is revelation (understood as the Word of God, the Word of Scripture, and the Word of proclamation), rather than the anthropological and psychological or the pneumatological aspects of faith. Haendler suggests that in Melanchthon's work there is an emphasis on the relationship between *fides historica* (*notitia*) and *fides iustificans* (*fiducia misericordiae*) rather than a strict distinction; for Melanchthon, faith always includes a cognitive or an intellectual quality. Where such knowledge becomes trust in the mercy of God for the sake of Christ, there is true faith (*fides iustificans*). Where such knowledge remains mere *notitia*, unmoved by grace to appropriate the effect of the history [*effectum historiae*], true faith is lacking. "Melanchthon formulates this fact in such a way that he defines *fiducia misericordiae* (in which *notitia historiae* becomes saving faith) as a reference to the effect of that history [*effectus jener Geschichte*] (as its *telos*), to which that knowledge is related. Faith orients itself toward the history of Christ [*historia Christi*] and in it on the forgiveness of sins as the goal, the *causa finalis*, the effect of this history [*effectus dieser Geschichte*]; or, to take up the earlier expression: it orients itself toward Christ and his history [*Geschichte*] and therein on the benefits of Christ." Ibid., 69. In terms of salvation history, "faith must see, understand, and believe this history as salvation history. If it does not, it mistakes it and it does not become salvation history for it [*nicht zur Heils-, sondern zur Unheilsgeschichte*]." Ibid., 68. For a more extensive discussion of *notitia historiae*, *fides iustificans*, and the relationship between faith and salvation history in Melanchthon's theology, see Haendler's dissertation, published as *Wort und Glaube bei Melanchthon*. Haendler also maintains that the distinction between *fides historica* and *fides iustificans* is analogous to the distinction between law and gospel and between letter and spirit. He refers this discussion to an article by Eberhard Buder on *fides historica* and *fides iustificans* in the context of the Augsburg Confession. Buder maintains that the history of Christ, because it is directed first toward knowledge and not toward faith, cannot be called "gospel" in the strictest sense. Haendler rejects this interpretation as missing Melanchthon's point that faith always includes the intellectual or cognitive assent to the historical fact of the earthly Jesus, even as it moves beyond mere knowledge to saving faith. Haendler, "Offenbarung – Geschichte – Glaube," 67. See Buder, "Fides iustificans und fides historica." Karl Barth would agree with Haendler that faith as trust cannot be isolated from faith as assent and knowledge as Melanchthon understands those terms, and Barth makes precisely this point in his critique of Wobbermin's references to Luther and Melanchthon in his doctrine of faith. Wobbermin, conversely, would find agreement with Buder's position. See pp. 146–147.

53. Wobbermin, *Richtlinien*, 131.

Erfahrung und Glaube

vation history with such limited doctrine, Wobbermin prefers to speak of the "biblical history of religion" as that which serves Christian faith as salvation history. The biblical history of religion serves this function because in and through it one finds the revelation of God present for those who read Scripture or hear it proclaimed:

> That Word which God has spoken in the past to men and women becomes present when faith grasps it as the revelation of God.
> Therefore everything for evangelical faith finally depends on Holy Scripture, because the Word of God becomes present to it through Holy Scripture.[54]

Here Wobbermin makes an important distinction between Scripture and the Word of God. The two must not simply be equated as if there were no distinction; the Word of God is contained *in* Scripture, but Scripture is not therefore simply identical to it. The Word of God always remains prior and superior to Scripture, which serves as both the document *of* and the witness *to* the divine revelation. This distinction is especially important in light of modern historical criticism of the Bible, which undermined confidence in the authority of Scripture by the results of its investigation of biblical texts.[55] Two basic alternatives emerged in light of criticism of the Bible: either reject the methods of historical criticism out of hand as secular encroachment on a sacred text, or accept the results of historical criticism of the Bible and reconfigure the doctrine of revelation in light of those results. Roman Catholic and Protestant confessional and orthodox theologians and biblical scholars generally chose the former option, while many of the so-called "mediating theologians" and liberal theologians and biblical scholars chose the latter option. The former group maintained various versions of the doctrine of verbal inspiration, which referred not

---

54. "*Das Wort, das Gott in der Vergangenheit zu Menschen geredet hat, wird zur Gegenwart, wenn der Glaube es als Offenbarung Gottes ergreift. Auf die Heilige Schrift kommt deshalb für den evangelischen Glaube schließlich alles an, weil ihm durch sie das Wort Gottes vergegenwärtigt wird.*" Ibid., 132. "Biblical history of religion" is another term that Wobbermin introduces without offering anything more than a very brief definition. In this case, he simply states that the biblical history of religion of the Old and New Testaments serves Christian faith as salvation history. ["*Dem christlichen Glauben gilt allerdings die biblische Religionsgeschichte Alten und Neuen Testaments als Heilsgeschichte.*"] Ibid., 131. There is no explanation of just what constitutes the biblical history of religion.

55. For two general studies of historical criticism in English, see Harrisville and Sundberg, *The Bible in Modern Culture* and Baird, *History of New Testament Research*.

only to the Bible as a whole but also to individual words and phrases of the Bible as directly and infallibly inspired by God. Those who affirmed the verbal inspiration of Scripture argued that, because Protestant Christianity is irreducibly biblical (as Luther himself maintained), the Bible must be the unconditional authority for Protestant Christianity. The Bible assumes this unconditional authority because God, who is absolutely unconditioned, speaks God's Word in the Bible. Wobbermin suggests that to this point the doctrine of verbal inspiration is grounded in sound Protestant principles. The problem, as he sees it, is the theological use of Scripture in Protestant orthodoxy. These theologians, he argues, understood the Christian faith to be a system of doctrines derived directly from Scripture as itself the unconditional, literal Word of God. The result, he claims, is decidedly un-Protestant: the Bible becomes, in his words, a "paper pope" [*papierenen Papst*]:

> The decisive mistake is that the unconditional authority that must be ascribed to Holy Scripture is understood as external and mechanical, so external and mechanical that it becomes completely parallel to Roman inerrancy, so that the significance of the personal conviction and experience of faith disappears.[56]

In contrast to the older Protestant orthodoxy, Wobbermin ascribes significant importance to Scripture as testimony.[57] In an essay on the Word of God and Protestant faith, he argues that God's Word and faith are not merely conceptually related, but stand in an *essential* relationship to one another.[58] There is a Word of God, strictly speaking, only for faith. In other words, the Word of God is comprehensible *qua* Word of God only by faith. Conversely, faith is saving faith (*fides iustificans*) only when it is oriented toward the Word of God. Wobbermin refers to Luther's commentary on Rom 10:17[59] and the second Smalcald Article, where Luther

---

56. "*Die Inspirationslehre macht nun die Bibel tatsächlich, wie man scherzhaft gesagt hat, zu einen papierenen Papst. Der entscheidende Fehler aber ist der, daß die unbedingte Autorität, die der Heiligen Schrift allerdings zugeschrieben werden muß, äußerlich-mechanisch gefaßt wird, so äußerlich-mechanisch, daß sie nun eben eine volle Parallele zur römischen Unfehlbarkeit wird, daß also die Bedeutung der eigenpersönlichen Glaubensüberzeugung und Glaubenserfahrung verloren geht.*" Wobbermin, *Richtlinien*, 133.

57. Ibid., 140.

58. Wobbermin, *Wort Gottes*, 5.

59. Luther, "Romanos," 102–4 [ET: *Romans*, 92].

argues that God's Word alone shall establish articles of faith,[60] to support his contention that faith must be oriented toward God's Word alone.

Although faith and the Word of God stand in a correlative relationship, the Word of God is prior to faith in an ontological sense.[61] God's Word must be spoken before it is grasped by faith, and God's Word is spoken concretely in and through the Bible. For Protestant faith, then, the Bible is the document of the divine revelation. Protestant orthodoxy also affirmed that the Bible is God's revelation, but orthodox theologians emphasized revelation as a system of doctrine and simply equated Scripture and the Word of God without distinguishing between the two. In opposition to this primarily intellectual understanding of revelation, Wobbermin suggests that God's revelation is directed toward the entire existence of the human being, so that revelation is to be understood existentially rather than intellectually or cognitively.[62] The Word of God meets men and women in their personal existence and makes of them new creatures, initiating a "complete conversion of the human being."[63] The divine revelation is not something merely past, completed in ancient events and recorded in Scripture. For Wobbermin, the divine revelation remains efficacious beyond the historic events in which it was originally expressed: "it is rather a personal salvific act of God occurring throughout all history."[64]

The content of God's revelation is Jesus Christ, the Word made flesh,[65] who, as a historic figure, remains active and efficacious throughout history. In addition to its status as the document of the divine revelation (a status that is always primary for Wobbermin), Scripture is also a witness to this original revelation in Jesus Christ, a revelation that is not fixed in

---

60. "Die schmalkaldische Artikel," 420 [ET: "The Smalcald Articles," 304].

61. Wobbermin, Wort Gottes, 9.

62. Wobbermin, Richtlinien, 105.

63. "Sie will den Menschen in der ganzen Existenz seines persönlichen Lebens treffen, eine völlige Umwandlung desselben herbeiführen und aus dem Menschen eine neue Kreatur machen." Wobbermin, Wort Gottes, 15.

64. "Sie ist vielmehr das durch die ganze Geschichte hin erfolgende persönliche Heilswirken Gottes." Ibid., 15. Wobbermin's position here is not unlike that of Wolfhart Pannenberg on salvation history and universal history. See, e.g. Pannenberg, "Heilsgeschehen und Geschichte" [ET: "Redemptive Event and History"].

65. John 1:14, which Wobbermin describes as "the fundamental proposition of evangelical Christian knowledge of God" ["der Fundamentalsatz evangelisch-christlicher Gotteserkenntnis"]. Wobbermin, Wort Gottes, 15.

the past but remains active and efficacious throughout history. The Bible is therefore both the document of God's revelation in Jesus Christ and the early church's testimony of its faith in Christ.[66] There is therefore in Scripture itself the religio-psychological circle between religious experience and objective historic fact, between the faith of the early Christian community and the divine revelation in Jesus Christ.

Because of this religio-psychological circle operative within Scripture itself, Wobbermin demands a sharp distinction between the existential and the intellectual or the cognitive in the doctrines of revelation and Scripture. Revelation is directed toward the whole human being in his or her concrete personal life, and the only appropriate response to God's revelation is obedient faith. Knowledge and understanding, he suggests, proceed only from such obedient faith and remain secondary to it, as Anselm expressed in his famous claim, "Credo ut intelligam."[67] The divine revelation is the unconditional authority in matters of faith, and this revelation takes place in history, becomes historic, and has its own history.

Because the divine revelation assumes historic form, first in Jesus Christ and then also in Scripture, it is open to the full range of historical research. Historical investigation of Scripture is required precisely because of the historic character of revelation, and for this reason historical research is an essential part of the theological task: "[Scripture] requires for its appropriate understanding the meticulous employment of means that are given to us by God for understanding historic facts and developments, thus – said simply – historical research."[68] Historical research serves an essential preliminary function, but it alone can never provide the foundation for faith. The most that can emerge from historical investigation of Scripture is *fides historica*, which is not yet saving faith. Such faith will always be a human work and faith in an improper object – in this case the results of historical research or the pronouncements of historians – rather than the God who is revealed in Jesus Christ.[69]

---

66. Ibid., 16.

67. Wobbermin, *Richtlinien*, 23. See Anselm, *Proslogion*, cap. 1.

68. "Sie verlangt damit zu ihrem sachgemäßen Verständnis die sorgfältige Anwendung aller der Mittel, die uns von Gott zum Verständnis geschichtlicher Tatsachen und Entwicklungen geschenkt sind, also kurz gesagt: die historische Forschung." Wobbermin, *Wort Gottes*, 18.

69. See Chapter 2 for a more detailed evaluation of Wobbermin's complex position on historical criticism.

Erfahrung und Glaube

Experience and Faith: Toward an Existential Theology

Historical research and its results are always directed toward the intellect and remain objects of knowledge and understanding. But Protestant faith, as Wobbermin consistently maintains, is an orientation of the whole human being toward God in Christ: "Theological thought in the sense of evangelical faith – and therefore in opposition to intellectualistic scholasticism – must, as a matter of fact, be *existential* thought."[70] Wobbermin acknowledges the dominant strain of existentialism within modern Protestant thought, reaching back to Kierkegaard and coming into vogue in the 1920s and 30s in the work of Martin Heidegger and Rudolf Bultmann, but he appeals to Schleiermacher as the best example of the marriage of existential thought and the psychology of religion.[71]

Referring to Schleiermacher, Wobbermin offers two definitions of existential thought. First, existential thought is "defined fundamentally by means of the comprehensive, highest point of view of the acknowledgement of the absolute dependence of our existence."[72] He also offers a more detailed definition of existential thought that explicitly draws the connection between faith and religious experience:

> This principle of Schleiermacher's stands in the closest relation to the basic approach of the Reformation: thinking from faith – faith not as mere *fides historica*, but rather true evangelical faith with the elements of obedience, decision, and experience – everything in daily struggle against despair, sin, and guilt. *Such thought is existential thought.*[73]

---

70. "*Denn theologisches Denken im Sinne evangelischen Glaubens und damit im Gegensatz zu intellektualistischer Scholastik, muß tatsächlich **existentielles** Denken sein.*" Wobbermin, Wort Gottes, 20. Emphasis in original.

71. See pp. 133–140.

72. "*Ein Denken, das grundsätzlich durch den übergreifenden obersten Gesichtspunkt der Anerkennung schlechthinniger Abhängigkeit unserer gesamtem Existenz bestimmt wird, – daß ist existentielles Denken.*" Ibid., 21.

73. "*Dieses Prinzip Schleiermachers steht in engster Beziehung zum Grundansatz der Reformation: aus dem Glauben heraus denken, - dem Glauben nicht als bloßer* fides historica, *sondern dem vorher besprochenen wahrhaft evangelischen Glauben mit dem Momenten Glaubensgehorsam, Glaubensentscheidung, Glaubenserfahrung – das alles in täglichen Kampf gegen Anfechtung, Sünde und Schuld.* **Solches Denken ist existentielles Denken.**" Ibid. Emphasis in original.

Wobbermin, like Karl Barth,[74] is skeptical of theology becoming too dependent on any one philosophical school, "not even one from which it can learn very much."[75] Despite his admiration for Heidegger's work and his agreement with Heidegger on many important points, Wobbermin prefers Schleiermacher as his primary source of insight for existential thought. Perhaps Wobbermin misses an opportunity to learn from Heidegger's distinction between *Geschichte* and *Historie* as such a distinction is made within existential philosophy,[76] but by referring primarily to Schleiermacher he is able to combine his existential thinking with an emphasis on religious experience and the psychology of religion that is missing in Heidegger.

For Wobbermin, existential thought is particularly interested in the personal experience of faith, so much so, he argues, that the concept "Word of God" is accessible only to religio-psychological and existential thought.[77] The correlative relationship (i.e., the religio-psychological circle) between personal experience and Scripture is analogous to the correlative relationship between faith and the Word of God. Holy Scripture, as both the document of the divine revelation and the early church's testimony of faith, represents this correlative relationship within itself. Scripture as the document of divine revelation, as the unconditioned authority in matters of faith, can be the only source for Protestant dogmatics.[78] Scripture as the early church's testimony of faith (as a testimony of

---

74. In a letter to Rudolf Bultmann dated December 24, 1952, Barth criticizes Bultmann for what he considers to be Bultmann's inappropriately high estimation of existential philosophy: "The most triumphant expansion of that philosophy over the whole earth could not make the slightest impression on me. . . . I am not an enemy of philosophy as such, but I have hopeless reservations about the claim to absoluteness of any philosophy, epistemology, or methodology." "Karl Barth, Basel, to Rudolf Bultmann, Marburg, December 24, 1952," in Barth, *Karl Barth - Rudolf Bultmann Briefwechsel*, 193 [ET: *Karl Barth - Rudolf Bultmann Letters*, 105].

75. Wobbermin, *Wort Gottes*, 20.

76. Wobbermin does mention Heidegger's "noteworthy" work on the distinction between *Geschichte* and *Historie*, and he claims that its use by younger theologians has helped to alleviate some of the difficulties he originally faced when he first wrote on the distinction in 1911. Despite the noteworthiness of Heidegger's work on the distinction, Wobbermin merely mentions it and moves on without additional commentary. Wobbermin, *Richtlinien*, 130–31. See Heidegger, *Sein und Zeit* [ET: *Being and Time*], especially §§6, 73, and 76.

77. Wobbermin, *Wort Gottes*, 21.

78. Wobbermin, *Richtlinien*, 138.

religious experience itself) is a record of the religious experience of the early community and remains secondary to Scripture as the document of divine revelation. Religious experience, therefore, is an essential resource for dogmatics but never its source. As God is ontologically prior to faith, Scripture as God's self-revelation in Christ (i.e., as the Word of God) is ontologically superior to Scripture as the early church's testimony of its faith in Christ, and Scripture as the document of God's self-revelation in Christ is therefore ontologically prior to personal religious experience. This interaction between personal religious experience and Scripture represents the religio-psychological circle "in its special application to the dogmatic task."[79]

Wobbermin's emphasis on personal religious experience recalls Luther's emphasis on individual experience of God's grace over against a *fides implicita* or Melanchthon's *fides historica*. Faith, in Luther's understanding, always concerns trust in God's promise to be gracious. Trust implies a personal decision of the individual, a giving of oneself to God despite the lack of any objective proof. Faith as trust, in other words, necessarily includes an element of risk. Assent and knowledge, while not absent from Luther's understanding of faith, are subordinated to trust. As Wobbermin puts it, "*fiducia* forms the proper essential element of evangelical faith."[80]

Wobbermin suggests that there are two pairs of relationships within Luther's doctrine of faith. On the one hand, faith is both obedience [*Glaubensgehorsam*] and decision [*Glaubensentscheidung*], and on the other hand faith is both obedience and experience [*Glaubenserfahrung*].[81] Within these two pairs of relationships Wobbermin finds both the essential Protestant harmony between the objective and subjective poles of faith and the origins of the religio-psychological circle. Faith as obedience is trust in the one true God who is revealed in Jesus Christ and in Scripture. Faith is also always a personal decision for God, "and only in this way, always deciding for God anew, in daily struggle against despair,

---

79. "Diese Wechselbeziehung – der religionspsychologische Zirkel in der speziellen Anwendung auf die dogmatische Aufgabe – entspricht dem Korrelatverhältnis, in dem, wie wir sahen, Wort Gottes und Glaube wesensmäßig stehen." Wobbermin, Wort Gottes, 22.

80. "Die fiducia bildet den eigentlichen Wesenskern des evangelischen Glaubens." Ibid., 11.

81. Ibid., 12.

sin, and guilt, does one obey God's will."⁸² In terms of the second relationship, faith is also a personal experience "to the degree to which as a gift of God it takes root in the core of the person, in the spiritual life."⁸³ Or as Wobbermin paraphrases Melanchthon in Article XX of the Augsburg Confession, "The frightened conscience experiences such comfort, standing with certainty that it has a gracious God for the sake of Christ."⁸⁴

Perhaps the clearest statement by Luther anticipating what Wobbermin calls the religio-psychological circle is found in Luther's foreword to his exposition of the Magnificat:

> In order to understand this holy song of praise properly, it must be noted that the most blessed virgin Mary speaks of her own experience, in which she has been enlightened and taught by the Holy Spirit. No one may understand God or God's Word rightly without the mediation of the Holy Spirit. No one can have it except by the Holy Spirit; one experiences it, seeks it, and feels it. And in the same experience the Holy Spirit teaches as in its own school, outside of which nothing is taught – only mock words and idle chatter.⁸⁵

For Wobbermin, this personal experience of faith "becomes the *testimonium spiritus sancti internum*, the witness for the working of the Holy Spirit in and on the individual soul."⁸⁶ Without the inner testimony

---

82. "*Und nur dadurch, daß er sich stets von neuem für Gott entscheidet, im täglichen Kampf gegen Anfechtung, Sünde und Schuld – gehorcht er Gottes Willen.*" Ibid.

83. "*daß der Glaube in dem Maße, wie er sich als Geschenk Gottes in den Personkern des seelichen Lebens einwurzelt, zur eigenpersönlichen Glaubenserfahrung wird.*" Ibid.

84. "*Es erfahren die erschrockenen Gewissen solchen Trost,* cum certo statuunt, *daß sie um Christus willen einen gnädigen Gott haben.*" Ibid., 10. The extended Latin text includes an explicit reference to faith: "Moreover, although this teaching is held in contempt by the ignorant, nevertheless pious and terrified consciences experience the greatest consolation offered them, consciences that cannot be restored to tranquility by any works, but only by faith, standing with certainty that they have a placated God for the sake of Christ." "Confessio Augustana," 77–78 [ET: "The Augsburg Confession," 55].

85. Luther, "Das Magnificat verdeutschet und ausgelegt," 546 [ET: "The Magnificat Translated and Expounded," 299].

86. "*Indem so die eigenpersönliche Glaubenserfahrung dem Gläubigen zum Zeugnis für das Gericht und die Gnade Gottes wird, wird sie ihm zum* testimonium spiritus sancti internum, *zum Zeugnis für die Wirkung des heiligen Geistes in und an der eigenen Seele.*" Wobbermin, *Wort Gottes*, 13. Wobbermin's use of the word "becomes" [*wird*] here is an unfortunate way of expressing this point. The word "becomes" suggests that religious experience is somehow prior to the inner testimony of the Holy Spirit, which is a claim Luther never would have made. Perhaps "signifies" [*bedeutet*] would be a more appropri-

Erfahrung und Glaube

of the Spirit, one can only respond to Scripture with *fides historica* or *fides implicita*. The casual reader of the Bible, untouched by the Holy Spirit, can only accept the truth of the historical data of salvation history (that Jesus of Nazareth was crucified, died, was buried, etc.). Such knowledge of historical facts includes neither the experience of faith, nor the obedience of faith, nor the decision of faith. It remains implicit faith at best; it has not yet become *fides iustificans*. Luther's discussion of the role of the Spirit and of experience in the doctrine of faith maintains the relationship between the objective and the subjective elements of faith and, Wobbermin suggests, corresponds to the correlative relationship between the *fides quae creditur* and the *fides qua creditur*, which is decisive for the religio-psychological approach.[87]

The Spirit "teaches" the individual soul, the individual standing within history as a historic being. The interaction between soul and Spirit, between subject and object, is a historic event. Because the religio-psychological circle is ultimately concerned with the relationship between the individual and the *effects* or *efficacy* of historic facts as immediately available to religious experience prior to historical research of those facts, it finally lies beyond the realm of *Historie*, the role of which is merely to uncover or reveal the effects or efficacy of those historic facts. For the successful operation of the religio-psychological circle, a strict distinction between *Geschichte* and *Historie* is essential.

GESCHICHTE AND FAITH: THE HISTORIC PICTURE OF CHRIST

For Wobbermin, Christian faith stands in the center of the religio-psychological circle between religious experience and historic facts. Here again Luther provides the foundation for Wobbermin's discussion. For his understanding of religious experience Wobbermin appeals to Luther's use of the term "experience of faith" [*Glaubenserfahrung*], which Wobbermin defines as "an experience in which faith gains its relation to the living God."[88] This religious experience, in which faith gains its relation to the

ate choice here than "becomes."

87. Ibid., 14.

88. Wobbermin refers to Luther's use of the concept of experience as forming the foundation of his work in systematic theology: "As I see in personal religious experience the indispensable methodological presupposition for the scientific treatment of the question of the essence and truth of Christianity, I understand religious experience funda-

living God, is a historic phenomenon that always occurs in and through *Geschichte*. *Geschichte* plays a vital role in the religio-psychological circle for three reasons: first, Christianity is a historic religion; second, human beings are historic individuals; and third, Jesus Christ is a historic figure, the self-revelation of God within *Geschichte*.

The historic character of Christianity is rooted in the historic picture of Jesus Christ, which "radiates outward" [*entgegenleuchten*] from the New Testament.[89] In his essay on *Geschichte* and *Historie*, Wobbermin defines *Historie* as "scientifically investigated *Geschichte*."[90] The historic picture of Christ must not be an exception to this definition, and Wobbermin maintains that the New Testament picture of Christ must be open to the full range of historical investigation.[91] That the man Jesus of Nazareth actually existed is a basic presupposition of the Christian faith, and therefore the question of Jesus' historicity must be posed and investigated by historical research.[92] Wobbermin concludes that this question must be answered affirmatively for at least two reasons: first, the texts of the New Testament provide sufficient historical evidence for such an affirmation; second, and more importantly,

> We are joined with the oldest Christianity through an unbroken connection of spiritual-historic life. And every link to that oldest Christianity points us back to the person of Jesus Christ as the

mentally in Luther's sense as the experience of faith, i.e., as an experience in which faith gains its relation to the living God." ["*Indem ich in der persönlichen religiösen Erfahrung die unentbehrliche methodische Voraussetzung für die wissenschaftliche Behandlung der Fragen nach Wesen und Wahrheit des Christentums sehe, fasse ich die religiöse Erfahrung grundsätzlich im Sinne Luthers als Glaubenserfahrung oder Glaubenserlebnis, d.h. als ein Erleben, in dem der Glaube seine Beziehung zum lebendigen Gott gewinnt.*"] Wobbermin, *Wesen und Wahrheit*, vii.

89. Wobbermin, "Psychologie und Erkenntniskritik der religiösen Erfahrung," 349.

90. Wobbermin, *Geschichte und Historie*, 5.

91. The seventh chapter of the third volume of Wobbermin's systematic theology ("Der Christusglaube der christliche Religion") is dedicated to this type of historical investigation. Wobbermin, *Wesen und Wahrheit*, 265–314.

92. Ibid., 266. Wobbermin's position in the third volume of his systematic theology on the historicity of Jesus and its importance for faith has evolved from that of *Geschichte und Historie*, where he claimed that the historicity of Jesus of Nazareth can be affirmed with the "best historical conscience" but is ultimately irrelevant for Christian faith. Wobbermin does not give any reason here for the change in his position, nor does he acknowledge that his position has changed at all. But it appears that he is more willing now to affirm the necessity of the historicity of Jesus of Nazareth than he was in his earlier work.

Erfahrung und Glaube

one through whose influence its life made its decisive turn. So too does the total historic existence of Christianity bear witness to the historic existence of the person of Jesus Christ. We may therefore lay claim to historical certainty for the reality of his historic existence.[93]

For Wobbermin, then, the continued existence of Christianity affirms the historical existence of Jesus. But historical certainty always remains relative and hypothetical, never absolute. Faith is not based on historical certainty after all. It is enough for Wobbermin to rest assured that historical research will continue to support the claims of faith rather than contradict them.[94]

This appears to be little more than wishful thinking on Wobbermin's part. He is content to assume that because the Christian tradition has survived and flourished for almost two thousand years it must have its roots in a historic figure. But there is no guarantee that this is in fact the case, which is a possibility Drews had raised so forcefully in *Die Christusmythe*. Nor is there any reason why Christianity could not have survived and flourished had there been no Jesus of Nazareth. It is highly unlikely, but it is a possibility. Wobbermin does not here consider the effect on his entire theological project of irrefutable historical evidence that Jesus of Nazareth never existed. He is content simply to proceed with the confidence that no such evidence will ever appear.[95]

Nevertheless, for Wobbermin the historic existence of the man Jesus of Nazareth is only one side of the issue. Much more important for him is the other side, namely "that we have before us in this Jesus Christ of the

---

93. "Wir sind ja mit der ältesten Christenheit durch einen ununterbrochenen Zusammenhang geistig-geschichtlichen Lebens verbunden. Und alle Glieder jener ältesten Christenheit weisen uns zurück auf die Person Jesu Christi als diejenige, durch deren Eindruck ihr Leben die entscheidende Wendung erhalten habe. So bezeugt auch der geschichtliche Gesamtbestand der Christenheit die Geschichtlichkeit der Person Jesu Christi. Deshalb dürfen wir für ihre Geschichtlichkeit historische Sicherheit in Anspruch nehmen." Ibid., 274.

94. Ibid., 275.

95. Again, this confidence is inconsistent with Wobbermin's contention in *Geschichte und Historie* that faith is ultimately unconcerned with the affirmation or negation of the historical existence of Jesus of Nazareth. Perhaps here he is attempting to step back from such bald assertions of the complete irrelevance of the historicity of Jesus that he tentatively made in the concluding section of *Geschichte und Historie*.

gospels . . . a man whose religious-moral content of life is unconditionally available beyond the level of the generally human."[96]

The Resurrection of Jesus as the Historic Foundation of the Christian Religion

The decisive element of the New Testament picture of Christ is the resurrection, an "event" that is presupposed by every text of the New Testament and is the most basic presupposition of the Christian faith. Without the resurrection of Jesus from the dead there is no Christian faith; the interests of faith and history meet most directly and decisively in this question of the resurrection of Jesus.

Wobbermin's first task in terms of the resurrection is to define precisely the point at which faith and history meet in this question.[97] The resurrection event itself cannot provide this point at which faith and history meet because, according to the New Testament itself, there were no witnesses of the actual event and it is never described anywhere in the New Testament. Wobbermin concludes that "the resurrection, in the sense of the resurrection event, is not a historically comprehensible event."[98]

The empty tomb also cannot provide this point of contact between faith and history because the empty tomb raises serious historical difficulties. There is ample evidence in the New Testament itself to disregard the empty tomb tradition as evidence for the resurrection, as the point at which faith and history most directly meet. Paul, as the earliest author in the New Testament, is especially important for deciding the question of the resurrection, even more so because Paul attempts to base the entire Christian faith on the resurrection in general and on the resurrection of Jesus in particular. 1 Cor 15 is the primary source of Paul's discussion of the resurrection, and it is significant that he never mentions the empty tomb in his argument for the reality of the resurrection.[99] Despite the

---

96. "*Aber das ist doch nur eine Seite des Sachverhalts. Die andere ist die, daß wir in eben diesem Jesus Christus den Evangelien, . . . einen Menschen vor uns haben, dessen religiös-sittlicher Lebensgehalt über das Maß des gemein-menschlichen unbedingt hinausliegt.*" Wobbermin, *Wesen und Wahrheit*, 277.

97. Ibid., 280.

98. "*Die Auferstehung im Sinne des Auferstehungsvorganges ist also kein historisch faßbares Ereignis.*" Ibid., 282.

99. For a more recent study of the empty tomb tradition and its insufficiency as proof of the resurrection of Jesus, see Dalferth, "Volles Grab, leerer Glaube?"

Erfahrung und Glaube

lack of discussion (it is not clear whether Paul was aware of an empty tomb tradition at all), Paul's claim that "flesh and blood cannot inherit the kingdom of God" (1 Cor 15:50) invalidates any appeal to an empty tomb insofar as that tradition presupposes a physical resuscitation or revivification of a corpse.[100]

If neither the resurrection event itself nor the empty tomb provides the point at which faith and history meet, there must be another tradition within the New Testament that provides this point:

> *In fact, the New Testament leaves no doubt that the disciples' conviction that their Lord lives on the basis of the appearances of the risen one to them represents this point.* That the disciples had gained this conviction, that Jesus Christ had conquered death and lives, that is really a historically comprehensible historic fact; and also, that this conviction developed on the basis of the appearances, in which Jesus Christ proclaimed himself as the risen one to their faith.[101]

Wobbermin acknowledges that the tradition of the appearances of the risen Christ is by no means consistent or unambiguous. Nevertheless, accounts of the appearances appear in each of the four gospels[102] as well as

---

100. Ibid., 284.

101. "*Vielmehr läßt das Neue Testament keinen Zweifel darüber zu, daß diesen Punkt die Überzeugung der Jünger vom Fortleben ihres Herrn auf Grund der ihnen zuteil gewordenen Erscheinungen des Auferstandenen darstellt. Daß die Jünger die Überzeugung gewonnen haben, Jesus Christus hat den Tod überwunden und lebt: das ist wirklich eine historisch zu fassende geschichtliche Tatsache; und ebenso das andere, daß ihnen diese Überzeugung erwachsen ist auf Grund von Erscheinungen, in denen sich ihrem Glauben Jesus Christus als der Auferstandene kundtat.*" Ibid., 285–86. Emphasis in original. That the disciples had gained a conviction is, as Wobbermin argues, a fact that is historically [*historisch*] comprehensible. But his further claim that the basis of this conviction in the appearances of the risen Christ is also a historically comprehensible fact is a completely different claim. That the disciples *claimed* that the appearances were the basis of their conviction of faith is a historically [*historisch*] comprehensible fact. But the appearances themselves are not a historically [*historisch*] comprehensible fact, despite the fact that Wobbermin conflates the two claims and declares both to be historically [*historisch*] comprehensible.

102. Wobbermin does not pause here to consider the location of the appearance narratives in the gospel of Mark, all of which appear in the longer ending (Mark 16:9ff). That there are in fact two (or more) endings of Mark (the original ending does not include any mention of the appearances of the risen Christ) was suggested by the 1830s, as D. F. Strauss notes in *The Life of Jesus Critically Examined*, 716. Strauss himself rejects the theory of two distinct endings of the gospel of Mark, but he does note that Heinrich Eberhard Gottlob Paulus and Carl August Credner had already made such an observation. William Baird notes that another nineteenth-century biblical critic, Heinrich

in Paul's first letter to the Corinthians and in his account of his conversion in the letter to the Galatians. Wobbermin notes two important elements within Paul's discussion of the appearances of the risen Christ: first, Paul claims that he stands in a long line of believers to whom the risen Christ has appeared; second, he regards the appearance of the risen Christ to him on the Damascus Road as a revelatory act of God: "It pleased God to reveal his Son in me" (Gal 1:15–16).[103]

The accounts of the appearances in the gospels raise important historical and scientific questions. According to the gospels, the crucified Jesus was laid in a tomb and on the third day emerged with a transformed body. Wobbermin suggests that the evangelists' accounts of the resurrection succumb to "the most serious doubts, and not only logical doubts and difficulties in understanding, but, more importantly, also ethical and internal religious doubts."[104]

At issue here is the reality of the death of Jesus, if one is to take the gospel accounts of the resurrection literally. Rehearsing the debates of the 18th and early 19th centuries, Wobbermin offers two alternatives in light of a literal reading of the gospel narratives: either Jesus really died, in which case he could not have emerged from the tomb with his earthly (but transformed) body intact, or, if the latter is in fact the case, he did not really die but only appeared to die.[105] The only alternative in this scenario is an appeal to a miracle of the omnipotent God, a miracle in which the process of bodily decomposition is halted and reversed. But, Wobbermin

---

August Wilhelm Meyer, had also claimed as early as the 1840s that there are two distinct endings of the gospel of Mark. See Baird, *History of New Testament Research*, 1:368. It is unclear whether Wobbermin was unaware of these text-critical developments (this would seem unlikely) or whether he was aware of them and determined that the text-critical issues were theologically unimportant.

103. This is my translation of Wobbermin's quotation of the German text. The NRSV translation of the entire passage reads, "But when God, who had set me apart before I was born and called me through his grace, was pleased to reveal his Son *to* me, so that I might proclaim him to the Gentiles, I did not confer with any human being, nor did I go up to Jerusalem to those who were already apostles before me, but I went away at once into Arabia, and afterwards I returned to Damascus" (Gal 1:15–17). Emphasis mine.

104. "*Diese Vorstellung der Evangelien von den Erscheinungen und die mit ihr gegebene Vorstellung von der Art und Weise der Auferstehung unterliegt aber den schwersten Bedenken, und zwar nicht etwa nur logisch-verstandesmäßigen, sondern durchaus und gerade auch ethischen sowie innerreligiösen Bedenken.*" Wobbermin, *Wesen und Wahrheit*, 287.

105. Ibid.

suggests, "in this case the omnipotent miracle as reversal of the already begun process of decomposition would have the character of an arbitrary miracle."[106] Such a miracle, understood in physical or natural terms, belongs to the realm of magic and mythology and can have no religious significance. This, at best, is the judgment of the matter from a modern, physiological perspective. According to Wobbermin, however, to the first disciples the bodily resurrection remained a possibility and was accepted as a miracle.[107]

The second and more difficult question is that of the nature of the resurrection body. If there is a necessary natural or physical continuity between the crucified Jesus and the risen Christ, then this continuity must be manifested in the body of Jesus. This is the suggestion of the evangelists, but their descriptions of the resurrection body raise more questions than they answer. The risen Lord appears in locked rooms (John 20:19), declines to be touched (John 20:17), and disappears before the disciples' eyes (Luke 24:31), and yet he also eats with them (Luke 24:42) and shows them his wounds (Luke 24:39–40; John 20:20, 27). For Wobbermin this entire presentation moves into the realm of magic and mythology and cannot serve as the point at which the interests of faith and history meet.[108]

It is finally to Paul that Wobbermin turns to understand the religious significance of the appearances of the risen Christ, and the key is Paul's description of his own encounter with the risen Lord: "It pleased God to reveal his Son in me" (Gal 1:15–16). Wobbermin suggests that it is this "in me" that provides the key to understanding the appearances in their religious significance.[109] The gospel narratives emphasize the external,

---

106. "*In dem vorliegenden Falle würde aber das Allmachtswunder als Rückgängigmachen der bereits eingetretenen Naturprozesse den Charakter des Willkürwunders tragen.*" Ibid., 288.

107. Ibid.

108. Ibid. The nature of the resurrection body, especially as Paul describes it in 1 Cor 15, was the subject of an early debate between Barth and Bultmann. See Barth, *Die Auferstehung der Toten* [ET: *The Resurrection of the Dead*] and Bultmann, "Karl Barth, *Die Auferstehung der Toten*" [ET: "Karl Barth, *The Resurrection of the Dead*"].

109. Wobbermin, *Wesen und Wahrheit*, 291. Wobbermin's argument here hangs on the preposition "in," which is the preposition used in the German text from which he quotes and which is a more literal translation of the original Greek phrase, "ἀποκαλύψαι τὸν υἱὸν αὐτοῦ ἐν ἐμοί," than the NRSV translation, which renders "ἐν ἐμοί" as "to me."

objective side of the appearances and require an acceptance of miracle in order to believe in the resurrection. Paul emphasizes the internal, subjective element of an inner experience of the Lord's resurrection, thus potentially eliminating the necessity of an intellectual sacrifice in order to believe in the resurrection. In two passages Wobbermin summarizes the importance of inner experience with respect to the appearances of the risen Christ as they are effective for the emergence of faith in the disciples. First:

> We may not conceive the appearances of Jesus Christ as being of a physical and bodily nature as such, but rather we must understand them as inner experiences through which the disciples became convinced of the continuing life and activity of their Lord.[110]

And second:

> A misunderstanding must be avoided – we speak according to the emphatic statements of Paul as the oldest witness in terms of this question of inner experience, not of illusions, but rather of inner experience on the basis of a self-attestation of the risen one, inas-

---

110 "*Wir dürfen die Erscheinungen Jesu Christi nicht als solche sinnlich-leiblicher Natur fassen, sondern müssen sie als innere Erfahrungen oder innere Erlebnisse verstehen, durch welche die Jünger vom Fortleben und Fortwirken ihres Herrn überführt wurden.*" Ibid., 290. Like the English word "history," the word "experience" corresponds to two distinct words in German, each with a different shade of meaning. Wobbermin often uses "Erfahrung" and "Erlebnis" together when referring to religious experience. Hans-Georg Gadamer discusses the history of "Erlebnis" and its relationship to "Erfahrung" in some detail in *Truth and Method*. Gadamer notes that for most of the history of the German language, "Erfahrung" was the only word for experience, at least until the 19th century. He traces the use of the word "Erlebnis" to Hegel, who coined the word in a letter. It appeared with some frequency in biographical literature beginning in the 1870s, most notably in an essay by Dilthey on Goethe (first published in 1877). See Dilthey, *Gesammelte Schriften*, vol. 26, *Das Erlebnis und die Dichtung* [ET: *Selected Works*, vol. 5, *Poetry and Experience*]. Gadamer suggests that the origins of the word "Erlebnis" in the Romantic Movement within philosophy, theology, and art is significant. Experience as *Erlebnis* (literally "something that is lived through") is thus opposed to the rationalism and mechanical detachment of the Enlightenment and, as Gadamer puts it, "implies a connection with totality, with infinity." *Erfahrung*, on the other hand, has a much older history, yet, as Gadamer laments, it is "one of the most obscure [concepts] we have." The history of the term "Erfahrung" as it had been used in modern German philosophy and especially in hermeneutics was, according to Gadamer, entirely oriented toward scientific analysis at the expense of the "inner historicity of experience." It is not clear how Wobbermin understands the distinction between *Erfahrung* and *Erlebnis*, nor whether he even intends one, but it is not insignificant that he was a student of Dilthey's at the time of the latter's popularization of the term "Erlebnis." See Gadamer, *Truth and Method*, 60–70; 346–62.

Erfahrung und Glaube

much as the disciples' experience was reckoned to their faith as the self-attestation of the risen one.[111]

The point at which faith and history most directly meet is the disciples' experience of the self-attestation of the risen Christ. Here Wobbermin attempts to unify the objective (the self-attestation of the risen Christ) and the subjective (the disciples' inner experience, their conviction that Jesus lives). The meeting point of faith and history, then, is not limited to an objective fact, nor is it limited to subjective experience; it includes and requires the interaction of both.[112]

The disciples' experience of the self-attestation of the risen Christ (if not that self-attestation itself) can be evaluated by historical investigation, and Wobbermin suggests that two conclusions may be drawn from a historical analysis. First, the appearance narratives "are testimonies of the steadfastness and absolute certainty of the disciples' conviction of the resurrection of Jesus Christ." Secondly, "at the same time they are testimonies for the fact that this conviction was the fundamental condition for the emergence of Christian faith and of Christianity in general."[113] These two historic facts – the disciples' conviction that Jesus lives and the emergence of Christian faith on the basis of that conviction – represent the decisive historic foundation of Christian faith and of Christianity. Moreover, these two facts stand in a correlative relationship to one another, and it is this

---

111. "*Aber nun muß hier ein Mißverständnis abgewehrt werden. Wir sprechen nach Maßgabe der ausdrücklichen Aussage des Apostels Paulus als des ältesten Zeugen in dieser Frage von inneren Erlebnissen, nicht etwa von Illusionen, sondern von inneren Erlebnissen auf Grund einer Selbstbezeugung des Auferstandenen, sofern jedenfalls dem Glauben der Jünger ihre Erlebnisse als Selbstbezeugung des Auferstandenen galten.*" Wobbermin, *Wesen und Wahrheit*, 291.

112. Despite the fact that the appearances of the risen Christ as his "self-attestation" [*Selbstbezeugung*] stand at the center of Wobbermin's interpretation of the resurrection, he never explicitly defines what this self-attestation entails or of what it consists beyond a general claim that it is the revelation of God to faith. The appearances as the self-attestation of Christ are consistently defined on the basis of the disciples' experience, thus from the subjective side. There is finally very little objective content in this particular "objective pole." In fact, Wobbermin expressly rejects a purely objective understanding of the appearances, arguing that they would then be reduced to "visions" and therefore to mere "illusions." Ibid.

113. "*Sie sind erstlich Zeugnisse für die Festigkeit und unbedingte Sicherheit der Überzeugung der Jünger von der Auferstehung Jesu Christi. Sie sind andererseits zugleich Zeugnisse dafür, daß diese Überzeugung die Grundbedingung für das Zustandekommen des christlichen Glaubens und also des Christentums überhaupt war.*" Ibid., 292.

relationship that proves decisive for the continued existence and persistence of the Christian faith.[114]

Experiencing the Historic Christ:
Geschichte and the Religio-Psychological Circle

These two historic facts (the disciples' conviction that Jesus lives and the emergence of Christian faith on the basis of that conviction) are decisive because they provide the foundation for Christian faith and because they provide the point of contact between Christian faith and the historic picture of Christ. The disciples' conviction of faith emerged as a result of their experience of the continuing efficacy of the historic Christ. Both this conviction and the picture of Christ as the self-revelation of God were recorded in the New Testament, and it is the same picture of the historic Christ as the self-revelation of God that confronts Christians of every time and place in the New Testament. For this picture of the historic Christ to be efficacious for faith – just as it was efficacious for the emergence of the disciples' faith – it must be immediately available and accessible to religious experience. Should Christian faith be made to depend *solely* on the results of historical analysis of the historic picture of Christ in the New Testament, rather than on the continuing efficacy of the risen Christ, faith would be reduced to a mere *fides historica* and would no longer be the Easter faith of the disciples.[115] There would then be an irreparable

---

114. Ibid., 293. This deduction of the historic foundation of Christianity from a historical investigation of the New Testament serves to illustrate Wobbermin's positive use of historical criticism, in spite of his protests against making faith in any way dependent on the results of historical research. In this case, historical criticism serves the vital purpose of uncovering the kernel or essence of the origins of Christian faith. Faith is not thereby made *dependent* on the results of historical research; the foundation of faith exists prior to historical investigation of it. Even less is faith reduced to a mere *fides historica*. While Wobbermin's own attitudes concerning the positive role of historical research remain unclear, especially in his essay on *Geschichte* and *Historie*, his application of historical criticism to the biblical texts in his systematic theology indicates a positive and necessary use of historical research in his theology.

115. As it was suggested in the previous note, while Wobbermin does not, in theory, grant historical criticism any positive role in determining the historic picture of Christ as the object of faith and consequently labels any attempt to do so as a move toward a mere *fides historica*, in practice he does require a positive role for historical criticism. As he says elsewhere, historical criticism must be given complete freedom to investigate the New Testament picture of Christ in order to strip away false supports and allow the essential elements to emerge. If that is true, then there is a historical [*historisch*] element to Christian faith after all; it is, however, only a small part of Christian faith and alone

Erfahrung und Glaube

severing of the link between the faith of the disciples and the faith of the church. But this is not the case. Christian faith, *fides iustificans*, is always *fides apostolica*, the faith of the disciples who experienced the risen Lord and believed in him on the basis of his continuing presence and activity. And so it is and must be, according to Wobbermin, for Christians of every time and place.

Wobbermin argues that the historic Christ is the Christ who confronts each reader or hearer directly from the New Testament in precisely the same way as Christ was present to his disciples and has been present throughout the entire history of Christianity.[116] The constant in this case is *Geschichte* itself. Just as Jesus Christ is a historic figure – the self-revelation of God in history – so, too, is the relationship between modern Christians and the historic Christ a historic relationship, available and accessible directly to individual religious experience.

Again referring to Kant's claim that the *Historische* serves for the illustration rather than the demonstration of truth, Wobbermin amends that statement to emphasize the significance of the historic Christ:

> To faith, *Geschichte* serves not only for the illustration of religious truth, but rather for the invention of religious truth, its discovery and attainment, and, indeed, religious truth is and remains accessible to faith only through such mediation of *Geschichte*.[117]

In terms of faith in Christ, then, the salvific life, death, and resurrection of Christ is the norm of Christian faith and serves for the invention of faith in God by bringing God's self-revelation to expression.

---

remains insufficient. The more important element, for Wobbermin, is the experience of the present reality of Christ in his efficacy and influence, which is gained in and through *Geschichte* and is primarily a historic [*geschichtlich*] rather than a historical [*historisch*] reality.

116. Wobbermin, *Wesen und Wahrheit*, 294.

117. "*Dem Glauben dient also die Geschichte nicht nur zur Illustration der religiösen Wahrheit, sondern zur Invention derselben, zu ihrer Auffindung und Erlangung, und zwar so, daß ihm die religiöse Wahrheit fortlaufend nur durch solche Vermittlung der Geschichte zugänglich wird und zugänglich bleibt.*" Ibid., 309. Wobbermin uses the same terms, "Auffindung" and "Erlangung," in his critique of Bousset's attempts to base religion in reason. Wobbermin, *Geschichte und Historie*, 70. B. A. Gerrish suggests that with this concept of the discovery and attainment of truth Wobbermin offers a third way between demonstrating the truth of religion by historical research or by rational deduction. Gerrish, "Jesus, Myth, and History," 35.

The discussion of the disciples' conviction of faith in the risen Christ finally returns to the religio-psychological circle. For Christian faith to remain apostolic faith it must be possible for Christians of every time and place to have the same experience of the same historic facts as the disciples did. This possibility exists because of the religio-psychological circle encompassing individual religious experience and the historic facts recorded in Scripture. Just as the disciples' faith was directed toward the historic Christ in whom they regarded the self-revelation of God, modern Christians direct their faith toward the same historic Christ as he is represented in the New Testament. This same relationship is possible by virtue of the historic character of the picture of Christ in the New Testament. Just as the disciples experienced the presence and efficacy of the historic Christ as the self-revelation of God, so do modern Christians experience the historic Christ as he "radiates outward" from the New Testament, which is the document of the divine revelation as well as the early church's testimony of faith in Christ as the revelation of God. It is the same faith in the same Christ. It is the same correlative relationship between the experience and conviction of faith on the one hand and the objective fact of the historic Christ on the other. It is not the faith of historians but living, justifying faith, the faith of the disciples and of the whole church, a faith that is a gift of the gracious God. It is the faith that emerges within *Geschichte* on the basis of a living relationship with the historic Christ.

In this application of the religio-psychological circle, Wobbermin contends that the Reformation doctrine of faith is upheld. He is careful to distinguish between *Geschichte* and *Historie* in his discussion of faith and the religio-psychological circle in order to safeguard the integrity of *fides iustificans* and to avoid both what Melanchthon called *fides historica* and what Kähler called *Autoritätsglauben*. By emphasizing the correlative relationship between personal religious experience and the objective historic facts of the New Testament picture of Christ, Wobbermin hopes to have maintained the Reformation unity of the objective and subjective elements of faith, and by emphasizing the historic character of Christian faith and the present efficacy of the historic picture of Christ, immediately given in Scripture to men and women standing within history, he hopes to have maintained the Reformation doctrine of justification by faith alone. In so doing, he stands squarely within a tradition reaching back through Schleiermacher to Luther and Melanchthon, and forward, in many important respects, to Rudolf Bultmann and his students.

4

Zwischen den Zeiten

Wobbermin's Self-Identification within the History of Protestant Thought

"CAPTAIN OF THE LIBERAL REARGUARD"

B. A. Gerrish has suggested that Wobbermin's chief concern during the 1930s was to steer Protestant theology back to Luther through Schleiermacher.[1] Following the publication of his systematic theology, Wobbermin turned his attention to the historical-theological foundations of his religio-psychological method, leading to an extensive engagement not only with Schleiermacher, but with Luther and Kant as well. As he honed his theological method, he paid careful attention to its foundations in the history of Protestant thought. His attention to Luther, Kant, and Schleiermacher corresponds to his preoccupation with methodological questions, both in his own theology and in his debates with Karl Barth and the dialectical theologians.

Occupation with the relationship between these seminal Protestant[2] thinkers and his own theological method in the 1920s and early 1930s, in the midst of the decline of liberal theology and the rise of dialectical theology, places Wobbermin squarely "between the times" [*zwischen den Zeiten*].[3] Wobbermin was, as Gerrish has argued, a "captain of the liberal

---

1. Gerrish, "Doctor Martin Luther," 53. Gerrish regards Wobbermin as an "almost forgotten captain of the liberal rearguard," hence the title of this section.

2. While it may be difficult to label Kant a "Protestant thinker," Wobbermin could claim Kant as such (with reservations), sometimes calling him a *Philosoph des Protestantismus*. See Wobbermin, "Luther, Kant, Schleiermacher und die Aufgabe der heutigen Theologie," 104. See also p. 129.

3. This is an intentional reference to the journal of the same name that served as an

rearguard,"[4] among the last of the liberal theologians working in a generation increasingly dominated by the new dialectical theology. And yet Wobbermin was not simply a relic of a bygone theological era; some of his positions (e.g., on the importance of existential thinking, the benefits of a distinction between *Geschichte* and *Historie*, and the dangers of a one-sided objectivism or subjectivism) anticipate some of the questions that would also occupy the younger generation of German Protestant theologians, particularly Rudolf Bultmann. Wobbermin sought a return to Luther through Schleiermacher as a viable alternative to what he considered to be the errors of dialectical theology, while at the same time embracing some of the positions of existentialism and phenomenology that would underlie Bultmann's work.

As Michael Aune has shown, historians of the theology of the early twentieth century typically describe this period with terms that emphasize radical discontinuity, terms such as *Aufbruch, Epochenwende, wirkungskräftigste Zäsur, theologische Ansatz, der Neueinsatz der Theologie, Zeitenwende, die grosse Wende, Theologierevolution,* and *totale Umwälzung*.[5] And as Matthias Wolfes has demonstrated in his study of liberal theology after 1918, in the 1920s and 30s there were several signs of theological *continuity* with the long tradition of Protestant thought reaching back to Schleiermacher and Luther, and these latter-day liberal theologians continued to produce new constructive work in a period increasingly dominated by dialectical theology.

Wobbermin clearly belongs to this group of latter-day liberals, and during and after the First World War he turned his attention to the continuing viability of a liberal theological method (i.e. his religio-psychological method) as well as its roots in the work of the great Protestant thinkers of the past and its relationship to a new generation of theologians who rejected much of liberal theology as a dead end. His chief concern in the post-war period was the relationship between the objective and subjective elements of faith and what he perceived as the dangers of ei-

---

organ of early dialectical theology, edited by Georg Merz and published from 1923 to 1933.

4. Gerrish, "Doctor Martin Luther," 53.

5. These terms can be translated, respectively, as "departure," "turn of an era," "the most powerfully effective break," "theological point of departure," "the new entry of theology," "turn of the times," "the great turn," "revolution of theology," and "total overthrow." Aune, "Discarding the Barthian Spectacles, Part III," 391.

Zwischen den Zeiten

ther a one-sided historicism or a one-sided psychologism.[6] Wobbermin perceived a tendency toward a one-sided historicism in the work of many Ritschlians and some members of the *religionsgeschichtliche Schule* (especially Ernst Troeltsch), and also in the work of Karl Barth; he perceived a tendency toward a one-sided psychologism in some forms of Pietism, in many interpreters and followers of Schleiermacher, and in those theologies whose methods emphasized the use of empirical psychology.

Before the First World War, Wobbermin attempted to combat these tendencies primarily by means of a strict distinction between *Geschichte* and *Historie*.[7] But by the 1920s this distinction receded into the background of his work, giving way to a more specific occupation with the Protestant doctrine of faith, understood as the interrelation between the *fides quae creditur* and the *fides qua creditur*, between the objective and the subjective elements of faith.[8]

The primary motivation for this shift is the emergence of dialectical theology immediately following World War I, particularly as represented by Karl Barth and Emil Brunner.[9] Barth, Brunner, and the other dialectical theologians rejected theological liberalism as a dead end, citing, among other things, its often explicit approval of Wilhelmine foreign and domestic policy immediately before and during the First World War.[10]

---

6. As discussed in further detail in Chapter 3, a one-sided historicism is a methodological approach that emphasizes the objective element of faith to the exclusion of the subjective element, while a one-sided psychologism is an approach that emphasizes the subjective element of faith to the exclusion of the objective element. Wobbermin address both "dangers" in passing in *Richtlinien der evangelischen Theologie*, and more directly in the foreword to the Swedish edition. See Wobbermin, "Im Kampf gegen Historismus und Psychologismus." He also wrote the *RGG²* entry for *Psychologismus*.

7. See Chapter 2 for a discussion of this aspect of Wobbermin's thought.

8. While explicit discussions of the distinction between *Geschichte* and *Historie* become much less frequent in the period following World War I, it would be a mistake to assume that Wobbermin simply abandoned the distinction. He refers to it occasionally in later texts (e.g., *Richtlinien der evangelischen Theologie*) but, more importantly, the distinction is an essential presupposition of the religio-psychological circle in particular and therefore of his theological method in general.

9. Even though it was Friedrich Gogarten who issued the most dramatic public rejections of liberal theology, Wobbermin rarely mentions him as a representative of dialectical theology. See Moltmann, ed., *Anfänge der dialektischen Theologie* [Partial ET: Robinson, ed., *The Beginnings of Dialectic Theology*] for some of the seminal texts from this period, including several selections from Barth and Brunner.

10. Perhaps the most famous example of such a rejection is found in Barth's "Nachwort" to the *Schleiermacher-Auswahl* [ET: "Concluding Unscientific Postscript on

But there were, of course, theological reasons for their rejection of liberalism, specifically what Barth and Brunner considered the subjectivization of the Christian faith as a result of an emphasis on personal religious experience at the expense of the objective content of faith. Schleiermacher often looms behind these debates, especially those between Barth and Wobbermin. Barth's criticisms of nineteenth-century theology rarely stray far from Schleiermacher,[11] and Brunner fired a salvo against liberal theology with his study of Schleiermacher, *Die Mystik und das Wort*.[12]

Both in his debates with Barth and the dialectical theologians and in his constructive discussions of the nature of faith and its relation to his religio-psychological method, Wobbermin consistently returns to Luther, Kant and Schleiermacher, and specifically to what he calls their three great "Copernican revolutions" [*kopernikanische Umwälzungen*]: the Copernican revolution of religious thought (Luther),[13] the Copernican revolution of epistemology (Kant),[14] and the Copernican revolution of theological method (Schleiermacher).[15]

Although not a Luther specialist, Wobbermin nevertheless refers to Luther constantly in his work, and he also published two essays on Luther's exposition of the First Commandment in the *Large Catechism*.[16] His dissertation on inner experience as the foundation of a moral proof for the existence of God demonstrates his familiarity with Kant's critical philosophy,[17] and he served as one of the editors of the Royal Prussian

---

Schleiermacher."]. See also Barth, "Evangelical Theology in the 19th Century," 14.

11. Here one first thinks of Barth's Göttingen lectures on Schleiermacher, but Schleiermacher also stands at the center of Barth's historical-theological study of nineteenth-century theology, *Die protestantische Theologie im 19. Jahrhundert* [ET: *Protestant Theology in the Nineteenth Century*].

12. Brunner, *Die Mystik und das Wort*. Wobbermin responded to both editions of this book with critical reviews. See Wobbermin, review of *Die Mystik und das Wort*, by Emil Brunner and Wobbermin, review of *Die Mystik und das Wort*, 2nd ed., by Emil Brunner.

13. Wobbermin, "Luther, Kant, Schleiermacher," 111.

14. Ibid., 105.

15. Ibid., 117.

16. Wobbermin, "Die Frage nach Gott in Luthers großem Katechismus" and Wobbermin, "Wie gehören für Luther Gott und Glaube zuhaufe?"

17. Wobbermin, *Die innere Erfahrung als Grundlage eines moralischen Beweises für das Dasein Gottes*. Wolf-Ulrich Klünker suggests that Wobbermin's dissertation functions as a blueprint for his thought. Klünker, *Psychologische Analyse und theologische Wahrheit*, 22–27.

Academy of Science's critical edition of Kant's *Die Religion innerhalb der Grenzen der bloßen Vernunft* and *Die Metaphysik der Sitten*.[18] Finally, Wobbermin was a constant defender of Schleiermacher against what he perceived to be persistent misunderstandings and faulty interpretations of his work both in recent liberal theology and in the dialectical theology of the 1920s and 30s.[19]

The most important texts for an appraisal of Wobbermin's self-identification within the Protestant tradition are "Luther, Kant, Schleiermacher und die Aufgabe der heutigen Theologie" from 1924 and "Gibt es eine Linie Luther – Schleiermacher?" from 1931.[20] The most important texts for an appraisal of the debate between Wobbermin and the dialectical theologians (especially Barth) are "Der Streit um Schleiermacher in seiner Bedeutung für die heutige Gesamtlage der evangelischen Theologie" of 1928 and *Richtlinien der evangelischen Theologie zur Überwindung der gegenwärtigen Krisis* of 1929.

WOBBERMIN'S UNDERSTANDING OF HIS PLACE WITHIN THE "LUTHER-KANT-SCHLEIERMACHER LINE"

Martin Luther

The Berlin historian Karl Holl inaugurated what has been called a "Luther Renaissance" during World War I, sparking renewed interest in Luther's theology and its relevance for the theology of the early twentieth century.[21] Wobbermin also showed more interest in Luther following World War I, returning to the Reformer to find support for his religio-psychological method. While Holl was primarily interested in Luther's understanding

---

18. Kant, *Gesammelte Schriften*, Werke VI, *Die Religion innerhalb der Grenzen der bloßen Vernunft; Die Metaphysik der Sitten*.

19. See e.g. Wobbermin, *Schleiermacher und Ritschl* and Wobbermin, "Schleiermacher," *RGG*² 5.

20. Wobbermin, "Gibt es eine Linie Luther – Schleiermacher?"

21. Holl's 1917 lecture on Luther's understanding of religion is generally considered to mark the advent of the Luther Renaissance, and it is not insignificant that 1917 also marked the 400th anniversary of the publication of Luther's 95 Theses, marking what is generally considered to be the beginning of the Reformation. For the first edition of this essay, see Holl, *Was verstand Luther unter Religion?* For a broader study of the place of Luther (and Melanchthon) in nineteenth- and twentieth-century histories of theology, see Gestrich, "Luther und Melanchthon in der Theologiegeschichte des 19. und 20. Jahrhunderts."

of religion and his doctrine of justification, Wobbermin was primarily interested in Luther's more general description of the relationship between the believer and God. He refers to Luther's insight into the relational quality of faith in God as one of his major contributions to Christian thought, calling it Luther's "Copernican revolution of religious thought."[22]

As Wobbermin sketches the problem, in the late medieval period the existence of God was understood by many theologians (particularly the Scholastic theologians) to be objectively established because it is rationally demonstrable, and these rational demonstrations were codified in Church dogma. In this case, then, the doctrines of the Church are the objects of faith, and faith is understood as *assensus* or *fides implicita* and as *notitia*.[23] Luther rejected the possibility of a purely rational demonstration of the existence of God and, more importantly, he rejected the definition of faith as *fides implicita*.[24] Luther argued that human beings gain a relation to God only through faith and in faith; the objective content of this relationship is then formed into an idea of God by means of reason. The existence of God is incomprehensible apart from faith; God is comprehensible and accessible to human beings only through faith. Rather than being a purely rational or cognitive assent and knowledge, faith is for Luther a living personal relationship between the human being and God. He expresses this most clearly in his exposition of the First Commandment in the *Large Catechism*, in his answer to the question, "What is a god?"

> A god means that to which we are to look for all good and in which we are to find refuge in all need. Therefore, to have a god is nothing other than to trust and believe in that one from the heart, as I have often said that the trust and faith of the heart alone make both God and idol. If your faith and trust are right, then your God is the true one, and in turn where your trust is false and wrong, there you do not have the true God. For the two belong together [*gehören zuhaufe*], faith and God. Anything on which your heart relies and depends, I say, that is really your god.[25]

---

22. Wobbermin, "Luther, Kant, Schleiermacher," 108.
23. Ibid., 108–9.
24. Ibid., 109.
25. Luther, "Der große Katechismus," 560 [ET: "The Large Catechism," 386].

Zwischen den Zeiten

Wobbermin refers to this passage as Luther's decisive turn toward the subject, his "Copernican revolution of religious thought."[26] Rather than emphasizing the objective reality of God independent of the human subject, Luther emphasizes the *relationship* between the human subject and the objective reality of God. Furthermore, Luther makes another decisive turn toward what Wobbermin prefers to call the "religio-psychological perspective."[27] It is the faith and trust of the heart that make both God and idol. God is not objectively established by rational proofs that require assent and implicit faith; rather, the objective reality of God is subjectively appropriated by the faith and trust of the heart. Faith is now understood primarily as *fiducia*.[28]

There is a danger of misunderstanding the relationship between objectivity and subjectivity in this relationship between faith and God: it could be construed as suggesting that God has no objective reality outside the believing subject. Wobbermin argues that Luther is very careful to emphasize the objective "pole" of this relationship, even as he starts with the subjective "pole":

> Luther begins from subjective personal experience. But he evaluates this religious experience from the perspective of its objective

---

26. Wobbermin, "Luther, Kant, Schleiermacher," 109–10.

27. Ibid. See also Wobbermin, "Gibt es eine Linie Luther – Schleiermacher?" 254.

28. Wobbermin takes this opportunity to offer a preemptive response to critics who might suggest that Luther here falls into the pure subjectivism that formed the basis of Ludwig Feuerbach's criticism of religion: "Isn't the necessary consequence of Luther's position the opinion of Feuerbach, who saw nothing other than illusion even in faith in God? No, absolutely not, in no possible way! . . . The trust and faith of the heart, Luther says, make both God *and* idol. Feuerbach could not say this; he could allow no distinction. Rather, he had to make an indiscriminate judgment: the faith and trust of the heart makes God – or even: it makes an idol. . . . In fact, both were the same for Feuerbach. For even the word "God" is for him only a linguistic expression for an idol. There is for him no factual distinction between God and an idol." ["*Ist nicht die notwendige Konsequenz dieser Betrachtung Luthers die Ansicht Feuerbachs, die eben im Gottesglauben nichts als Illusion sieht? Nein, das doch ganz und gar nicht, in gar keiner Weise! . . . Das Trauen und Glauben des Herzens, sagt Luther, macht beide, Gott und Abgott. So könnte Feuerbach nicht sprechen; er könnte keinen Unterschied zulassen, er müßte vielmehr unterschiedslos urteilen: das Trauen und Glauben des Herzens macht Gott – oder auch: es macht den Abgott. . . . Sachlich aber wäre für Feuerbach beides das Gleiche. Denn auch das Wort Gott ist für ihn nur ein sprachlicher Ausdruck für den Abgott. Es gibt für ihn keinen sachlichen Unterschied zwischen Gott und Abgott.*"] Ibid., 110. Emphasis in original. See Feuerbach, *Das Wesen des Christentums* [ET: *The Essence of Christianity*] and Feuerbach, "Das Wesen des Glaubens im Sinne Luthers" [ET: *The Essence of Faith according to Luther*].

content. The question of the objective content or the objective corresponding pole is for him the comprehensive and decisive main question.[29]

According to Wobbermin, Luther insists that subjective religious experience cannot be divorced from its objective content. The two belong together in the closest possible relationship: "This objective content is completely inseparable from religious experience; it belongs to the constancy of religious experience itself: the two belong together, faith and God."[30]

Although Wobbermin never expresses this particular thought in classical Lutheran terms, he is in fact making a classical Lutheran (and Melanchthonian) argument for the primacy of the *pro nobis*. Just as Luther was more concerned with the knowledge that we have a gracious God than with any speculative philosophical proofs for God's existence, and just as Melanchthon was more concerned to know the benefits (the work) of Christ rather than anything about Christ's nature (his person) in itself,[31] Wobbermin is more concerned with the accessibility and comprehensibility of God to faith and personal religious experience than with the external, objective reality of God outside of faith.[32]

---

29. "*Luther geht aus von der subjektiv-persönlichen religiösen Erfahrung. Aber er beurteilet diese religiöse Erfahrung unter dem Gesichtspunkt ihres Objektgehaltes. Die Frage nach dem Objektgehalt oder dem objektiven Gegenpol ist für ihn von vornherein die übergreifende und entscheidende Hauptfrage.*" Wobbermin, "Luther, Kant, Schleiermacher," 110–11. Wobbermin prefers to name the two elements of faith (the subjective side and the objective side) "Gegenpole" – literally "antipoles," "opposite poles," or "corresponding poles."

30. "*Dieser Objektgehalt ist ihm von der religiösen Erfahrung gar nicht zu trennen; er gehört ihm zum Bestand der religiösen Erfahrung selbst hinzu: die zwei gehören zu Haufe, Glaube und Gott.*" Ibid., 111.

31. "To know Christ is to know his benefits, not . . . to look upon his nature and mode of incarnation." Melanchthon, "Loci Communes (1521)," 85.

32. Although Wobbermin never refers to this theme, his position here recalls Luther's concept of the "hidden God" [*Deus absconditus*], especially in Luther's commentary on Genesis: "For one must debate either about the hidden God or about the revealed God. With regard to God, insofar as God has not been revealed, there is no faith, no knowledge, and no understanding. And here one must hold to the statement that what is above us is none of our concern. For thoughts of this kind, which investigate something more sublime above or outside the revelation of God, are altogether devilish. With them nothing more is achieved than that we plunge ourselves into destruction; for they present an object that is inscrutable, namely, the unrevealed God." Luther, "Vorlesung über 1. Mose," 458–59 [ET: "Commentary on Genesis," 44].

Zwischen den Zeiten

For Wobbermin, everything here returns to Luther's exposition of the First Commandment in the *Large Catechism*. In his essay on the question of God in the *Large Catechism*, Wobbermin provides a detailed analysis of the structure and content of the *Catechism* as a whole and in its parts in an effort to ground his own religio-psychological method in Luther's thought.

For Luther, the First Commandment is the chief commandment, the commandment on which all others are based: "If the heart is right with God and this commandment is kept, all the rest will follow on their own."[33] Wobbermin refers to Luther's exposition of the First Commandment as a "red thread" that weaves its way through the entire *Catechism*, providing the basis for all that follows.[34] It is especially significant for Wobbermin that Luther's answer to the question of all religion ("What is a god?") also marks his decisive, "epoch-making" turn toward the subject.[35]

Unlike the late medieval Scholastic theologians, Luther does not turn to speculative philosophy or rational demonstrations, nor does he appeal to the doctrinal tradition of the Church to answer the question of God. Rather, according to Wobbermin, Luther turns to subjective, personal religious experience by relating the objective content of this experience to Scripture. Anticipating possible criticisms of his interpretation,[36] Wobbermin questions whether Luther does not in fact retreat to a

---

33. Luther, "Der große Katechismus," 572 [ET: "The Large Catechism," 392].

34. Wobbermin, "Die Frage nach Gott in Luthers großem Katechismus," 418.

35. Ibid., 421.

36. In at least one case, Wobbermin anticipated rightly. It is precisely at this point that Karl Holl raises an objection to Wobbermin's interpretation of Luther. In a revised edition of his lecture on Luther's understanding of religion, Holl criticizes Wobbermin for suggesting that Luther attempted to secure the objective importance of religious experience (i.e., the certainty that religion is not an illusion) by relating it to the objective historic foundation of religion (in this case, Scripture). Holl denies that Luther ever made such a connection in this context, instead focusing on Luther's use of the term "right confidence" in his exposition of the First Commandment: "The decisive point is accordingly what he means by 'right' confidence. In any case, what is meant is not 'complete' confidence, for the latter could also refer to a false god: 'To have a god means to have something in which the heart reposes complete confidence.' The difference between 'right' and 'wrong' confidence must be found at a deeper level. . . . 'Right' confidence is . . . characterized by two moments: first, the confidence must be directed to a God who is truly transcendent, beyond the visible world; second, the 'confidence' must be free from earthly wishes. . . . Luther regards the knowledge of the transcendent God himself as immediately given with the *syntheresis*, the conscience." Holl, *What Did Luther Understand by Religion?* 64 [The German original is "Was verstand Luther unter Religion?" 54]. The transcendent

reliance on a purely external authority with his insistence that Scripture is the final authority by which the idea of God is gained and evaluated:

> The religious experience of the individual may not claim to act as the norm of religious life and thought. On the other hand, religious experience should not bow to any mere external authority, not even to that of biblical revelation. Rather, the idea of God expressed in the biblical revelation should be normative only insofar as it corresponds to religious experience and satisfies the religious need. It is thus, to speak conceptually, the religio-psychological circle between individual-subjective religious experience and the objective historic revelation of God, which Luther establishes as the criterion for answering the question of God.[37]

For Luther, Scripture is authoritative because it is the Word of God, specifically because it is the primary witness to and mediation of the gospel. The gospel is understood primarily as "a discourse about Christ, that he is the Son of God and became man for us, that he died and was raised, that he has been established as Lord over all things."[38] Again, the gospel is "a book of divine promises in which God promises, offers, and gives us all his possessions and benefits in Christ."[39] Christ becomes present in the gospel, "for the preaching of the gospel is nothing else than Christ coming to us, or we being brought to him."[40]

God *in se*, however, is for Luther the hidden God [the *Deus absconditus*] and has no relation at all to trusting faith. Neither Holl nor Wobbermin make this connection, but it would seem to support Wobbermin's position more than Holl's in this instance.

37. "*Nicht die religiöse Erfahrung des Einzelnen darf beanspruchen, als Norm des religiösen Lebens und Denkens aufzutreten. Andrerseits soll sich die religiöse Erfahrung keiner bloß äußeren Autorität beugen, auch nicht derjenigen der biblischen Offenbarung. Vielmehr hat der Gottesgedanke dieser biblischen Offenbarung nur insofern normativ zu gelten, als er der religiösen Erfahrung entspricht und dem religiösen Bedürfnis Genüge leistet. Es ist also, begrifflich zu sprechen, der religionspsychologische Zirkel zwischen der subjektiv-eigenen religiösen Erfahrung und der objektiv-geschichtlichen Gottesoffenbarung, den Luther als Kriterium für die Beantwortung der Frage nach Gott aufstellt.*" Wobbermin, "Die Frage nach Gott in Luthers großem Katechismus," 424.

38. Luther, "Eyn kleyn unterricht, was man ynn den Euangelijs suchen und gewartten soll," 9 [ET: "A Brief Instruction on What to Look for and Expect in the Gospels," 118].

39. Ibid., 13 [ET, 120].

40. Ibid., 13–14 [ET, 121]. Despite constant references to the centrality and primacy of Scripture in Lutheran theology, the Lutheran Confessions (unlike the Reformed Confessions, for example) contain no article devoted solely to Scripture and its doctrinal authority. The closest any of the Confessions come to a clear declaration of Scripture's authority is Luther's argument in the article on the Mass in the Smalcald Articles that

In each of these definitions of the gospel, Luther emphasizes the relationship between objective content and subjective experience. In the first definition, the gospel is described as a story about how Christ came *for us*, in the second the gospel is defined as a record of God's promises and benefits given *to us*, and in the third the proclamation of the gospel is described in almost sacramental language as the means by which Christians are united with Christ. The unifying element in each of these three cases is faith. It is by faith – itself a gift of the gracious God through the gospel – that the promises and benefits of the gospel are received.

Again with particular reference to the *Large Catechism* Wobbermin discusses the relationship between faith and God in the context of what he calls Luther's "Trinitarian monotheism,"[41] which, he argues, must be understood simultaneously as retrieving the Trinitarian thought of the early church and as representing a point of departure for an entirely new understanding of the Trinity.[42] In the *Large Catechism*, Luther treats the Trinity most extensively in his exposition of the Apostles' Creed: "One God and faith, but three persons, therefore also three articles or confessions."[43] Wobbermin suggests that Luther's relating of the three persons to the three articles of the Creed represents a reciprocal understanding of the objective and subjective elements, or *Gegenpole* of faith:

> Objectively (theocentrically): God created us in order to redeem and sanctify us. Thus the thought here moves from the first article through the second and to the third. Subjectively (anthropocentrically) evaluated, the order is reversed: it moves from the third article through the second and to the first. Were it not revealed to us through the Holy Spirit, we would know nothing of Christ; and without the Lord Christ, who is a mirror of the heart of the Father, we could never come to know the Father's love [*Hulde*] and grace, where except for Christ we see nothing but a wrathful and terrible judge. Thus this direction and sequence is crucial for the origins of faith. In this respect it is the more important one for Luther.[44]

"the Word of God shall establish articles of faith and no one else, not even an angel." The paragraph containing this passage was added by Luther for publication only after it was presented and signed at Smalcald. "Die Schmalkaldische Artikel," 421 [ET: "The Smalcald Articles," 304].

41. See Wobbermin, "Luthers trinitarischer Monotheismus."
42. Wobbermin, "Die Frage nach Gott in Luthers großem Katechismus," 427.
43. Luther, "Der große Katechismus," 647 [ET: "The Large Catechism," 432].
44. "*Objektiv (theozentrisch): Gott hat uns dazu geschaffen, daß er uns erlöste und hei-*

In both directions – from the objective to the subjective and from the subjective to the objective – the second article serves as the lynchpin of the Creed not only formally but also materially. Objectively understood, God's reconciling activity (what Wobbermin calls "the crowning of God's creative work") is realized in the redemption accomplished by Jesus Christ and is "brought home" [*heimgebracht*] by the Holy Spirit. Considered subjectively, the Holy Spirit leads human beings to Christ, who is the "mirror of the heart of the Father," in whom human beings may know the Father's love. In both cases, the second article (and Christ, the content of the second article) serves as the mediating element both formally and materially.[45]

For Luther, "the total divine essence, will and work" [*das ganze göttliche Wesen, Willen und Werk*] is portrayed in the doctrines of creation, redemption, and sanctification that constitute the essential basis of the Creed in particular and the Christian faith in general. Wobbermin suggests that this "total divine essence, will and work" must be understood both objectively (theocentrically) and subjectively (anthropocentrically) if Luther's Trinitarian monotheism is to be retained. Wobbermin prefers to express this relationship between the theocentric and the anthropocentric elements of Luther's Trinitarian thought in terms of the religious experience of the Christian, of the correspondence between subjective experience and the objective reality of God:

> *According to Luther's understanding of faith, these three elements therefore belong to the essence of God.* They correspond to God's ways of agency as they are experienced in the religious experience of Christians. But for this reason faith must properly attribute them to the essence of God and think of them as fixed in God's essence. Otherwise, with their objective ontological reality the objective ontological reality of God himself would be endangered. Therefore Luther most strenuously emphasizes that Trinitarian faith pertains

---

ligte. So geht hier der Gedanke vom ersten Artikel über den zweiten zum dritten. Subjektiv (anthropozentrisch) beurteilt ist dagegen die Reihenfolge die umgekehrte: sie führt vom dritten Artikel über den zweiten zum ersten. Wo es uns nicht durch den heiligen Geist offenbart würde, könnten wir von Christus nichts wissen; und ohne durch den Herrn Christus, der ein Spiegel ist des väterlichen Herzens, könnten wir nimmermehr dazu kommen, daß wir des Vaters Hulde und Gnade erkenneten, da wir außer Christus nichts sehen denn einen zornigen und schrecklichen Richter. Für die Begründung des Glaubens ist also diese Richtung und Reihenfolge die ausschlaggebende. Sie ist insofern für Luther die wichtigere." Wobbermin, "Die Frage nach Gott in Luthers großem Katechismus," 429.

45. Ibid., 430.

to the "total divine essence, will and work," given that God has "revealed and opened the deepest abyss of his fatherly heart" in the three articles.[46]

In these appeals to Luther, Wobbermin hopes to establish his religio-psychological circle on the basis of Luther's thought, particularly his doctrines of God and faith. His references to Luther's work remain limited almost exclusively to Luther's *Large Catechism*; for example, he does not retain Luther's Eucharistic theology or his emphasis on the proclamation of the gospel. Because Wobbermin relies almost exclusively on Luther's exposition of the First Commandment in the *Large Catechism*, he does not take advantage of the many additional places in Luther's theology where he could find substantial support for his religio-psychological circle. It is quite curious that Wobbermin does not consider the Eucharist and preaching as important examples of the religio-psychological circle at work in the lives of Christians and in the life of the church, especially since these are precisely the two events in which, according to Luther, Christ is immediately present for faith.

While there is no significant engagement with the doctrine of the Eucharist and its potential implications for the religio-psychological circle in Wobbermin's work, he does follow Luther in his high regard for Scripture and its role in awakening faith. However, Wobbermin's references to Scripture as the objective, historic revelation of God often fail to account for the *proclamation* of Scripture, which, as Luther puts it, "is nothing else than Christ coming to us, or we being brought to him."

It is even more curious that in Wobbermin's many discussions of the doctrinal authority of Scripture and its status as one half of the religio-psychological circle he never elaborates on *how* Scripture serves this important function other than to repeat that Scripture is the historic document of the divine revelation and the early church's testimony of faith. He simply suggests that the historic picture of Christ "radiates outward" from the New Testament, remaining present and efficacious in the

---

46. "*Diese drei Momente gehören folglich nach dem Glaubensverständnis Luthers zum Wesen Gottes. Sie entsprechen den in der religiösen Erfahrung vom Christen erlebten Wirkungsweisen Gottes. Ebendeshalb aber muß der Glaube sie auf das Wesen Gottes selbst zurückführen, sie zu diesem gehörig und in ihm verankert denken. Denn sonst würde mit ihrer objektiv-ontologischen Wirklichkeit diejenige Gottes selbst gefährdet sein. Daher denn Luther auch aufs stärkste betont, daß der trinitarische Glaube das 'ganze göttliche Wesen, Willen und Werk' betrifft, da Gott in den drei Artikeln 'den tiefsten Abgrund seines väterlichen Herzens offenbart und aufgetan' hat.*" Ibid., 430–31. Emphasis in original.

Christian community and becoming accessible and comprehensible only to faith.[47]

Wobbermin's appeals to Luther, especially his arguments for a relational understanding of faith, demonstrate his desire to ground his method in the Lutheran theological tradition. This desire represents a significant development in Wobbermin's thought, marking an increased awareness of his place within the broader Protestant tradition and a self-conscious attempt to provide historical support and justification for his theological method. It is not insignificant that this increased interest in and attention to the historical foundations of his theological method corresponds to both the "Luther Renaissance" of Holl and the so-called theological *Epochenwende* and the rise of dialectical theology immediately following the First World War.

Immanuel Kant

The 200th anniversary of Kant's death in 1904 sparked a renewed interest in Kant and his philosophy, and many Protestant theologians also returned to Kant to find philosophical support for their work.[48] Many of these theologians were even prepared to anoint Kant the *Philosoph des Protestantismus*, the "philosopher of Protestantism."[49] Wobbermin was also prepared to grant Kant this title, albeit with certain reservations. He admits that such a description certainly has its merit, or at least contains a significant element of truth. But "it may not be understood primarily that Kant had brought the fundamental religious position of Protestantism to a purely philosophical form. He did not do that at all. But that description nevertheless contains an important kernel of truth."[50]

---

47. Perhaps this emphasis on the presence of Christ in the Christian community is ultimately based on Schleiermacher's description of the church as the community of fellowship with the Redeemer. See, e.g., Schleiermacher, *Der christliche Glaube*, §14 and the Second Section of the Second Aspect of the Second Part, "On the Constitution of the World with Respect to Redemption," encompassing §113–163. There are similarities between the two positions, but Wobbermin never explicitly refers to Schleiermacher's ecclesiology in these passages.

48. On the theological reception and use of Kant in this period, see Graf and Tanner, "Philosophie des Protestantismus."

49. This title was first bestowed upon Kant by Friedrich Paulsen in *Kant, Der Philosoph des Glaubens*.

50. "*Sie darf vor allem nicht dahin verstanden werden, Kant habe die religiöse Grundposition des Protestantismus zu reiner philosophischer Ausprägung gebracht. Das*

Zwischen den Zeiten

Kant's significance for Protestant theology, in Wobbermin's estimation, is rooted in his epistemology, particularly as he developed it in his critical philosophy.[51] Wobbermin highlights two related themes of Kant's epistemology in particular as especially representative of Kant's significance for Protestant theology: the possibility of rational knowledge of God and the cognition of objects.

Kant famously exposed the "abyss" spanning the distance between the thinking subject and the "unconditioned necessity," or God: "The unconditioned necessity, which we need so indispensably as the ultimate sustainer of all things, is for human reason the true abyss."[52] God is not available to cognition because God is not an object of possible experience,[53] and the possibility of experience provides cognitions with their objective reality.[54] Kant rejected speculative theology and the traditional proofs for the existence of God precisely because human reason cannot span this abyss.[55]

In his epistemology Kant transferred the emphasis from the object of cognition to the cognizing subject. This, for Wobbermin, represents Kant's "Copernican turn":

> Thus Kant turned according to the manner of Copernicus, who no longer permitted the sun to revolve around the earth but the

---

hat er ganz und gar nicht getan. Aber doch enthält jene Bezeichnung einen wichtigen Wahrheitskern." Wobbermin, "Luther, Kant, Schleiermacher," 104.

51. Wobbermin also refers to Kant's ethics as a second major influence on Protestant thought, and he traces the roots of Kant's ethics back to what he considers to be Luther's imperative ethics or "doctrine of duty" [*Pflichtenlehre*]. Ibid., 107–8. This second area of influence, however, lies beyond the scope of this study.

52. Kant, *Critique of Pure Reason*, 574 [The German original is *Kritik der reinen Vernunft*].

53. "No *a priori* cognition is possible for us except solely of objects of possible experience." Ibid., 264.

54. Ibid., 282. Again, "The conditions of the possibility of experience in general are at the same time conditions of the possibility of the objects of experience, and on this account have objective validity in a synthetic judgment *a priori*." Ibid., 283.

55. Ibid., Chapter 3, Section 3: "The grounds of proof of speculative reasons for inferring the existence of a highest being," 559–63; Section 4: "On the impossibility of an ontological proof of God's existence," 563–69; Section 5: "On the impossibility of a cosmological proof of God's existence," 569–78; Section 6: "On the impossibility of a physico-theological proof," 578–83; and Section 7: "Critique of all theology from speculative principles of reason," 583–89.

earth around the sun.[56] [Kant] directed the view from the objects [*Gegenständen*] of cognition initially to the subjects of cognition. He showed that up to that point all assumptions toward objects [*Objekte*] are dependent on the subjects, namely on their cognition, on the manner and conditions of their cognition. Accordingly he began to clarify these conditions in detail and thereby laid the foundation on which critical thought in the precise sense can be constructed.[57]

God and the world are not immediately accessible to rational cognition. In an often misunderstood passage in his preface to the second edition of the *Critique of Pure Reason*, Kant declares that he must deny knowledge to make room for faith:

> Thus I cannot even assume God, freedom and immortality for the sake of the necessary practical use of my reason unless I simultaneously deprive speculative reason of its pretension to extravagant insights; because in order to attain to such insights, speculative reason would have to help itself to principles that in fact reach only to objects of possible experience, and which, if they were to be applied to what cannot be an object of experience, then they would always actually transform it into an appearance, and thus declare all practical extension of pure reason to be impossible. Thus I had to deny knowledge in order to make room for faith; and the dogmatism of metaphysics, i.e., the prejudice that without criticism reason can make progress in metaphysics, is the true source of all unbelief conflicting with morality, which unbelief is always very dogmatic.[58]

Kant's statement concerning the need for faith can be interpreted to advocate a certain dogmatism or faith in authority, an interpretation

---

56. See Copernicus, *On the Revolutions of the Heavenly Spheres*. See also Vollmann, *Uncentering the Earth*.

57. "So kehrt Kant nach Art des Kopernikus, der die Sonne sich nicht mehr um die Erde, sondern die Erde sich um die Sonne drehen ließ, den Standpunkt der bisher üblich gewesenen Betrachtung geradezu um. Er lenkt den Blick von den Gegenständen der Erkenntnis zunächst auf die Subjekte des Erkennens. Er zeigt, daß allen bisherigen Annahmen entgegen die Objekte abhängig sind von den Subjekten, nämlich von ihrem Erkennen, von der Art und den Bedingungen ihres Erkennens. Demgemäß hat er dann den Anfang gemacht, diese Bedingungen im einzelnen klarzustellen und hat damit den Grund gelegt, auf dem kritisches Denken im strengen Sinne aufgebaut werden kann." Wobbermin, "Luther, Kant, Schleiermacher," 105.

58. Kant, *Critique of Pure Reason*, 117.

Wobbermin is quick to reject. Kant himself precludes this interpretation much later in the first *Critique* when he distinguishes between having an opinion, believing, and knowing. According to Kant, having an opinion is taking something to be true despite its being subjectively and objectively insufficient. Knowing is when taking something to be true is both subjectively and objectively sufficient. Believing, on the other hand, is when taking something to be true is subjectively sufficient but objectively insufficient.[59]

Believing, as Kant defines it, is analogous (but certainly not identical) to Wobbermin's description of the "corresponding poles" of faith. The objective reality of God, according to Wobbermin, is inaccessible to human beings apart from faith. In other words, there can be no independent, objective knowledge of God outside the believing subject. This does not mean that God does not *exist* outside the believing subject; rather, it means that the objective reality of God cannot be subjectively appropriated apart from faith. For Wobbermin, faith is always related to the historic revelation of God, specifically the historic picture of Christ. The divine revelation is directed toward the entire existence of the human being, never toward the intellect or reason alone. Although Kant does not relate faith to revelation in any traditional sense of the term, he, too, anchors faith somewhere other than the intellect or reason. Faith, for Kant, is a personal conviction finally anchored in the conscience.[60]

Wobbermin counts Kant an ally of Protestant theology on this point, especially against the rationalism of Catholic and Protestant Scholastic theology. But it cannot be said that Kant's doctrine of faith is in any way intrinsically "Protestant." Furthermore, it is open to certain misunderstandings, specifically in terms of the relationship between objectivity and subjectivity in the doctrine of faith. Kant's definition can be understood as a retreat to a pure subjectivism in which the reality of God is based exclusively on the individual's believing, a conclusion that, in Wobbermin's estimation, would be a misinterpretation of Kant.

---

59. Ibid., 686.
60. Wobbermin, "Luther, Kant, Schleiermacher," 106. It is interesting that Karl Holl emphasizes the relationship between the transcendent God and the conscience in his critique of Wobbermin's interpretation of Luther. Wobbermin does not discuss the role of the conscience in the relationship between God and faith at all, except in this summary of Kant's position.

The seeds of such misinterpretations are present in Kant's treatment itself. Kant does not make any distinctions – at least within the first *Critique* – between believing in general and Christian faith in particular.[61] Neither does he define faith in terms of certainty, preferring to limit any constructive idea of God to a "postulate," e.g., as a postulate of pure reason[62] or, in the *Critique of the Power of Judgment*, as the giver of the moral law.[63] For Kant there can be no certainty in faith precisely because it is never objectively sufficient, and this is one important reason why faith is to be distinguished from knowledge. Wobbermin also distinguishes between faith and knowledge, specifically within the doctrine of revelation in his *Richtlinien evangelischer Theologie*, where he argues that revelation is not directed toward the enrichment of knowledge but to the entire existence of the human being.[64] But Wobbermin, unlike Kant, is willing to secure a degree of certainty for faith in its relation to the objective historic divine revelation in Scripture, specifically in the historic picture of Christ.

Kant's epistemological "Copernican turn" toward the subject remains open to the criticism of being a retreat into pure subjectivism. Wobbermin's interpretation of the relationship between the subjective and objective "poles" of faith is most directly based on his interpretation of Schleiermacher, and it is his interpretation of Schleiermacher and his affinity for Schleiermacher's theological method that comes most consistently under attack in the post-war period.

Friedrich Schleiermacher

Wobbermin was occupied with Schleiermacher throughout his career, and he wrote more about Schleiermacher than about any other theologian.[65] He constructed his three-part systematic theology on the foun-

---

61. Kant does discuss Christianity at length in *Die Religion innerhalb der Grenzen der bloßen Vernunft* [ET: *Religion within the Boundaries of Mere Reason*], but even there he does not propose a specifically Protestant doctrine of faith.

62. Kant, *Critique of Pure Reason*, 584–89.

63. Kant, *Critique of the Power of Judgment*, 318 [The German original is *Kritik der Urteilskraft*].

64. Wobbermin, *Richtlinien*, 105.

65. See the following of Wobbermin's essays and articles on Schleiermacher: *Schleiermacher und Ritschl*; *Schleiermachers Hermeneutik*; "Luther, Kant, Schleiermacher"; "Ist Schleiermacher wirklich ausgeschöpft?"; "Zum Streit um Schleiermacher"; "Schleiermacher in der Zeit seines Werdens"; "Der Streit um Schleiermacher"; "Gibt es eine Linie Luther-Schleiermacher?"; "The Doctrine of Grace in Evangelical German

dation of what he calls Schleiermacher's religio-psychological approach, and in his post-war debates with the dialectical theologians he constantly returned to Schleiermacher for support. It would not be an exaggeration to call Wobbermin's theology "Schleiermacherian," primarily because he consistently appeals to Schleiermacher in support of his positions, but also because his theological method displays some striking similarities to Schleiermacher's method in the *Glaubenslehre*.[66]

Wobbermin's systematic theology is based on what he calls the "Schleiermacher-Jamesschen Problemstellung," with its emphasis on the interrelation of faith and religious experience.[67] But to understand Wobbermin's appeals to Schleiermacher in support of his theological method, especially against the criticism of the dialectical theologians, his occasional writings on Schleiermacher are more instructive. These occasional writings can be divided into two categories: the first category comprises those texts in which Wobbermin traces the roots of his method to the great Protestant thinkers of the past, and the second category comprises those texts in which Wobbermin defends his interpretation and use of Schleiermacher against his critics, specifically Karl Barth.

Schleiermacher's two great theological works, the *Reden* and the *Glaubenslehre*, best represent Schleiermacher's basic religious and theological positions. The *Reden* already reveal the important role of religious experience in Schleiermacher's thought, and the *Glaubenslehre* represents the height of his methodological and theological thought.[68] In both texts, religious experience and the psychological and logical structure of religious consciousness serve as the foundation of Schleiermacher's theology.

Theology from Schleiermacher Onwards"; "Schleiermacher in der Theologie des englischen Sprachgebiets"; "Die anthropologische Gedanken in der Theologie Luthers und Schleiermachers"; "Schleiermachers protestantische und vaterländische Sendung"; and "Schleiermacher," *RGG*² 5.

66. In the introduction to the second volume of his systematic theology, Wobbermin adopts the motto, "Back to Schleiermacher! and from Schleiermacher forward!" ["*Zurück zu Schleiermacher! und von Schleiermacher aus vorwärts!*"] Wobbermin, *Das Wesen der Religion*, vi [ET: *The Nature of Religion*, xi].

67. See Chapter 3, "Systematic Theology According to the Religio-Psychological Method." Despite the reference to James in his discussion of the foundations of his religio-psychological theology, Wobbermin overwhelmingly favors Schleiermacher over James when providing support for his method.

68. Given the priority of feeling and religious consciousness in the *Reden*, it is quite surprising that Wobbermin does not engage them at all in his discussions of the religio-psychological method.

But it is the *Glaubenslehre* that represents the pinnacle of Schleiermacher's theological work, and it is to the *Glaubenslehre* that Wobbermin most consistently turns for support in his own work.

The *Glaubenslehre* serves as an important resource for Wobbermin's work in two respects. First, in it Schleiermacher analyzes the essence of religion in general and Christianity in particular, an analysis that forms the basis of Wobbermin's own investigation of those topics in his systematics. Second, Schleiermacher's emphasis on religious experience and the psychological and logical structure of religious consciousness serves as a model for Wobbermin's religio-psychological method.[69]

For Wobbermin, Schleiermacher's major contribution to the history of Christian thought is his "Copernican revolution" of theological method. First, Schleiermacher defines the essence of all piety[70] as being conscious of oneself as absolutely dependent, or being conscious of being in relation to God.[71] Second, Schleiermacher defines Christian doctrines as accounts of the Christian religious affections brought to speech, so that the task of dogmatics is to express these religious affections in descriptively didactic speech.[72]

Schleiermacher's "Copernican turn" is often misunderstood as a retreat to a pure subjectivism in which only the subjective experience of the believer is considered as the basis for Christian faith. Wobbermin suggests that Schleiermacher's relational language is (as it was with Luther) the cause of this misunderstanding. Consciousness of being in relation to God is often misinterpreted as indifference toward the objective reality of God outside the consciousness of the believing subject.[73] But,

---

69. See Chapter 3, "Systematic Theology according to the Religio-Psychological Method," for a more detailed discussion of the importance of psychology in Wobbermin's theological method in the systematics.

70. "Piety . . . is, considered purely in itself, neither a knowing nor a doing, but a determination of feeling, or of immediate self-consciousness." Schleiermacher, *Der christliche Glaube*, §3. Wobbermin discusses this proposition at some length in his entry on Schleiermacher in the *RGG*²: "Feeling is for him identical to immediate self-consciousness. This expression allows one to know more clearly what Schleiermacher means. He does not mean a unique spiritual function alongside others, but a unifying basis of the human spiritual life." When Schleiermacher refers to feeling, he does not mean any arbitrary feeling, but a *determination* of feeling that is then more precisely defined as the feeling of absolute dependence. Wobbermin, "Schleiermacher," 172.

71. Schleiermacher, *Der christliche Glaube*, §4.

72. Ibid., §15.

73. Schleiermacher himself addresses this misunderstanding in his first letter to Dr.

as Wobbermin emphasizes, the relationship between the believer and God, and thus between subjective experience and objective reality, must be held together to avoid either a pure subjectivism or a pure objectivism. And, according to Wobbermin, Schleiermacher successfully avoids both dangers by always emphasizing the relational character of religious consciousness:

> *Clearly this relationship is such that it is not arbitrarily effected by us; rather, it is established by God and can only be established by God. Therefore Schleiermacher prefixes the concept of the feeling of absolute dependence. But this feeling of absolute dependence has an objective content or an objective corresponding pole just as self-evidently and as unconditionally as the trust and faith of the heart in Luther.*[74]

This "objective content" in Schleiermacher is not primarily understood in terms of Kant's *Gegenstände* – as objects of the senses – but rather as an objective content that is accessible only to personal religious experience.[75] It is not primarily an object acquired by the imagination; it is "a reality of a higher order," accessible only through personal experience of the relationship itself.[76] In other words, the objective reality of the feeling of absolute dependence is available only to one who is conscious of being absolutely dependent, that is, only to one who is conscious of being in relation to God. Wobbermin suggests that Schleiermacher's discussion of the feeling of absolute dependence unites the "religious inwardness" of Luther and the critical thought of Kant. That Schleiermacher himself did not fully appreciate this synthesis provides Wobbermin with his

---

Lücke: "It is said that my 'God-consciousness' should not be confused with 'consciousness of God,' and immediately afterward it is also said that the God-consciousness in humans is supposed to be God itself! Poor me! Even when I believe I have made every effort to be most grammatically precise, the result turns out to be the exact opposite." Schleiermacher, *On the Glaubenslehre*, 45–46.

74. "*Freilich ist dieses Beziehungsverhältnis ein solches, das nicht von uns willkürlich herbeizuführen ist, das vielmehr von Gott gesetzt ist und nur von Gott gesetzt werden kann. Deshalb stellt Schleiermacher den Begriff des schlechthinnigen Abhängigkeitsgefühls voran. Aber dies schlechthinnige Abhängigkeitsgefühl hat einen Objektgehalt oder objektiven Gegenpol genau so selbstverständlich und genau so bedingungslos wie bei Luther das Trauen und Glauben des Herzens.*" Wobbermin, "Luther, Kant, Schleiermacher," 117–18. Emphasis in original.

75. Ibid., 117.

76. Ibid., 118.

task of establishing the "Luther-Kant-Schleiermacher line" in Protestant thought.[77]

According to Schleiermacher, the feeling of absolute dependence is the basis of all religion. Wobbermin argues that Schleiermacher's analysis of the feeling of absolute dependence and the essence of religion constitutes an application of the religio-psychological circle between religious experience and the objective reality of God.[78] And, as for Luther, the key to this circle is faith. Schleiermacher also indicates the importance of faith and experience with the epigraph to his *Glaubenslehre*, taken from Anselm's *Proslogion*: "Nor do I seek to understand in order that I may believe, but I believe in order that I may understand. For the one who does not believe does not experience, and the one who does not experience does not understand."[79] By equating the feeling of absolute dependence with the consciousness of standing in relation to God, Schleiermacher "intended to show the way to achieve objectivity through subjectivity"[80] much as Luther did in his exposition of the First Commandment.[81]

---

77. Ibid., 119. Wobbermin notes that Albrecht Ritschl attempted such a synthesis of Kant and Schleiermacher by returning through them to Luther's thought. But Wobbermin concludes that, while Ritschl's desire for a deliberate synthesis is laudable, his synthesis faltered on methodological grounds, specifically in terms of Ritschl's emphasis on the theory of value judgment [*Werturteil*], which failed to carry on the "Copernican revolutions" of Luther, Kant, and Schleiermacher. Ibid. See also Wobbermin, *Schleiermacher und Ritschl*.

78. Wobbermin, "Gibt es eine Linie Luther – Schleiermacher?" 257.

79. Schleiermacher, *Der christliche Glaube*, 1:1. See Anselm, *Proslogion* I; De fide trin. 2.

80. "*Sie will den Weg zeigen, durch die Subjektivität hindurch zur Objektivität zu gelangen.*" Wobbermin, *Schleiermacher und Ritschl*, 28.

81. Wobbermin concludes his article on the "Luther-Schleiermacher line" with a summary of the methodological similarities between Luther and Schleiermacher and his own religio-psychological approach: "To summarize, the fundamental theological direction of Schleiermacher's thought tends toward a religio-psychological, existential theology that seeks to make the correlative relationship between the *fides quae creditur* and the *fides qua creditur* into the methodologically decisive authority.... But insofar and inasmuch as Schleiermacher represents that intention, he returns to Luther's basic Reformation position and attempts to make this the basis of theological and dogmatic work. In this sense one can speak of a 'Luther-Schleiermacher' line. It is the line of religio-psychological existential theology." ["*Zusammenfassend ist also zu sagen, daß die theologisch grundlegende Gedankenführung Schleiermachers auf eine religionspsychologisch-existentielle Theologie tendiert, die das Korrelatverhältnis von fides quae creditur und fides qua creditur zur methodisch entscheidenden Instanz zu machen sucht.... Aber sofern und soweit Schleiermacher jene Intention vertritt, kehrt er zu der reformatorischen Grundposition*

Zwischen den Zeiten

Wobbermin consistently returns to Schleiermacher's definition of Christian doctrines as an important foundation for the religio-psychological method. For Schleiermacher, Christian doctrines are accounts of the religious affections brought to speech. The ultimate subject matter of dogmatics is not merely the objective content of revealed doctrine, as it was for the Protestant Scholastic theologians. The subject matter is also not merely the subjective experience of the Christian, as it is for empirical psychologists of religion. The proper subject matter of dogmatics, according to Schleiermacher, is the Christian's subjective experience of the objective reality of the transition from a state of being in need of redemption to a state of being redeemed (the movement from sin to grace), a transition made possible by fellowship with the Redeemer in faith.

Faith in the Redeemer is accompanied by assumption into the fellowship of the Redeemer's blessedness, the Christian community. Schleiermacher emphasizes the presence of Christ in the Christian community in terms similar to Wobbermin: the Christian community is the community of fellowship with the Redeemer, the community of his enduring presence and influence. Although Schleiermacher does not distinguish in any systematic way between *Geschichte* and *Historie* in his Christology,[82] his description of the presence of the Redeemer in the Christian community is similar to Wobbermin's description of the present efficacy of the historic portrait of Christ throughout the history of the Christian tradition. For Schleiermacher, one important way the Redeemer is present in the community is through the testimony of Christians to their experience of redemption in Christ:

> [All direct Christian preaching] can always only take the form of testimony; testimony of one's own experience, which shall arouse in others the desire to have the same experience. But the impression that all later believers received in this way from the effect [*Bewirkten*] of Christ, namely from the common Spirit communi-

---

Luthers zurück und versucht, diese zur Basis der theologisch-dogmatischen Arbeit zu machen. In diesem Sinne ist von einer Linie 'Luther-Schleiermacher' zu reden. Es ist die Linie religionspsychologisch-existentieller Theologie."] Wobbermin, "Gibt es eine Linie Luther-Schleiermacher?" 257–58. Emphasis in original.

82. Although Schleiermacher does not distinguish between *Geschichte* and *Historie*, his lectures on the life of Jesus stand at the beginning of a long line of historical research into the life of Jesus that ultimately provided the basis for such a distinction. See Schleiermacher, *Friedrich Schleiermacher's sämmtliche Werke*, div. 1, vol. 6, *Das Leben Jesu* [ET: *The Life of Jesus*].

cated by him and from the whole communion of Christians, supported by the historic representation [*geschichtliche Darstellung*] of his life and essence, was just the same impression that his contemporaries received from him directly.[83]

For Wobbermin, the historic portrait of Christ available in the New Testament and present throughout the history of the Christian tradition constitutes the objective pole of the religio-psychological circle. The religious experience of Christians (the subjective pole) is always related to and dependent on this objective reality of the present historic Christ.

Wobbermin's doctrine of Scripture is essential for understanding the religio-psychological circle. Schleiermacher also relates faith in Christ to Scripture, which he defines, like Wobbermin, as revelation and as testimony:

> The efficacy [*Wirksamkeit*] of Christ therefore consists solely in the human communication of the Word, but only insofar as it advances [*fortbewegt*] the Word of Christ, the indwelling divine power of Christ himself. This is in perfect accord with the truth that, in the consciousness of a person in the grip of conversion, every sense of human intermediation [*Zwischenwirkung*] vanishes, and Christ is immediately present in all his redeeming and atoning activity.... [T]hese divine workings of grace are supernatural insofar as they depend upon and actually proceed from the being of God in the person of Christ; at the same time, they are historic [*geschichtlich*] and formative of history [*geschichtsbildend*], and they are natural in so far as they are in general bound to the historic [*geschichtlich*] life of Christ; and in detail each working that establishes a new personality is bound up with the historic coherence [*geschichtlichen Zusammenhang*] of Christ's effects.[84]

Schleiermacher's distinction between the supernatural and the natural within the "divine workings of grace" corresponds very closely to Wobbermin's definition of Scripture as both the divine revelation and the early church's testimony of faith in Christ, the religio-psychological circle operative within Scripture itself. This religio-psychological circle within

---

83. Schleiermacher, *Der christliche Glaube*, §14.1, 1:96 [ET *The Christian Faith*, 69]. The consistency of this impression, the fact that it is the same basic experience in the present as it was for the disciples themselves, is especially significant for Wobbermin's treatment of the resurrection and Easter faith. See Chapter 3, "The Resurrection of Jesus as the Historic Foundation of the Christian Religion."

84. Ibid., §108.5, 2:167 [ET, 492].

Scripture is also extended more broadly to include the religious experience of the individual Christian as it is related to the objective revelation of God in the historic portrait of Christ available in the New Testament and in the history of the Christian tradition. Both applications of the religio-psychological circle are rooted in the corresponding relationship between the objective and the subjective elements of faith, the *fides quae creditur* and the *fides qua creditur*. It is this relationship between the two elements of faith and the prominent role it plays in both Schleiermacher's and Wobbermin's theology that marks the most significant point of contention between Wobbermin and the dialectical theologians.

WOBBERMIN AND POST-WAR THEOLOGY

The dialectical theologians, particularly Karl Barth, considered liberal theology to be an abject failure for at least two important reasons. First, they considered liberal theology's turn toward the subject to be an abandonment of any objective basis for the Christian faith and a sacrifice of theology in favor of an anthropology merely masquerading as theology.[85] Second, the dialectical theologians considered liberal theology to have forfeited its critical voice by too readily accommodating the bourgeois culture of the nineteenth century, which, in their estimation, implicates many of the liberal theologians and, by extension, liberal theology itself in the horrors of the First World War.[86]

Karl Barth

It is well known that Barth regarded Schleiermacher with a combination of deep respect and harsh criticism. His Göttingen lectures on Schleiermacher reveal a profound admiration for Schleiermacher, even as

---

85. Consider Barth's famous critique of what he considered to be the anthropocentrism of liberal theology: "Speaking of God means something *other* than speaking of human beings in a somewhat higher tone." Barth, *Das Wort Gottes und die Theologie*, 164. The only available English translation is rather different: "[O]ne cannot speak of God simply by speaking of man in a loud voice." Barth, *The Word of God and the Word of Man*, 196. In his reflections marking the discontinuation of the journal, *Zwischen den Zeiten*, Barth also uses the term *Menschgott* ("human-God") to indicate the anthropocentrism he detects in liberal theology. Barth, Thurneysen, and Merz, "Abschied von *Zwischen den Zeiten*," 313.

86. This charge is one of the roots of the pejorative description of liberal theology as *Kulturprotestantismus*. On Barth and "Culture-Protestantism" see Ruddies, "Karl Barth im Kulturprotestantismus."

he is consistently critical of Schleiermacher's method and the directions his thought was taken in the nineteenth century:

> I certainly have no reason to conceal the fact that I stand with personal *mistrust* against Schleiermacher and all that Protestant theology essentially became through him, that I do *not* regard the decision in Christian matters that was made in that intellectually and culturally significant time as a happy one, that the result of my engagement with Schleiermacher thus far can be summed up in that saying of Goethe: "Behold, his spirit calls to you from the cave: Be a man and do *not* follow me!"[87]

One of Barth's fundamental criticisms of Schleiermacher concerns his turn toward the subject in the *Glaubenslehre*, or what Wobbermin calls Schleiermacher's "Copernican revolution of theological method."[88] This turn toward the subject also constitutes the main point of contention between Barth and Wobbermin.

Barth is suspicious of Schleiermacher's description of the "givenness" of the feeling of absolute dependence, which is presupposed in the Christian self-consciousness. This presupposition of the feeling of absolute dependence and the definition of the "whence" of that feeling as God represents for Barth an irreversible move away from the objective to a

---

87. Barth, *Die Theologie Schleiermachers*, 6 [ET: *The Theology of Schleiermacher*, xv]. Emphasis in original. Here Barth paraphrases the epigraph to the second edition of Goethe's *The Sorrows of Young Werther*: "Sieh, dir winkt sein Geist aus seiner Höhle; Sei ein Mann und folge mir nicht nach." Goethe, *Goethes Werke*, vol. 4, *Die Leiden des jungen Werthers* [ET: *Goethe's Collected Works*, vol. 11, *The Sorrows of Young Werther, Elective Affinities, Novella*].

88. Barth also refers to Schleiermacher's method in the *Glaubenslehre* as his "Copernican revolution": "This is the great Copernican revolution with which Schleiermacher has drawn the undoubtedly correct and unavoidable conclusions from the history of Protestant theology since the Reformation and with which he has made and still makes a school in spite of all the attempts of the so-called positivists to kick against the pricks. So long and so far as we do not perceive this revolution to be a fundamental mistake and fundamentally reverse it; so long as the opinion remains intact that with it (1) Schleiermacher has honored the true legacy of *Luther* in theology, and (2) he has given theology right of place on the soil of Kant's critical philosophy (of which Schleiermacher all his life spoke with sovereign *spite*!), so long as the title is felt at a first glance to be right and not wrong (and who among us feels otherwise?), Schleiermacher *is* in fact the master, with no less authority than *Melanchthon* and *Calvin* had in the 16th and 17th centuries." Barth, *Die Theologie Schleiermachers*, 333 [ET: *The Theology of Schleiermacher*, 187]. Emphasis in original. It is especially interesting that Barth draws the same conclusions as Wobbermin regarding Schleiermacher's synthesis of Luther's theological legacy and Kant's critical philosophy.

pure subjectivism. Barth traces one of the roots of this move to what he considers to be Schleiermacher's deficient doctrine of the Word:

> To anticipate, nothing remained of the belief that the Word or statement is as such the bearer, bringer, and proclaimer of truth, that there could indeed be such a thing as a Word of God. Schleiermacher, too, knows the concept of the *kerygma*, but it is a kerygma that only *depicts* [*darstellt*] and does not *bring*, that only *states* or *expresses* and does not *declare*. Truth does not come in the spoken Word; it remains in speaking feeling.[89]

For Schleiermacher, as for Wobbermin, proclamation as testimony is possible only on the basis of one's personal experience of redemption through the influence of Christ. The Christian gives testimony concerning religious experience in the hopes of eliciting that same experience in others. Without this personal experience of redemption, the Word remains something purely external and unrelated to one's own experience. To put it in Wobbermin's terms, others must be drawn into the religio-psychological circle between religious experience and the objective revelation of God in order to have a similar experience. This is one of the primary purposes of the church as the community of fellowship with the Redeemer and the locus of his enduring redemptive influence, and this is also one of the primary purposes of the ministry of the Word. For Schleiermacher and Wobbermin, the Word is God's revelation directed toward the entire existence of the human being, and it is accessible only by faith. Schleiermacher's doctrines of revelation and Scripture presuppose a relationship between the subjective experience of the Christian and the objective reality of the divine revelation. As Schleiermacher puts it, "Faith in Christ cannot be grounded in the reputation [*Ansehen*] of Holy Scripture; rather, [faith] must already be presupposed in order to grant a specific authority to Holy Scripture."[90]

Barth is most emphatically critical of Schleiermacher's understanding of God as the "whence" of the feeling of absolute dependence. For Barth, a definition of God that is rooted in the subjective experience of God – the feeling of absolute dependence – shifts the focus of theological work from

---

89. Ibid., 373 [ET, 210]. Emphasis in original. For more on the Word of God in Schleiermacher's theology, see DeVries, "The Word of God in the Theology of Friedrich Schleiermacher."

90. Schleiermacher, *Der christliche Glaube*, §128, 2:284 [ET: *The Christian Faith*, 591].

the divine to the human and represents an abandonment of theology for anthropology. Barth's puzzlement at this most fundamental position of Schleiermacher's is expressed in the second of five two-part questions in his epilogue to the 1968 edition of the *Schleiermacher-Auswahl*:

> In Schleiermacher's theology or philosophy, do persons feel, think, and speak (1) in relationship to an indispensable Other, in accordance with an *object* that is superior to their own being, feeling, perceiving, willing, and acting, an object toward which adoration, gratitude, repentance, and supplication are concretely possible and even imperative? Were that the case, then I would prick up my ears and be joyfully prepared to hear further things about this Other, in the hopes of finding myself fundamentally at one with Schleiermacher....
>
> Or, for Schleiermacher, do persons feel, think, and speak (2) in and from a sovereign consciousness of their own being together, and indeed essentially *being one*, with everything that might possibly come into question as something or even someone different from them? If that were the case, then the door between him and me would indeed be latched, and substantial communication would then be impossible.[91]

---

91. Barth, "Nachwort," 308 [ET: "Concluding Unscientific Postscript on Schleiermacher," 275–76]. In his study of the early Barth's liberal roots and the development of his "critically realistic" dialectical theology, Bruce McCormack has shown that Barth's earliest theological writings are steeped in the liberalism of his teacher Wilhelm Herrmann, including an emphasis on personal religious experience and a subjective appropriation of the objective reality of God and God's revelation in Christ. McCormack, *Karl Barth's Critically Realistic Dialectical Theology*, 31–125. Three essays are especially significant for understanding Barth's early liberalism. The first two essays are part of a brief debate concerning the fitness of "modern" pastors for mission work that played out in the *ZThK*: "Moderne Theologie und Reichgottesarbeit" and "Antwort an D. Achelis und P. Drews." The third essay is a reflection on Ernst Troeltsch's *Die Bedeutung der Geschichtlichkeit Jesu für den Glauben*: "Der christliche Glaube und die Geschichte." Barth's affinity for liberal theology was shattered in 1914 when so many of his former teachers supported the German war effort. McCormack suggests that these events led Barth to the conclusion that the theology of experience too easily became a "*Kriegstheologie*" that sought God's blessings on Germany's war. He cites a letter from Barth to Wilhelm Herrmann in which Barth challenges his former teacher to defend his theological support for the war: "Especially with you, Herr Professor (and through you with the great masters – Luther, Kant, and Schleiermacher), we learned to acknowledge 'experience' as the constitutive principle of knowing and doing in the domain of religion. In your school it became clear to us what it means to 'experience' God in Jesus. Now, however, in answer to our doubts, an 'experience' which is completely new to us is held out to us by German Christians, an allegedly religious war 'experience'; i.e. the fact that German Christians 'experience' their war as a holy war is supposed to bring us to silence,

Zwischen den Zeiten

While Barth's final questions to Schleiermacher remain unanswered, there is no such hesitation in his condemnation of Wobbermin. Whereas Schleiermacher's theology remains in some sense redeemable in Barth's estimation, Wobbermin's is beyond redemption.[92] Barth is rarely as consistently critical as he is in his rejection of Wobbermin's positions, which often call to mind the acerbity of Barth's later debate with Emil Brunner on the possibility of a natural theology.[93] Barth's criticisms of Wobbermin generally fall into two related categories: his appeals to Luther and Schleiermacher in support of his religio-psychological method, and his doctrine of faith.

The majority of Barth's criticisms of Wobbermin are found in the first volume of his *Kirchliche Dogmatik*. There Barth takes issue with Wobbermin's appeal to Luther's exposition of the First Commandment, specifically as Wobbermin interprets it to indicate a correlative relationship between faith and the Word of God:

> There is really no point in building one's understanding of Luther or one's whole theology on this popular preamble. Neither in the *Large Catechism* nor elsewhere did Luther teach the God thus defined, but only the true God of true faith, and in the question of this God he never referred to faith as such or its immanent correctness nor did he ever raise it to the dignity of a "counterpole" or partner of God's Word. . . . In my view terms like circular or reciprocal or correlative relation are very imprecise descriptions of what Luther meant to say and did say in this matter.[94]

---

if not demand reverence from us. Where do you stand in relation to this argument and to the war theology which lies behind it?" Karl Barth to Wilhelm Herrmann, November 4, 1914, cited in McCormack, *Karl Barth's Critically Realistic Dialectical Theology*, 113. This letter helps to clarify why Barth remained a vehement critic of theological subjectivism and of appeals to personal religious experience wherever he found them, particularly in the work of Wobbermin.

92. The animosity between Barth and Wobbermin extended beyond the professional and into the personal realm. Matthias Wolfes notes that when Barth left the University of Göttingen in 1925, Wobbermin (who had been on the faculty since 1922) bought Barth's house on the Nikolausberger Weg. The transaction was fraught with complications, and Barth and Wobbermin exchanged a series of letters with one another and with the university administration to resolve the issue. See Wolfes, *Protestantische Theologie*, 298, n. 127.

93. See Brunner, *Natur und Gnade* and Barth, *Nein!* [ET of both texts: Brunner and Barth, *Natural Theology*]. This exchange marks a breach of what had been to that point a close theological alliance. See Hart, *Karl Barth vs. Emil Brunner*.

94. Barth, *Die Kirchliche Dogmatik*, I.1, 245–46 [ET: *Church Dogmatics*, I.1, 233–34].

Wobbermin's use of the term "correlative" is, according to Barth, a misunderstanding and betrayal of Luther's intention,[95] as well as a dangerous move toward making the existence of God and the authority of God's Word dependent on faith. Wobbermin himself never makes such a move in an ontological sense, and he warns against understanding it in this way.[96] Faith and God are interdependent only for the believing subject. Or, as Wobbermin puts it, "the understanding of the object of faith, the *fides quae creditur* (thus of God and his revelation in Jesus Christ) is not possible without consideration of the *fides qua creditur*, of the personal conviction and experience of faith."[97]

Wobbermin, following Luther and Melanchthon, defines faith primarily as *fiducia*, as trust. Faith as trust signifies an existential decision that must never be regarded as completed.[98] The religio-psychological

---

95. Barth accuses Wobbermin of misquoting Luther in his discussions of the correlative relationship between God and faith: "The other [saying of Luther's] is in the Lectures on Romans and, as every reader of Wobbermin knows, it runs: *fides et promissio sunt relativa* (Wobbermin persistently writes *correlativa* for this. . .)." Ibid., 244 [ET, 232]. Barth is correct in this instance. Luther's own words are, "Quia fides et promissio sunt relatiua." Luther, "Romanos," 45 [ET, *Romans*, 39]. See also p. 89, n. 43.

96. "This is clearly not interdependence in an ontological sense, not that the existence of God depends on human faith – it is interdependence only for us: God gives himself to us in his revelation to be grasped only through the mediation of faith – and accordingly we approach God only on the way of faith." ["*Die Wechselbeziehung freilich nicht im ontologischen Sinne, nicht so, daß die Existenz Gottes vom Glauben der Menschen abhinge. Wohl aber die Wechselbeziehung für uns: Gott gibt sich uns in seiner Offenbarung nur zu fassen durch Vermittlung des Glaubens – und demgemäß kommen wir an Gott nur heran auf dem Wege des Glaubens.*"] Wobbermin, *Richtlinien*, 21–22.

97. "*Das Verständnis des Glaubensgegenstandes, der* fides quae creditur *(also Gottes und seiner Offenbarung in Jesus Christus) ist nicht möglich ohne Berücksichtigung der* fides qua creditur, *der eigenpersönlichen Glaubensüberzeugung und Glaubenserfahrung.*" Ibid., 22.

98. Barth is quite critical of Wobbermin's use of existential thinking in his later work, wryly remarking that it is "not without humor." He accuses Wobbermin of merely following the most recent theological fad, made even more insincere by Wobbermin's apparent lack of interest in Kierkegaard, to whose work Barth traces the theological existentialism of the 1920s. See Barth, *Kirchliche Dogmatik* I.1, 18 [ET: *Church Dogmatics* I.1, 20]. Wobbermin does acknowledge Kierkegaard's influence on existential thought, but he prefers to base his existential thinking on Schleiermacher, a preference he explains in some detail in *Wort Gottes*, 20ff. It is especially important to note that Kierkegaard's work was only available in Danish until the late nineteenth century, when the first German translations appeared. The first collection of Kierkegaard's works in German translation was prepared by Hermann Gottsched and Christoph Schrempf and published in 12 volumes between 1913 and 1925, and by all accounts this translation was far from

Zwischen den Zeiten

circle is a dynamic process rather than a static structure, and faith must always find its relation to its object in every new situation. The relation between faith and its object is always understood from the side of the believing subject, a move Schleiermacher had already made. Barth, however, criticizes Wobbermin's similar move as completely antithetical to the intentions of the Reformers:

> It should now be quite comprehensible that the interpretation of faith as *fiducia*, trust, or confidence as we find it in the Reformers and the whole of the older Protestant theology . . . has nothing whatever to do with a displacement of the reality of faith from its object to the believing subject. . . . Certainly faith is first faith

---

reliable. A more accurate translation of the bulk of Kierkegaard's work was not available in German until after World War II, when Emanuel Hirsch's translation was published in thirty-six volumes between 1950 and 1969. This collection remained the standard German Kierkegaard source for much of the twentieth century. For more on the translation of Kierkegaard into German and the role his thought played in the theology of the mid-twentieth century, see Morgan, "Adorno's Reception of Kierkegaard." The retrieval of Kierkegaard as a theological resource by the dialectical theologians represents the blazing of a new path from the Reformation to the present. While Wobbermin took his stand in the "Luther-Kant-Schleiermacher line," many of the dialectical theologians (including Brunner, Bultmann, and Gogarten) took their stand firmly in the "Reformation-Kierkegaard line," bypassing Schleiermacher altogether. Ernst Troeltsch made much the same point (albeit it negatively) when he remarked that Gogarten had thrown an "apple from the tree of Kierkegaard" into the midst of German liberal Protestantism. Troeltsch, "Ein Apfel vom Baume Kierkegaards" [ET: "An Apple from the Tree of Kierkegaard"]. The extent of Barth's indebtedness to Kierkegaard is still debated. Eberhard Jüngel, for example, thinks Barth's development during the period of the *Romans* commentaries is best understood in terms of his immersion in Kierkegaard during the same period. See Jüngel, "Von der Dialektik zur Analogie." Bruce McCormack, however, thinks Jüngel overestimates Kierkegaard's influence on Barth during this period. McCormack acknowledges Kierkegaard's influence on the early Barth, but he is careful not to overemphasize this influence: "We overestimate Kierkegaard's importance if we wish to see in him the decisive influence on Barth's thought in this phase." McCormack, *Karl Barth's Critically Realistic Dialectical Theology*, 235–240. For more on Barth's relationship to Kierkegaard, see an early study by Gemmer and Messer, *Sören Kierkegaard und Karl Barth*. However, in recent years there has also been a resurgence of interest in the relationship between Kierkegaard and Schleiermacher. See Crouter, "Schleiermacher: Revisiting Kierkegaard's Relationship to Him" and Cappelørn et al., eds., *Schleiermacher und Kierkegaard*. It is interesting that it was precisely Kierkegaard's emphasis on the "infinite qualitative distinction" between God and human beings that Barth found so appealing, while recent work on the relationship between Schleiermacher and Kierkegaard is uncovering important points of contact precisely in terms of their shared interest in the subjective character of Christian faith. It is therefore all the more regrettable that Wobbermin never paid serious attention to Kierkegaard.

when it is *fiducia*. *Notitia* and *assensus* alone would not be faith, but only that *opinio historica* which the ungodly can have too. But how can faith be *fiducia* without also being, even as *fiducia*, *notitia* and *assensus*, *fiducia promissionis*, trust in the mercy of God that encounters us as *misericordia promissa*, i.e., in the objectivity [*Gegenständlichkeit*] of the Word, which has form and even a form of words, and therefore has also a form of knowledge [*Erkenntnisgestalt*], of acceptance of its truth, in the faith which receives it?[99]

Barth further suggests that any subordination of *assensus* or *notitia* to *fiducia* would have been unthinkable to the Reformers, especially Melanchthon, who would have insisted instead that all three elements of faith must be subordinated equally to their object.[100] For Wobbermin, faith that is not understood primarily as *fiducia* threatens to become a mere *fides historica* (which is rooted in *historiae notitia* or *opinio historica*) or a mere *fides implicita* rather than the "trust of the heart" that Luther describes in the *Large Catechism*. Faith, for Wobbermin, must be understood in terms of obedience, decision, and experience. These existential categories preclude the primacy of the cognitive elements of faith [*notitia* and *assensus*] and instead point to the primacy of *fiducia*.[101]

The debate concerning Wobbermin's appeals to Luther and Melanchthon serves only as prologue to the most significant debate between Barth and Wobbermin, the debate concerning Schleiermacher. Many of Wobbermin's essays and articles on Schleiermacher written in the 1920s and 30s are directed against Barth and the dialectical theologians, specifically toward their criticism of Schleiermacher and what they perceived as the subjective tendencies or blatant subjectivism of liberal theology.[102] In 1928, Wobbermin declared the Schleiermacher debate to be a "controversy" [*Streit*],[103] and one year later he declared this contro-

---

99. Barth, *Kirchliche Dogmatik* I.1, 246–47 [ET: *Church Dogmatics* I.1, 234–35].

100. Ibid., 247 [ET, 235].

101. Wobbermin, *Wort Gottes*, 12–13.

102. In some cases, these tendencies developed into a pure subjectivism, and Wobbermin suggests that moving beyond such subjectivism constitutes one of the primary tasks of evangelical theology in the 1930s. See Wobbermin, "Gibt es eine Linie Luther-Schleiermacher?" 250.

103. See Wobbermin, "Der Streit um Schleiermacher."

versy to have developed into a "crisis" [*Krisis*] that threatened the very foundations of contemporary Protestant theology.[104]

This controversy, focused as it was on the theological legacy of Schleiermacher, was ultimately a controversy about the principal questions and basic problems of theology in general. It was a controversy between the dialectical theology of Barth, Brunner, and Gogarten on the one hand and the religio-psychological theology of Wobbermin and his students on the other.[105] Both schools take their name from their methods, and Wobbermin suggests that the entire debate finally has to do with the competing methodological points of departure of these two schools rather than with Schleiermacher's own method.[106]

The essential point of conflict between these two schools, in Wobbermin's estimation, is their respective attitudes toward the *fides qua creditur*. Dialectical theology wants to disregard the subjective, personal experience of faith as a methodological point of departure, while religio-psychological theology wants to take it as a basic methodological principle. Based largely on his interpretation of Luther and Schleiermacher, Wobbermin insists that the fundamental methodological position of Protestant theology must take into account both the objective and subjective "corresponding poles" of faith (the *fides quae creditur* and the *fides qua creditur*). This relation between the objective and subjective poles must be taken into account because religious faith is essentially a relationship between the believer and God. The fact that the objective pole (God) is not directly accessible to human knowledge requires the use of the religio-psychological circle between the subjective experience of faith and the objective content of faith, primarily available in Scripture as the historic revelation of God culminating in Jesus Christ and as the historic objectification of religious conviction, as the testimony of the early church's faith in Christ.

Scripture is not to be equated with religious experience; it remains superior to religious experience because God first speaks in and through Scripture, thereby awakening the personal experience of faith.[107] Scripture,

---

104. See Wobbermin, *Richtlinien*.

105. For some examples of Wobbermin's students' religio-psychological work, see Schmidt, Winkler, and Meyer, eds., *Luther, Kant, Schleiermacher in ihrer Bedeutung für den Protestantismus*.

106. Wobbermin, "Der Streit um Schleiermacher," 281–82.

107. Ibid., 282.

therefore, is the sole source for Christian doctrine in the Protestant tradition. Personal religious experience serves as an indispensable methodological aid for understanding the divine revelation in Scripture; it is only through the *fides qua creditur* that the *fides quae creditur* is appropriated and understood. Dialectical theology's rejection of this interaction between the objective and subjective elements leads, in Wobbermin's opinion, to what he calls a theology of false alternatives:

> *Barth's dialectical theology proceeds from a false alternative and consequently leads in many cases to false alternatives.* It is thus most accurately characterized *as a theology of false alternatives.* This is already based in its initial approach, for this first, fundamental approach, which is decisive for all further work, rests on a false alternative inasmuch as it rips the *fides quae creditur* apart from the *fides qua creditur* in the false opinion that only in this way can the majesty of God (the *fides quae creditur*) adequately be emphasized.[108]

These "false alternatives" are not unique to dialectical theology. Wobbermin traces their roots to Ritschl and even to Schleiermacher himself. The objective pole (God) must be further divided into a transcendent side (God *in se*) and an immanent side (God's revelation in history). Schleiermacher and Ritschl both intended to base their methodological points of departure on the relationship between the objective and subjective poles, but both failed adequately to carry out their intentions. Wobbermin suggests that Schleiermacher overemphasized the subjective pole, which in his followers became a pure subjectivism or psychologism.[109] Ritschl, on the other hand, overemphasized the immanent side of the objective pole (the revelation of God in history) which in his fol-

---

108. "*Barths dialektische Theologie geht demgegenüber von einer falschen Alternative aus und führt infolgedessen auch weiterhin vielfach zu falschen Alternativen. Sie ist gerade so am treffendsten zu charakterisieren: als Theologie der falschen Alternativen. Das ist schon in ihrem ersten Ansatz begründet. Denn bereits dieser erste, grundlegende und für alles weitere entscheidende Ansatz beruht auf einer falschen Alternative, sofern er* fides quae creditur *und* fides qua creditur *auseinander reißt, in der falschen Meinung, nur so sei das Majestätsrecht Gottes (die* fides quae creditur*) zur vollen Geltung zu bringen.*" Ibid., 283. Emphasis in original.

109. Wobbermin mentions two representatives of the Erlangen school – Johann Christian Konrad von Hofmann and Franz Hermann Reinhold Frank – as examples of this type of pure subjectivism.

lowers became a pure objectivism or historicism.[110] Dialectical theology takes both sides of the objective pole alone as its methodological point of departure, sacrificing the subjective pole altogether, which results in what Wobbermin calls a "false objectivism."[111] Religio-psychological theology, on the other hand, seeks its point of departure in the relationship between the objective and the subjective poles "in such a way that the relationship to the transcendent side [of the objective pole] is found through the immanent side." In this way it seeks to overcome both a false and pure objectivism or historicism and a pure subjectivism or psychologism.[112]

The key to this middle way sought by Wobbermin is found in Schleiermacher's definition of doctrines and dogmatics. Doctrines are accounts of the Christian religious affections brought to speech, and dogmatic statements are propositions of faith [*Glaubenssätze*]. These propositions bring the convictions of faith to speech and, according to Wobbermin, have the character of convictions of faith themselves. Any other statement, be it purely historical, rational, or speculative, has no place in Protestant dogmatics. Therefore Schleiermacher defined his dogmatics as a *Glaubenslehre* (doctrine of faith) and called it simply, "The Christian Faith presented as a coherent whole according to the basic principles of the Evangelical Church."

Wobbermin suggests that Schleiermacher's definition of doctrines and dogmatics remains true to the Reformation doctrine of faith, while

110. Ernst Troeltsch serves as Wobbermin's example of this type of thinking.

111. Ibid., 284.

112. Ibid. Emil Brunner offers a similar critique of historicism and psychologism but comes to a radically different conclusion on the only way forward than the way proposed by Wobbermin. Brunner suggests that the entire history of liberal theology led inevitably to these twin dangers and therefore must be abandoned. He puts it specifically in terms of the historical-critical method, which "has had its time and its right. . . . But it has lost the sense for the nonhuman-objective. It has completely surrendered the gospel to history and psychology. . . . With inner necessity its work was forced to both "highpoints" at which we now see it to have arrived, in the icy historical relativism of a Troeltsch and the opulent, stuffy psychologism of Heiler." Brunner, *Erlebnis, Erkenntnis und Glaube*, 2. It is interesting that Brunner does not mention Wobbermin at all in this study except for a brief reference in the midst of a discussion of empirical and transcendental psychology, where he refers to the first volume of Wobbermin's systematic theology as the "most significant" systematic study of the psychology of religion written by a German theologian. There he agrees with the judgment of Wilhelm Koepp, who concludes that, despite the merits of Wobbermin's work, the transcendental-psychological method must be judged a failure. Koepp, *Einführung in das Studium der Religionspsychologie*, 30. See Brunner, *Erlebnis, Erkenntnis und Glaube*, 40–41, n. 2.

Barth and Brunner reject Schleiermacher's method as a pure subjectivism that betrays the intentions of the Reformers. Wobbermin contends that this judgment is based on a misunderstanding of Schleiermacher's definition of Christian religious affections. He suggests that Barth and Brunner understand "affections" as a merely subjective condition distinct from convictions of faith. Schleiermacher, according to Wobbermin, understood the religious affections to be convictions of faith rather than something distinct from them. Convictions of faith have an objective content, namely God and God's revelation. In this relationship between the conviction of faith and its objective content, Wobbermin detects the corresponding relationship between the *fides qua creditur* and the *fides quae creditur*.[113]

Wobbermin contends that Schleiermacher cannot simply be abandoned or relegated to the history of Protestant thought as though he could be of no value for addressing the problems of contemporary theology. He considers Schleiermacher to be a valuable ally against the objectivizing tendencies of dialectical theology and a rich resource for theology in the post-war period. Furthermore, Wobbermin suggests that Schleiermacher is especially relevant because he anticipated two of the popular philosophical and theological trends of the first half of the twentieth century, namely phenomenology and existentialism.

Wobbermin interprets Schleiermacher's attempt at overcoming the contemporary *Identitätsphilosophie* (traces of which, he suggests, remain in Schleiermacher's work as a result of his reliance on other contemporary philosophers) as a move toward the phenomenological approach popularized in the work of Edmund Husserl.[114] He defines Schleiermacher's nascent phenomenology as an approach to thinking that combines Kant's critical thought with a tendency against pure subjectivism and an intention toward the objective content of thinking. It is based on the conviction that objectivity and subjectivity must not be separated, even in the act of thinking itself. Wobbermin expresses it with an obvious reference to Luther's exposition of the First Commandment:

> Νόημα and νόησις belong together, complement one another, and determine one another. Νόημα and νόησις, i.e., the content

---

113. Ibid., 286–87.

114. See, e.g., Husserl, *Logische Untersuchungen* [ET: *Logical Investigations*] and Husserl, *Ideen* [ET: *Ideas*].

of thinking and the execution of thinking, the objective content of thinking and the act of thinking. For human beings there is no νόημα other than by means of νόησις; on the other hand, all νόησις has a necessary relation to a νόημα, to an objective content.[115]

Schleiermacher anticipated this phenomenological approach by insisting on a reciprocal relationship between the conviction of faith and its objective content, ultimately going back to Luther's description of the reciprocal relationship between faith and God. Wobbermin offers that the proto-phenomenology of Luther and Schleiermacher finds its fullest theological expression in the religio-psychological circle, in the "constant reciprocal relationship between the *fides quae creditur* and the *fides qua creditur*."[116]

Rudolf Bultmann

In his essay *Wort Gottes und evangelischer Glaube*, published in 1931, Wobbermin, perhaps recognizing the directions in which contemporary Protestant theology was moving, suggests that all Protestant theological thought must be existential thought. This does not mean, however, that theological thought must be bound to one or another philosophical school (e.g. Heidegger's philosophy of existence);[117] rather, theological existential thought must be rooted in the Protestant theological tradi-

---

115. "Νόημα und νόησις gehören zusammen, ergänzen und bestimmen sich gegenseitig. Νόημα und νόησις, d.h. Gedankengehalt und Denkvollzug, Objektgehalt des Denkens und Akt des Denkens. Für uns Menschen gibt es kein νόημα anders als durch die νόησις hindurch; andererseits aber alle νόησις hat eine notwendige Beziehung auf ein νόημα, auf einen Objektgehalt." Wobbermin, "Der Streit um Schleiermacher," 293.

116. Ibid.

117. It would appear that Wobbermin and Barth find common ground on this issue. In a letter to Barth, Bultmann criticizes Barth's refusal to incorporate a philosophical perspective into his theology: "You have a sovereign scorn for modern work in philosophy, especially phenomenology. What point is there in saying occasionally that the dogmatician must also be oriented to philosophical work if the presentation finds no place for this orientation...? It seems to me that you are guided by a concern that theology should release itself from dependence on philosophy. You try to achieve this by ignoring philosophy. The price you pay for this is in fact that of falling prey to an outdated philosophy. For because faith is the faith of a *believer*, i.e., an existent person (I can also say: because the justified person is the *sinner*), dogmatics can speak only in existential-ontological terms." "Rudolf Bultmann, Marburg, to Karl Barth, Münster, June 9, 1928," in Barth, *Karl Barth – Rudolf Bultmann Briefwechsel*, 82 [ET: *Karl Barth – Rudolf Bultmann Letters*, 38–39]. Emphasis in original.

tion. Wobbermin finds this basis in the work of Schleiermacher, with his emphasis on personal religious experience. For Wobbermin, religio-psychological thought is an essential component of any valid theological existentialism, and it is precisely at this point that he cannot agree with the theological existentialism of someone like Bultmann, who bases his existentialism on a combination of Heideggerian philosophy and theological-historical analysis of the New Testament.[118]

Despite this disagreement about the proper methodological foundations of existential theology, there are important ways in which Wobbermin's thought anticipates some of Bultmann's positions. The most striking similarity concerns the distinction between *Geschichte* and *Historie* and its use as an interpretive principle in theological work, especially within Christology.

The similarity between Wobbermin's and Bultmann's use of the distinction between *Geschichte* and *Historie* is just one example of the continuity between liberal theology and the new generation of German theologians after World War I, an example that calls into question the prevailing wisdom of a radical *discontinuity* between these two generations. The continuity is only emphasized by the fact that Bultmann did not adopt the distinction between *Geschichte* and *Historie* from Wobbermin or any other liberal theologian. It had been used before Wobbermin and outside of liberal theology by Kähler, and it was an essential component of Heidegger's philosophy of existence, especially in his *Sein und Zeit*. Bultmann never refers to Wobbermin's work on the distinction, and yet the similarities are striking.

Both Wobbermin and Bultmann share a similar definition of the historical Jesus, which they define as the Jesus who is the subject and product of historical research, and both define *Geschichte* as that in the person of Jesus that has meaning and significance for Christian faith in the present.[119] The *historisch* is only of interest to historians, while the *geschichtlich* continues to influence the present and the future. This

---

118. Wobbermin accuses Bultmann of failing to understand the religio-psychological basis of theological existentialism, which leads him (according to Wobbermin) to an untenable speculative position. Wobbermin, *Wort Gottes*, 20.

119. The similarities and the differences between Wobbermin's and Bultmann's understandings of the distinction between *Geschichte* and *Historie* are many and complex, and it is a topic worthy of further exploration. Anything more than a brief sketch here, however, is beyond the scope of the present study.

distinction is uniquely important in terms of the resurrection of Jesus. Neither Wobbermin nor Bultmann is willing to define the resurrection as a historical event [*ein historisches Ereignis*]; both prefer to define it as a historic event [*ein geschichtliches Ereignis*]. For Wobbermin, "the resurrection, in the sense of the resurrection event, is not a historically comprehensible event."[120] The historical element is found in the disciples' conviction of faith, which "is really a historically comprehensible historic fact."[121] Similarly for Bultmann, "the event of Easter as the resurrection of Christ is not a historical event; the only thing that can be comprehended as a historical event is the Easter faith of the first disciples."[122]

The primary difference between Wobbermin and Bultmann on the resurrection concerns the character of the event itself. Wobbermin is content to define it as a historic event that produced the Easter faith of the disciples, which is the foundation of the Christian faith and the Christian church.[123] Bultmann agrees with this assessment of the Easter event, but further defines it as an eschatological act of God in which the cross is revealed to be the cross *of Christ*, the salvation event.[124] Wobbermin does not define the resurrection in explicitly eschatological terms, although he does approach an eschatological interpretation by defining the historic Christ as God's self-revelation in history, remaining present and efficacious in the New Testament picture of him and throughout the history of Christianity.[125] Another important difference concerns the role of proclamation in presenting the risen Christ for faith. While Wobbermin never explicitly mentions preaching or the kerygma in his discussions

---

120. "*Die Auferstehung im Sinne des Auferstehungsvorganges ist also kein historisch faßbares Ereignis.*" Wobbermin, *Wesen und Wahrheit*, 282.

121. "*Das ist wirklich eine historisch zu fassende geschichtliche Tatsache.*" Ibid., 286.

122. The language Bultmann uses is almost identical to Wobbermin's: "*Das Osterereignis als die Auferstehung Christi ist kein historisches Ereignis; als historisches Ereignis ist nur der Osterglaube der ersten Jünger faßbar.*" Bultmann, "Neues Testament und Mythologie," 46–47 [ET: "New Testament and Mythology," 39–40.]

123. The resurrection, for Wobbermin, is an unhistorical historic event insofar as it is unverifiable by historical research but as it nevertheless produces an effect (e.g., the faith of the disciples and the confession of Christ as Lord) within history. Here again, Wobbermin's position would be strengthened by acknowledging explicitly what remains implicit in his understanding of history, namely, a threefold distinction between *Historie*, *Geschichte*, and *Wirkung*.

124. Bultmann, "Neues Testament und Mythologie," 41–44 [ET: "New Testament and Mythology," 33–36].

125. Wobbermin, *Wesen und Wahrheit*, 294.

of the resurrection, for Bultmann the risen Christ is encountered in the church's kerygma and nowhere else. Nevertheless, for both Wobbermin and Bultmann the false historical supports for faith must be stripped away by a rigorous application of the historical-critical method, a task that is especially important in terms of the resurrection.[126] By distinguishing between the *historisch* and the *geschichtlich* in the resurrection, room is made for justifying faith that moves beyond what threatens to become a mere *fides historica*.

The role of historical-critical research in this area is crucial, and the misuse or misunderstanding of its proper role constitutes what Bultmann considers to be one of the signal failures of liberal theology. Bultmann cites the positive use of the historical-critical method within liberal theology as a means of providing support for faith as an important contributing factor to its demise as a theological movement.[127] Wobbermin also criticizes this positive use of historical criticism, both in terms of the doctrine of faith and in terms of the historical-critical method itself.[128] The historical-critical method, according to Wobbermin, is most effectively used in its *negative* function, specifically in stripping away the false supports for faith. Or, as Bultmann similarly argues,

> There can be no question of discarding historical criticism. But its significance must be grasped: it is needed radically to train us for freedom and veracity, not only by freeing us from a specific traditional view of history, but because it frees us from any possible view of history that is within the scope of scientific knowledge and

---

126. Bultmann, while insisting on a rigorous application of the historical-critical method, adds the additional task of demythologizing the New Testament kerygma. See, e.g., Bultmann, "Zum Problem der Entmythologisierung (1952)" [ET: "On the Problem of Demythologizing (1952)"] and Bultmann, "Zum Problem der Entmythologisierung (1960)" [ET: "On the Problem of Demythologizing (1960)"]. While Wobbermin occasionally mentions the mythical or mythological character of the New Testament accounts of the resurrection in the third volume of his systematic theology, he does not propose anything like Bultmann's program of demythologization. For Wobbermin, the historical-critical method itself is sufficient for interpreting these texts.

127. Bultmann, "Die liberale Theologie und die jüngste theologische Bewegung" [ET: "Liberal Theology and the Latest Theological Movement"].

128. Despite this explicit criticism, Wobbermin's own use of the historical-critical method reveals a more complicated position than he admits to having. See Chapter 2 for a discussion of Wobbermin's use of the historical-critical method.

Zwischen den Zeiten

brings us to the consciousness that the world that faith wills to grasp is absolutely unattainable by scientific knowledge.[129]

The importance of this negative function of historical criticism for Bultmann marks one of the most significant and enduring points of contact between Bultmann's thought and the liberal theological tradition. In 1956, as he was reflecting on his life in a short autobiographical reflection, he summarized his perspective on the fundamentally different understandings of religion in liberal theology and dialectical theology. He noted, however, that his allegiance to the new theological movement never led him to a wholesale condemnation of liberal theology: "On the contrary, I have endeavored throughout my entire work to carry further the tradition of historical-critical research as it was practiced by the 'liberal' theology and to make our more recent theological knowledge fruitful for it."[130]

Just as Wobbermin's use of the distinction between *Geschichte* and *Historie* is directly related to his religio-psychological method, Bultmann's insistence on the proper limits of historical-critical research is directly related to his existential and eschatological interest, particularly in terms of the relationship between faith and the kerygma.[131] Bultmann's early thinking on the doctrine of faith and the proper object of theology developed in conversation with the theology of the nineteenth century and is particularly evident in his lectures on theological encyclopedia.[132]

The basic question of the encyclopedia is that of theology's proper object, which leads to the question of faith and its constitutive elements.

---

129. Bultmann, "Die liberale Theologie," 4 [ET: "Liberal Theology," 31].

130. Bultmann, "Autobiographical Reflections," 288.

131. While Bultmann and Wobbermin similarly emphasize faith's character as *fiducia*, Bultmann further emphasizes faith's character as risk, especially in terms of the proper object of faith and any and all lack of objective proof of that object (especially through historical-critical research): "Those who want to believe in God as their God must know that they hold nothing in hand in which they can believe; that they are, as it were, poised in midair and can demand no proof of the word that has been spoken to them. For the ground and the object of faith are identical. Only the one who abandons all security can find security, only the one who – to speak with Luther – is prepared to enter into the inner darkness." Bultmann, "Zum Problem der Entmythologisierung (1952)," 207 [ET: "On the Problem of Demythologizing (1952)," 122]. This radical definition of faith is related to Bultmann's rejection of any attempt to "objectify" God as a return to mythological thinking. See Bultmann, "Welchen Sinn hat es, von Gott zu reden?" [ET: "What Does It Mean to Speak of God?"].

132. Bultmann, *Theologische Enzyklopädie* [ET: *What Is Theology?*].

Bultmann argues that the relationship between the *fides quae creditur* and the *fides qua creditur* was not properly understood in the nineteenth century, primarily because one was inevitably made prior or superior to the other in such a way that ultimately dissolved their proper relationship.¹³³ Liberalism tended to emphasize the *fides qua creditur* (the act of faith) to the exclusion of the *fides quae creditur* (the content of faith), leading to what Wobbermin calls a one-sided psychologism or a mere subjectivism, while orthodoxy tended to emphasize the *fides quae creditur* to the exclusion of the *fides qua creditur*, leading to what Wobbermin calls a one-sided historicism or a mere objectivism. Wobbermin attempts to maintain the interrelation of the *fides quae creditur* and the *fides qua creditur* by means of the religio-psychological circle, but he fails, according to Bultmann, because he made the alternation between the corresponding poles itself the object of faith¹³⁴ rather than God as seen in faith, which Bultmann suggests is the proper object of theology.¹³⁵

Despite their different emphases, Bultmann's definition of the object of theology is quite similar to Wobbermin's, insofar as both attempt to maintain the relationship between the *fides quae creditur* and the *fides qua creditur*. It is this interest that separates Bultmann from the dialectical theologians, for example, who were more interested in the objective side of the relationship while consistently minimizing the subjective side.¹³⁶

One early interpreter of Bultmann, Geraint Vaughan Jones, suggests that Bultmann's existentialism is merely liberalism in modern dress. Jones contends that it is the philosophical foundation rather than the theological approach that separates Bultmann from the liberal theologians, for both ultimately share the common denominator of personal experience.¹³⁷

---

133. Ibid., §5–6.

134. Ibid., §5.

135. Ibid., §15. Despite Bultmann's attempt to demonstrate Wobbermin's failure to maintain the objective content of faith as the proper object of theology, Wobbermin's own reflections on the proper object of theology suggest that Bultmann has perhaps misunderstood or at least misrepresented Wobbermin's position. Wobbermin is always careful to emphasize the ontological priority and superiority of the "objective pole," even as it is only grasped and comprehended from the subjective side. This, finally, is much closer to Bultmann's definition of the proper object of faith as "God as seen in faith" than Bultmann is willing to grant.

136. Ibid., §5.

137. Another shared quality, according to Jones, is the ultimate motive for emphasizing the subjective: "Indeed, it would seem that the constructive aspect of [Bultmann's]

Zwischen den Zeiten

While Bultmann is certainly no liberal theologian, his basic theological position does show some signs of continuity with the work of some of the later liberal theologians, including Wobbermin.[138] Bultmann's own "turn toward the subject" can be understood as a reaction against the threatening one-sided objectivism of the post-war Barth,[139] as Bultmann and Barth began to part ways in the 1920s with Barth's publication of the first volumes of his *Kirchliche Dogmatik* and with Bultmann's increasing interest in the possibility of a theology modeled after Heidegger's existential philosophy.[140]

By the 1920s it was clear that liberal theology's influence was waning, to be replaced by the dialectical theology of Barth, Brunner, and Gogarten. But no sooner had this new movement gained traction than new divisions arose between Barth and Gogarten, Brunner, and Bultmann, beginning in

---

work is designed to overcome the difficulty caused by his conviction that the historical approach to the gospel can provide no real basis for faith. In this, too, his attitude is similar to that of Liberals who, having abandoned myth and miracle and are alive to the effect of Biblical criticism on belief, are driven to find a more 'subjective' and experiential basis for it. The danger lurking in Bultmann's thought is that the historical is of little account and in holding that faith is virtually independent of 'history.'" Jones, "Bultmann and the Liberal Theology – II," 316–17. This is a common criticism of Bultmann's work, even by his own students, particularly Ernst Käsemann, who insisted that something more than the mere *Daß* of the historical Jesus must be known if faith is to have any objective basis outside the individual believer at all. See Käsemann, "Das Problem des historischen Jesus" [ET: "The Problem of the Historical Jesus"].

138. Other interpreters of Bultmann have also noticed his indebtedness to Schleiermacher and nineteenth-century liberal theology. See, for example, Evang, "Rudolf Bultmanns Berufung auf Friedrich Schleiermacher" and Jaspert, "Rudolf Bultmanns Wende."

139. Bultmann is particularly critical of any attempts to "objectify" God as an object of research or of observation like other mundane objects. See especially "Welchen Sinn hat es, von Gott zu reden?" [ET: "What Does It Mean to Speak of God?"] and "Zum Problem der Entmythologisierung (1952)" [ET: "On the Problem of Demythologizing (1952)"].

140. Jaspert refers to Bultmann's existential interest, the "red thread" woven throughout his entire body of work, as Bultmann's enduring point of contact with the liberal theological tradition. Jaspert, "Rudolf Bultmanns Wende," 43. Likewise it was Bultmann's existentialism that made any lasting alliance with Karl Barth impossible. By the 1950s the differences between the two men had become so significant that Barth could remark that they were like a whale and an elephant meeting "with boundless astonishment on some oceanic shore. . . . They do not have a common key to what each would obviously like to say to the other in its own speech and in terms of its own element." "Karl Barth, Basel, to Rudolf Bultmann, Marburg, December 24, 1954," in Barth, *Karl Barth – Rudolf Bultmann Briefwechsel*, 192 [ET: *Karl Barth – Rudolf Bultmann Letters*, 105].

the mid-1920s and intensifying in the 1930s.¹⁴¹ These latter two divisions were marked by retreats from what Brunner and Bultmann considered to be Barth's overemphasis on the objective at the expense of the subjective element of faith and religious experience. Once again, a new balance was sought between the objective and the subjective elements of faith.

---

141. Barth's conflict with each of these former colleagues is well documented in the primary literature of the period. Barth was shocked and dismayed by Gogarten's defection to the German Christians in the 1930s, a development that ultimately led to the demise of *Zwischen den Zeiten* (see Barth, Thurneysen, and Merz, "Abschied von *Zwischen den Zeiten*"). Barth's debates with Brunner over the possibility of a natural theology are well documented. Finally, Barth's debates with Bultmann, while never descending into bitterness or personal attacks, were nevertheless lively and at times quite heated. See, for example, Barth, *Rudolf Bultmann: Ein Versuch, ihn zu verstehen* [ET: "Rudolf Bultmann: An Attempt to Understand Him"] and the correspondence between Barth and Bultmann in *Karl Barth – Rudolf Bultmann Briefwechsel* [ET: *Karl Barth – Rudolf Bultmann Letters*].

5

Conclusion

Historical theology is according to its most basic definition a conversation with the theologies and theologians of the past for the sake of the theology of the present. It is a disciplined investigation of past attempts to express the truth of the Christian faith in a specific time and place. But historical theology also serves as the "royal road" to systematic and constructive theology, which are attempts to express the truth of the Christian faith in and for the present. Therefore historical theology is always both a historical and a theological task. Its historical interest grounds it in the concreteness of a particular time and place, and its present theological interest ensures its distinction from intellectual or social history.

The choice of the subject matter of historical theology says much about the interests and concerns of historical theologians themselves; rarely is the interest in this subject matter of a purely historical nature. There are often present concerns that inform the choice of the theology or theologian being studied, concerns that are shaped in part by the subsequent development of theology after the period in question. With historical distance comes a more comprehensive view of the terrain, of the figures and movements that helped to lay the foundation upon which we now do our own theological thinking. But looking back on the history of theology also enables the historical theologian to observe the many twists and turns in the road or roads that lead to the present, and to discover paths that perhaps met a premature dead end. At times these twists and turns were slow to develop, and the dead ends did not appear to be so until the road had already been traveled for some time. At other times the road ended suddenly and a new trail was blazed.

The early twentieth century witnessed just such a rapid dead end of the old path and the blazing of a new trail. At least this is the common interpretation of that period in the history of German Protestant theology. But with historical distance comes a broader view of the theological terrain of that period, and what we now see is a more complicated theological roadmap. Where earlier generations of historians have seen a dead end to the liberal theology of the late nineteenth and early twentieth century, some contemporary historical theologians are discovering signs that the road continued on, parallel to the new trail that had been blazed by Karl Barth and the dialectical theologians. Rather than meeting a dead end and finding a new beginning, we are now discovering a fork in the road. And if that road did indeed continue on, might we not discover it again, leading on into our own time?

Within the last ten years, more historical theologians have set off down this forgotten road to see where it might lead. In 1999 a conference was held at the University of York on "the future of liberal theology,"[1] and in the same year Matthias Wolfes published *Protestantische Theologie und moderne Welt*. In 2002 Mark Chapman published *Ernst Troeltsch and Liberal Theology*, in which he appeals for a more sympathetic understanding of liberal theology, and in 2004 Michael Aune began a series of articles entitled "Discarding the Barthian Spectacles," proposing a renewal of scholarly attention to the liberal theology of the early twentieth century.[2]

One traveler of this forgotten road was Georg Wobbermin, whose work presents a wealth of opportunities for exploring the liberal theology of the Weimar period. While his influence was cut short both by the rapid ascendancy of Barth and dialectical theology and by his own unfortunate political affiliations, perhaps Wobbermin still has something to say to us today.

Questions remain of the relationship between faith and history, particularly in terms of the historical Jesus,[3] and of the relationship of the contemporary Christian to the Bible. Claims of many modern people to be "spiritual but not religious" raise the question of how personal religious experience is to be related to and informed by the Christian tradition in a way that perhaps has been overlooked or at least underappreciated. Wobbermin and the liberal theologians offer an alternative to religion

---

1. Some of these papers were published in Chapman, ed., *The Future of Liberal Theology*.

2. The last installment of this series was published in 2007.

3. One need only consider the continuing popularity of the "Jesus Seminar" to recognize that these questions of faith and history are far from settled.

without personal engagement and to spirituality without anchors in history and tradition. By attempting to maintain a balance between the subjective and objective elements of Christian faith, Wobbermin offers one possible way forward that takes seriously both the personal experience of redemption and fidelity to Scripture and tradition.

Wobbermin also presents significant opportunities for historical theologians interested in the broader history of German Protestant thought. His interpretation of Luther, Kant, and Schleiermacher presents a particularly fruitful area for further research. These three masters remain indispensable for understanding the development of German Protestant theology, and Wobbermin's religio-psychological interpretation of the three "Copernican revolutions" accomplished by these figures affords unique insights into their work, possibly opening new avenues for interpretation. Additionally, renewed interest in Wobbermin and the interwar liberal theologians provides an opportunity for revising the common understanding of a radical departure from the theological tradition of the nineteenth century at the end of the First World War, potentially challenging decades of interpretation of that period of theology.

Finally, Wobbermin provides a foundation for a theological method that values interrelation and balance rather than dichotomy and contrast. As this study has shown, the key to Wobbermin's theology is the theme of interrelation, between the subjective experience of the believer and the objective reality of God, between the subjectivity of the individual Christian standing within history and the objective reality of the historic portrait of Christ that transcends mere historicity, and between the *fides qua creditur* and the *fides quae creditur*, the subjective and objective "corresponding poles" of faith. This method of interrelation, expressed in Wobbermin's religio-psychological circle, seeks a middle way between a theology that emphasizes the external reality of God and the divine revelation to the exclusion of the subjective appropriation of that reality and a theology that emphasizes personal religious experience to the exclusion of the objective reality of God and the historic divine revelation in Jesus Christ.

According to the liberal theological theory of theology proposed by Wolfes, "the essence and task of theology . . . consists precisely in helping the faith in a lively cultural milieu to come to a language of its own that is nonetheless understandable."[4] Wobbermin employed a method governed by precisely this concern. One contemporary appraisal of Wobbermin summarizes his significance as follows:

> One can predict with a fair degree of certainty that when a given time has passed, systematic theology will still have to contend with Wobbermin's method; Barth, however, will have become a significant – and for a particular bygone time important – historical figure.[5]

History has shown this prediction to have been mistaken, and it is Barth, not Wobbermin, who stands tall as a giant of twentieth-century theology. But perhaps the way forward provided by Wobbermin's method and by liberal theology in general was closed prematurely, and perhaps it is a road still worth traveling.

---

4. Wolfes, *Protestantische Theologie*, 585.

5. From an advertisement for Wobbermin's *Wort Gottes und evangelischer Glaube*, published by Vandenhoeck & Ruprecht. Cited in Klünker, *Psychologische Analyse und theologische Wahrheit*, 9.

APPENDIX 1

Fides Historica and *Fides Iustificans* in Melanchthon, Luther, and the Lutheran Confessions

MELANCHTHON: LOCI COMMUNES THEOLOGICI (1521)

PERHAPS THE FIRST INSTANCE of the theme *fides historica* in the Reformation is found in Melanchthon's 1521 *Loci communes*, where *fides historica* (or what is also called "mere *opinio*" or "*opinio historica*") is contrasted with *fides iustificans*, faith in the *misericordia dei*. In several places Melanchthon offers definitions of *fides historica* with examples from Scholastic doctrine:

> Therefore, that faith of the Sophists which they call both "incomplete" and "acquired," by which godless men assent to the gospel history [*historiae Evangelicae*] as we commonly give assent to the history of Livy or Sallust, is not really faith; it is opinion, that is, the uncertain, inconstant, and fluctuating deliberation of the mind on the Word of God.[1]

Later Melanchthon offers a second critique of *fides historica*, this time preferring to call it "opinion" instead of "faith":

> For obviously faith is not that opinion concerning beliefs or divine history [*divina historia*] which hypocrites have conceived without the Holy Spirit. . . . For the sake of teaching I used to call that which was acquired and incomplete "historical faith" [*historicam fidem*]; now I do not call it faith at all, but merely "opinion."[2]

Perhaps the best example of the use of *fides historica* in the 1521 *Loci* is Melanchthon's contrasting of *fides historica* and *fides iustificans*:

---

1. Melanchthon, "Loci theologici (1521)," 161 [ET: *The Loci Communes of Philipp Melanchthon*].
2. Ibid., 162.

It is not merely a matter of believing the history about Christ [*historiae de Christo credere*]; this is what the godless do. What matters is to believe why he took on flesh, why he was crucified, and why he came back to life after his death; the reason, of course, is that he might justify as many as would believe in him. If you believe that these things have been done for your good and for the sake of saving you, you have a blessed faith. Aside from faith of this kind, whatever they call "faith" is deceit, lying, and false madness.[3]

MELANCHTHON: LOCI THEOLOGICI GERMANICE (1555)

In the 1555 *Loci theologici germanice*, Melanchthon again contrasts *fides historica* and *fides iustificans*:

> Faith does not mean knowledge of history [*die Historien wissen*] alone, as the devils must confess: that it is true that the Son of God appeared, rose from the dead . . . but true faith is to hold as true every word of God that is given to us, and thus also the promise of grace, and is thus a heartfelt trust in the savior Christ, that God for the sake of his Son graciously forgives our sins, receives us, and makes us heirs of eternal blessedness. And this is the understanding of the word "faith" as Romans 4 clearly shows: "through faith we are justified."[4]

Melanchthon also addresses criticisms of his definition of true faith over against *fides historica*. In response to the question, "Since the devils also believe, how then can this faith be that through which one is justified?" he answers: "The devils only believe the history [*Historien*]; they do not believe that the Son of God has come to them for good." In response to a second question about the relationship between faith and knowledge, he emphasizes the character of gift and the role of the Holy Spirit in producing true faith:

> As far as heaven and hell are from one another, so far also is this true faith [*rechten Glauben*] distinguished from the knowledge [*wissen*] of the devils or the godless. And what true faith is, and how it is seen to shine in people, is learned only in trust, when we are quickened out of great angst and taken out of the vengeance of hell. . . . Thus this faith is not only a knowing and having an idea

---

3. Ibid., 177.

4. Melanchthon, "Loci theologici germanice (1555)," 329 [ET: *Melanchthon on Christian Doctrine*].

Fides Historica and *Fides Iustificans*

[*ein wissen vnd gedancken*] that one produces alone; it is rather a light and joy that the Son of God produces through the gospel and the Holy Spirit.[5]

MELANCHTHON: LOCI PRAECIPUI THEOLOGICI (1559)

In the last edition of the *Loci*, Melanchthon puts the distinction between *fides historica* and *fides iustificans* in more explicitly existential terms:

> Historical knowledge [*notitia historiae*] does not bring peace; on the contrary, it increases terror and desperation, as in the devils. ... "The just shall live by faith." Certainly no one lives by historical knowledge [*historiae notitia*].[6]

LUTHER: DIE EIN UND DREISSIGSTE PREDIGT, 29. JUNIJ AM TAGE PETRJ UND PAULJ (1538)

Luther also refers to *fides historica*, though not with Melanchthon's systematic clarity. The most explicit discussion of *fides historica* in Luther's works is in a sermon on the third chapter of John, where Luther contrasts true faith with the faith of Turks and the pope:

> See that you do not dispute this faith or disgrace or slander it, as the pope does, who says: "I also believe that Christ makes others blessed, but not me." The devil also knows that God has made Saint Peter blessed. Faith is not therefore an insignificant thing, as the pope despises it. Rather, it is a heartfelt trusting in God through Christ, that Christ's suffering and dying belong to you and shall be your own. The devil and the pope also have a faith, but it is only *fides Historica*.[7]

THE TORGAU ARTICLES (1530)

The *Torgau Articles* also include a section on the distinction between *fides historica* and *fides iustificans* ("Of Faith and Works"):

---

5. Ibid., 336.

6. Melanchthon, "Loci praecipui theologici (1559)," 365.

7. Luther, "Die ein und dreissigste Predigt," 92–93. See Krumwiede, *Glaube und Geschichte in der Theologie Luthers* on faith and history in Luther and his role in the development of German historical thought.

> But if any one adduce to the contrary that "also the devils and godless men believe, and yet are not righteous," our answer is this: The devils and godless men do not believe all articles; and especially the chief article, on account of which Christ has come, viz. the forgiveness of sins. To believe the Scripture is not only to have knowledge of the history, but to believe is to grasp this article: The forgiveness of sins. For, on that account, Christ has come, and the words: "The forgiveness of sins" are not put in the Creed in vain. And this faith comes in this manner, viz. when the heart is alarmed, and recognizes sins, and hears that grace through Christ has been promised, when it believes this promise, it receives consolation and joy and life, as Paul says: "Being justified by faith, we have peace with God," that is, a joyful conscience, "and feel that God is gracious and will help." It is right to learn to know him thus, to have confidence in him that he will help in all need, as his promise and word declare. And that this is faith, not only to know history, but to have such confidence in God, is clear from the words of Paul, who says: "Faith is the substance of things hoped for." Therefore faith is not only to be acquainted with the history, but to expect and hope for something from God.[8]

APOLOGY OF THE AUGSBURG CONFESSION (1531)

The distinction between *fides historica* and *fides iustificans* is treated in the fourth article of the *Apology of the Augsburg Confession* ("On Justification"):

> The opponents imagine that faith is nothing more than a knowledge of history [*notitiam historiae*], and so they teach that it can coexist with mortal sin. As a result they say nothing about the faith by which (as Paul so often says) we are justified, because those who are accounted righteous before God do not continue living in mortal sin. But the faith that justifies is not only knowledge of history [*notitia historiae*]; it is to assent to the promise of God, in which forgiveness of sins and justification are bestowed freely on account of Christ. To avoid the suspicion that it is merely knowledge, we will add further that to have faith is to desire and to receive the offered promise of the forgiveness of sins and justification. . . .

---

8. "The Torgau Articles," 87. There is some debate concerning the original version of The Torgau Articles. The recently published *Sources and Contexts of the Book of Concord* translates a different draft of the articles than that found in the Jacobs edition. For a very brief discussion of these text-critical issues, see the introduction to The Torgau Articles in *S&C*, 93.

> But faith signifies not merely knowledge of history [*historiae notitiam*] but the faith which assents to the promise, as Paul clearly testifies when he says righteousness "depends on faith, in order that the promise may . . . be guaranteed." He realizes that this promise cannot be received in any other way than by faith. . . . Thus it is not enough to believe that Christ was born, suffered, and was raised again unless we also add this article, which is the real purpose of the history [*causa finalis historiae*]: "the forgiveness of sins."[9]

AUGSBURG CONFESSION *VARIATA* (1540)

The 1540 *Variata* edition of the Augsburg Confession slightly amends the discussion of *fides historica* in the 1530 Augsburg Confession by including a reference to James 2:19 as the source of the necessary distinction between *fides historica* and *fides iustificans* (Article XX: "Of Faith and Good Works," A: "Of Faith"):

> When therefore we say: "We are justified by faith" [Rom 5:1], we do not mean that we are righteous on account of the worthiness of the virtue itself, but this is the meaning: that we obtain the forgiveness of sins and the imputation of righteousness by mercy for Christ's sake. But this mercy cannot be received unless by faith; and faith signifieth here not only a knowledge of the history, but it signifieth a belief of the promise of the mercy, which becomes ours on account of Christ as Mediator. And when faith is understood in this way concerning a confidence in mercy, James and Paul do not disagree. For when James saith "The devils believe and tremble" [Jas 2:19],[10] by faith he meaneth knowledge of the history; this doth not justify, for even the godless and the devils are acquainted with the history. But when Paul saith: "Faith is reckoned for righteousness" [Rom 4:5],[11] he speaketh of confidence in the mercy promised for Christ's sake; and his meaning is that men are pronounced righteous, that is, recognized through mercy, and not through our own worthiness; but that this mercy for Christ's sake ought to be received by faith.[12]

---

9. "Apologia Confessionis," 169–70 [ET: "Apology of the Augsburg Confession," 128]. The German translation of the Latin text translates "notitiam historiae" either as "Historien wissen" or "Wissen der Historien."

10. The NRSV translation of this passage reads, "Even the demons believe – and shudder."

11. The NRSV translation of this passage reads, "Faith is reckoned as righteousness."

12. "Variata," 116.

APPENDIX 1

THE LEIPZIG INTERIM (1548)

The topic is also treated briefly in *The Leipzig Interim* of 1548, where historical knowledge is contrasted with true faith that grasps the divine promise in Christ ("How Man Is Justified before God"):

> This true faith believes all the articles of faith. For it must recognize God correctly and believe along with the other articles of faith the following: "I believe in the forgiveness of sin, that it is conveyed to me and not only to others." For although many who live with a bad conscience also confess Christian teaching and boast of their faith, it is nevertheless not a living and justifying faith. For such a heart does not believe the forgiveness of sins is given to it, and it does not accept the promise but flees from God's presence and has no comfort and cannot call upon God. And there is no doubt that this devil's faith, which is terrified in the face of God's judgment, is a far different thing than the true faith. True faith accepts the promise and its gracious comfort, as Paul clearly testifies, Romans 4[:13]; there he speaks of this faith which accepts the promise, which is not only the knowledge that the devil or human beings who live with a bad conscience have, but this faith believes, together with the other articles of faith, in the forgiveness of sins. It accepts the promise and has in the heart a true trust in God's Son, who bestows trust and the ability to call on God and other virtues.[13]

EPITOME OF THE FORMULA OF CONCORD (1577)

Lastly, there is a brief discussion of the distinction in the third article of the *Epitome* of the *Formula of Concord* ("On the Righteousness of Faith before God"):

> We believe, teach, and confess that this faith is not a mere knowledge of historical facts [*Erkenntnus der Historien*[14]] about Christ. Rather, it is a gift of God, through which in the Word of the gospel we rightly know Christ as our redeemer and trust in him, that because of his obedience alone, by grace, we have the forgiveness of sins, are regarded as godly and righteous by God the Father, and are eternally blessed.[15]

---

13. "The Leipzig Interim," 186.
14. The Latin text reads "notitia historiae."
15. "Die Konkordienformel," 783 [ET: "The Formula of Concord," 495].

APPENDIX 2

National Socialism and the Aryan Paragraph

The Debate between Wobbermin and Bultmann

FRIEDRICH WILHELM GRAF HAS noted that many German liberal theologians ultimately took positions that were anything but "liberal" in the social or political sense of the term,[1] and Wobbermin certainly belongs to this group of liberal theologians. Highly critical of the conservative and confessional theological movements of the nineteenth and early twentieth century, Wobbermin nevertheless associated with extreme right-wing political organizations from a very early date. He enthusiastically supported German involvement in the First World War and was one of the subscribers to the "Appeal of German Churchmen and Professors to Protestant Christians in Foreign Lands" of September 4, 1914.[2] His primary motivation for subscribing to this statement was his conviction of the cultural superiority of German and Anglo-American Protestant culture.[3]

According to Matthias Wolfes, Wobbermin experienced Germany's defeat in World War I as nothing short of a catastrophe. He searched for a new political party for almost a year without success, until, in June of

---

1. Graf, "What Has London (or Oxford or Cambridge) to Do With Augsburg?" 24.

2. Other subscribers included Friedrich von Bodelschwingh, Adolf Deißmann, Adolf Harnack, Wilhelm Herrmann, Theodor Kaftan, Friedrich Loofs, and Wilhelm Wundt. This is the "Manifesto" cited by Barth as proof that liberal theology had abandoned its critical role and become a *Kriegstheologie* by uncritically accommodating the prevailing culture. For the text of the Appeal, see "Aufruf deutscher Kirchenmänner und Professoren."

3. See, for example, the foreword to the second edition of his translation of William James's *Varieties of Religious Experience*: James, *Die religiöse Erfahrung in ihrer Mannigfaltigkeit*, xxxi. See also Wobbermin, "Deutschland, Nordamerika und England als christliche-evangelische Kulturstaaten."

1919, he joined the monarchist, anti-democratic and anti-Semitic *Bund der Aufrechten* (literally the "League of the Upright").[4] Wolfes suggests that several of Wobbermin's publications from the 1920s contain allusions to the propaganda of the *Bund der Aufrechten*, most notably his frequent use of the term *Kampf* ("struggle," "battle," or "fight"):

> There is a noteworthy parallel between the propagandist language of the publications of the *Bund* and Wobbermin's theological publications of the twenties and early thirties in terms of the recurring use of the word *Kampf* and semantically associated words. Wobbermin always treated the most important theological debates as "*Kampf.*" Both his opponents from dialectical theology, especially Karl Barth, and also the theological antitypes historicism and psychologism appear as opponents in the battle. Even in his theological reasoning itself, Wobbermin frequently operated in a markedly militant mode, especially when responding to replies or controversial contributions to discussions directed toward his own statements. Even in the title of his 1929 theological manifesto on "overcoming the current crisis,"[5] Wobbermin falls back on the authoritarian instrument of "*Richtlinien*" ["directives" or "guidelines"] to indicate how he wanted his critical thought to be understood.[6]

Wolfes notes that Wobbermin regarded the Nazi seizure of power as the fulfillment of his greatest hopes for Germany. He had already voted for the National Socialists in the Reichstag elections of September 14, 1930, before the Nazis were the dominant right-wing political party in Germany.[7] By 1933 the National Socialists had assumed control of the Reichstag and Hitler had become Chancellor. Wobbermin officially joined the NSDAP on May 1, 1933, and over the next few years he also joined the NS-Dozentenbund (League of Docents), the NS-Lehrerbund (League of Teachers), the NS-Volkswohlfart (People's Welfare), the Reichsbund der Deutschen Beamten (Reich League of German Civil Servants), the

---

4. Wolfes, *Protestantische Theologie*, 290. On the *Bund der Aufrechten*, see Hofmann, *Wir sind das alte Deutschland*.

5. Wobbermin, *Richtlinien*.

6. Wolfes, *Protestantische Theologie*, 297.

7. For two socio-political analyses of the electoral politics of the late Weimar Republic and the Third Reich, see Allen, *The Nazi Seizure of Power* and Childers, *The Nazi Voter*.

National Socialism and the Aryan Paragraph

Reichsluftschutzbund (Reich Air Defense League), and the Kampfbundes für deutsche Kultur (League of Struggle for German Culture).[8]

On April 7, 1933, the Law for the Restoration of the Professional Civil Service was promulgated, signed by Hitler, Interior Minister Wilhelm Frick, and Finance Minister Lutz Graf Schwerin von Krosigk. Paragraph 3 of the Law, commonly called the "Aryan Paragraph," required that all civil servants of non-Aryan descent be dismissed from their positions:

1. Civil servants who are not of Aryan descent are to be retired; if they are honorary officials, they are to be dismissed from their official status.

2. Section 1 does not apply to civil servants in office from August 1, 1914, those who fought at the front for the German Reich or its allies in the World War, or those whose fathers or sons fell in the World War. Other exceptions may be permitted by the Reich Minister of the Interior in coordination with the Minister concerned or with the highest authorities with respect to civil servants working abroad.[9]

Wolfes notes that the reaction from the churches to this law was quite varied.[10] While the Roman Catholic reaction was more uniformly critical, the Protestant reaction ranged from vigorous support to silent acceptance to vocal criticism. In September of 1933 the General Synod of the Protestant Church of the Old Prussian Union adopted a version of the Aryan Paragraph for its churches. That version read in part:

2. Persons of non-Aryan descent or those married to a person of non-Aryan descent may not be called as clergy or officials of the general ecclesiastical body. Clergy and officials of Aryan descent who enter into marriage with a person of non-Aryan descent are to be dismissed.

3. Clergy or officials who are of non-Aryan descent or who are married to a person of non-Aryan descent are to be retired.[11]

---

8. Wolfes, *Protestantische Theologie*, 327.
9. "Gesetz zur Wiederherstellung des Berufsbeamtentums."
10. For general information on the churches in the Nazi period, see, e.g., Scholder, *Die Kirchen in das Dritte Reich* [ET: *The Churches and the Third Reich*] and Helmreich, *The German Churches under Hitler*.
11. Cited in Wolfes, *Protestantische Theologie*, 329–30.

Soon after the General Synod, a group of pastors approached the theological faculty of the University of Marburg to request a report on the recently adopted ecclesiastical law.[12] The faculty condemned the law as "irreconcilable with the essence of the Christian church as defined by the only proper authority of Holy Scripture and the gospel of Jesus Christ as attested by the Confessions of the Reformation."[13] They argued that the law relegated non-Aryan Christians to second-class status within the church, dissolving the fundamental equality of Christians in Christ. There were additional historical objections to the law, the most significant of which is the fact that Jesus of Nazareth, his disciples, and the earliest Christians were Jews.

A few days later, Bultmann drafted a condemnation of the law on specifically exegetical grounds. This response, to which several leading German New Testament scholars subscribed, was entitled "The New Testament and the Race Question."[14] The question of race is a modern question, argues Bultmann, and as such it is foreign to the New Testament. He turns to Paul and the many passages on the Jews for his exegetical basis. For Paul, the distinction between Jewish and Gentile Christians is not one of race or ancestry, but one of the significance of the rituals of the law. But insofar as Jewish and Gentile Christians are *Christians*, they are equal members of the body of Christ by virtue of their one baptism and one faith in the one Lord: "There is no longer Jew nor Greek, there is no longer slave nor free, there is no longer male and female; for all of you are one in Christ Jesus" (Gal 3:28). This unity in Christ extends to the pastoral and teaching offices. Bultmann concludes his condemnation of the new law with five propositions:

---

12. The report, entitled "Gutachten der Theologischen Fakultät der Universität Marburg zum Kirchengesetz über die Rechtsverhältnisse der Geistlichen und Kirchenbeamten," was presented by the professors and docents of New Testament studies at the University of Marburg and distributed to several German theological faculties. It was signed by Walter Bauer, Wilhelm Brandt, Rudolf Bultmann, Adolf Deißmann, Kurt Deißner, Johannes Gottfried Fitzer, Karl Heim, Joachim Jeremias, Adolf Jülicher, Alfred Juncker, Hans Lietzmann, Ernst Lohmeyer, Wilhelm Lueken, Wilhelm Lütgert, Albrecht Oepke, Heinrich Schlier, Karl Ludwig Schmidt, Otto Schmitz, Julius Schniewind, Hans von Soden, and Hans Windisch. Liebing, 9–15.

13. "Gutachten der Theologischen Fakultät der Universität Marburg," Liebing, 11.

14. Bultmann, "Neues Testament und Rassenfrage," Liebing, 16–19.

National Socialism and the Aryan Paragraph

1. According to the New Testament, the Christian church is a church of Jews and Gentiles who find themselves together visibly in one community.

2. According to the New Testament, faith and baptism alone are decisive for membership in this community; Jews and Gentiles can come to faith and be baptized in the same way.

3. According to the New Testament, Jews and Gentiles are suited to be public ecclesiastical officials in the same fundamental way. They are called to an ecclesiastical office by the church and only by the church, solely according to the measure of their faith, their conversion [*Wandeln*], and their personal aptitude.

4. This position is based on the fact that, according to the New Testament, the church owes its being [*Dasein*] in the world solely to the Holy Spirit. It is God who calls persons of all races and peoples into the one corporate church through the audible Word of proclamation and the visible sign of baptism, whose believers are the visible body of the invisible head, Christ, and who therefore are bound with one another in the visible community as his limbs.

5. We are therefore of the opinion that a Christian church may not renounce this position in its doctrine and in its action as a matter of principle.[15]

Wobbermin responded to the Marburg faculty and Bultmann's report with an article entitled "Two Theological Reports on the Aryan Paragraph, Critically Illuminated," published in the National Socialist newspaper, *Der Reichsbote*, on October 18, 1933.[16] His primary criticism of both reports concerns the extension of one's personal religious status *coram Deo* to include one's fitness for public ministry in the church. Bultmann contended that because one's relationship to the church is determined solely by one's faith and one's baptism, this criterion should therefore be the sole criterion for holding a public ecclesiastical office. Wobbermin makes a distinction between one's status as a Christian and one's fitness for ministry. Bultmann and the theological faculty of Marburg did not consider the question of Jews in the church to be a racial question, while Wobbermin considers the racial question to be the decisive question.

---

15. Ibid., 18.
16. Wobbermin, "Zwei theologische Gutachten," Liebing, 28–31.

Wobbermin considers Paul's prohibition of women's participation in the leadership of worship and the absence of any examples of female clergy in the New Testament to be clear indications that there is a distinction between one's status before God and one's fitness for leadership in the church. He interprets Gal 3:28 to refer solely to the status of the human being *coram Deo*; one's status in the church remains dependent on one's gender or, in this case, on one's race.

The question of non-Aryan leadership in the Protestant Church is, for Wobbermin, ultimately a question of the purity of the German spiritual life:

> The Evangelical Church had borne a substantial share of the guilt in this [current] emergency, which had been coming for some time. It had, in recent decades, accepted on a large scale the conversion of Jews to the Evangelical Church on purely social or similar grounds, even encouraging it to some extent. Indirectly and without intending it, the church thereby contributed to the enormous excess of Jewish impact and influence in German spiritual life that had come about and was always increasing – not the least in the universities, whose younger generations among *Privatdozenten* and assistants in many faculties already numbered 50 percent Jews, and in some cases even far more.
>
> Therefore the church may not now elude this common task and may not refuse to carry its share, as burdensome as it might be.[17]

Bultmann continued the debate with a response to Wobbermin entitled "The Aryan Paragraph within the Church."[18] According to Bultmann, the fundamental difference between his position and Wobbermin's concerns the relationship between civil and ecclesiastical law. For Wobbermin the church as a civil institution is bound to uphold the laws of the state, while for Bultmann the church must first question whether the laws of the state are consistent with the essence of the church. Bultmann contends that the question is whether the Aryan Paragraph is tolerable as an *ecclesiastical* law, that is, whether it is in accordance with the doctrine of the church expressed in Scripture and interpreted by the Confessions. The essence of the church, then, is the final criterion for judging any civil law concerning the functioning of the church and its ministry.

17. Ibid., 31.
18. Bultmann, "Der Arier-Paragraph im Raume der Kirche," Liebing, 32–45.

National Socialism and the Aryan Paragraph

The key to this question, according to Bultmann, is to be found in the ecclesiology of the New Testament and of the Lutheran Confessions. According to Paul, the church is the body of Christ, and there can be no distinctions within it. Wobbermin agrees that pastoral care and the Eucharist must be made available to all the baptized without distinction, but he does not agree that this basic equality extends to the right of any baptized person to hold a public ecclesiastical office. Bultmann rejects this distinction on the basis of the Confessions, specifically Article V of the Augsburg Confession (On Ministry):

> To obtain such faith, God instituted the office of preaching, giving the gospel and sacraments, through which, as through means, God gives the Holy Spirit, which works faith when and where it wills in those who hear the gospel, and which teaches that we have a gracious God, through Christ's merit and not our own, when we so believe.[19]

Bultmann suggests that this article is misunderstood if it is taken to define public ecclesiastical office solely as a matter of external order. Wobbermin understands it in precisely this way, which permits him to make a distinction between one's status before God and one's fitness for ministry in the church. Bultmann insists that there can be no absolute distinction, that the ministry itself is both a spiritual and a temporal office.[20]

Bultmann accuses Wobbermin of misunderstanding the essence of the pastoral office as something pertaining only to the external order of the church:

> On what within the church is the right to proclaim the Word based? Is it based on personal qualities such that a certain racial parentage [*völkische Abkunft*] should be reckoned to them? Or is it based singly and solely on the fact that each baptized Christian has the Spirit of Christ and therefore has the right to speak ac-

---

19. "Die augsburgische Konfession," 58 [ET: "The Augsburg Confession," 40]

20. There are some striking similarities between the debate concerning the Aryan Paragraph and the current debate within the Evangelical Lutheran Church in America concerning the ordination of men and women in committed same-sex relationships, particularly in terms of a gay or lesbian Christian's status *coram Deo* versus a gay or lesbian Christian's fitness for ordination. The ELCA has made several relevant resources available on its website under the heading "Journey Together Faithfully." Online: http://www.elca.org/What-We-Believe/Social-Issues/Social-Statements-in-Process/JTF-Human-Sexuality/Resources.aspx.

cording to the measure of the Spirit? Does the proclaimer of the Word then speak in the church on the basis of his or her ethnicity [*Volkstum*] or on the basis of the Spirit of Christ? . . . Moreover, according to the Reformation view, the preacher is not superior to the community as a priest; rather, the preacher is called by community, from the community. There exists a peculiar reciprocity [*Wechselverhältnis*], one that is certainly no "religio-psychological circle," but a real circle. But this circle is broken when Christians should be classified as members of the community but have their right to the office of preaching denied. The acceptance granted to them is then not genuine.[21]

Bultmann also rejects Wobbermin's appeal to the unity of German spiritual life as a criterion for the necessity of a racially "pure" clergy:

> Had Luther been an existential psychologist of religion, the Reformation never would have come, as it (as is widely known) tragically disrupted the unity of German spiritual life. May the church then understand itself from the perspective of its being a part of German spiritual life? Would that be an existential self-understanding? Or must it understand itself from the perspective of the transcendent, eschatological church of Christ?[22]

Wobbermin responded very briefly with an article entitled "Once Again the Aryan Question in the Church,"[23] in which he accuses Bultmann of completely misunderstanding his position by forcing a distinction between the situation in the church and the situation in the nation. Wobbermin insists that the "Jewish Question" in the church is directly related to the "Jewish Question" facing the German nation:

> The influence of Judaism in the higher vocations and therefore in the entire spiritual life had [in recent decades] increased to staggering numbers. And in the Jewish-cultural-Bolshevik literati this influence had a dangerous impact. It had brought Germany and its Evangelical Churches straight to the edge of the abyss of Bolshevism. The National Socialist movement of Adolf Hitler has, at the last moment, saved Germany and its Evangelical Churches from this danger.[24]

---

21. Bultmann, "Der Arier-Paragraph im Raume der Kirchen," Liebing, 33–34.
22. Ibid., 38–39.
23. Wobbermin, "Nochmals die Arierfrage in der Kirche," Liebing, 51–52.
24. Ibid., 52.

National Socialism and the Aryan Paragraph

Wolfes suggests that Wobbermin's position here is typical of the German Protestant bourgeoisie of the early 1930s, whose anti-Semitic attitudes were characterized by references to the "infiltration" of German cultural and intellectual life by the Jews. Wolfes describes this attitude as a "deeply rooted consciousness of inferiority" compared with the Jewish intellectual class. The Jews' sometimes disproportionate representation in the intellectual, cultural, and professional fields resulted in a defensive attitude among the bourgeoisie, an attitude the Nazis relentlessly exploited.[25] Wobbermin's warnings concerning the "danger" to German spiritual life posed by what he calls the "Jewish-cultural-Bolshevik literati"[26] is especially typical of this bourgeois attitude.

Wobbermin's last major publication was a small book entitled *Deutscher Staat und evangelische Kirche*, a study of the relationship of the Protestant Church to National Socialism.[27] His last years were spent mired in personal controversy, most notably with Karl Barth (whom Wobbermin accused of attempting to become pope of the Protestant Churches).[28] He experienced a bitter falling out with the German Christians while on the theological faculty of the University of Berlin, where he was called in 1937 and where he taught until his death in 1943.[29]

---

25. Wolfes, *Protestantische Theologie*, 333.
26. Wobbermin, "Zwei theologische Gutachten," Liebing, 31.
27. Wobbermin, *Deutscher Staat und evangelische Kirche*.
28. See Wobbermin, "Karl Barths Anspruch, als Papst aller evangelischen Kirchen zu gelten."
29. Wolfes, *Protestantische Theologie*, 403.

APPENDIX 3

Georg Wobbermin

A Brief Biography

Ernst Gustav Georg Wobbermin was born in Stettin, in Prussian Pomerania (now Szczecin, Poland) on October 27, 1869, the son of Albert Wobbermin, a teacher in the local *Gymnasium*, and Laura Quandt.[1] In his youth he attended his father's school and then the *Marienstiftsgymnasium*. After passing his *Abitur* in 1888, he matriculated at the University of Halle, intending to study philosophy and theology. In 1890 he moved to the Friedrich-Wilhelms University in Berlin to study under Wilhelm Dilthey, Adolf Harnack, and Julius Kaftan. While at Berlin he served for two years as a mission secretary before he received his doctorate in 1894. After receiving his licentiate the following year, he spent one year in compulsory military service.

Following his military service, Wobbermin traveled to Greece with the New Testament scholar, Hermann von Soden. While in Greece he visited the monastic communities on Mount Athos, where he discovered a collection of liturgical manuscripts from the eleventh century and a previously unknown letter of the Egyptian Bishop Serapion, a friend and supporter of Athanasius. Wobbermin published these manuscripts, along with a text-critical study, as *Altchristliche liturgische Stücke aus der Kirche Ägyptens*.[2]

---

1. For additional biographical information, see Klünker, *Psychologische Analyse und theologische Wahrheit*, 13–22; Wolfes, *Protestantische Theologie*, 253–403; Macintosh, Introduction to *The Nature of Religion*, v–vii; Wesseling, "Wobbermin, Ernst Gustav Georg"; Glaue, "Wobbermin, Georg"; Winkler, "Wobbermin, Georg"; Lohff, "Wobbermin, Georg"; and Pfleiderer, "Wobbermin, Georg."

2. Wobbermin, *Altchristliche liturgische Stücke* [ET: *Bishop Sarapion's Prayer-Book*].

Georg Wobbermin: A Brief Biography

In 1898 Wobbermin was promoted to professor of systematic theology and the philosophy of religion at Berlin. In 1906 he was called to Marburg as professor of systematic theology and in that same year he married Theodora Brockhausen, the daughter of a Berlin businessman. He remained at Marburg for only one year before being called to Breslau as a full professor. During this period Wobbermin was also granted an honorary doctorate by the Friedrich-Wilhelms University in Berlin. In 1907 he accepted an invitation to teach as visiting professor at Yale University. While teaching at Yale he also visited Harvard University, where he developed a friendship with William James.[3] Following his visit to the United States and his meetings with James, he published the first volume of his systematic theology in 1913.

With the outbreak of World War I, Wobbermin became engaged with political questions and began to assert the superiority of German Protestant culture. He was one of the subscribers to the "Appeal of German Churchmen and Professors to Protestant Christians in Foreign Lands" on September 4, 1914. In early 1915 he was called to Heidelberg to take Ernst Troeltsch's chair after Troeltsch had left to take a chair in philosophy in Berlin. He remained in Heidelberg throughout the war years and in 1922 was called to succeed Arthur Titius as professor of systematic theology and the philosophy of religion at Göttingen. While at Göttingen he lectured and provided seminars almost exclusively on themes related to the psychology of religion. Also during this time he published the second and third volumes of his systematic theology.

In 1925 he refused a call to Leipzig for unspecified personal reasons, and in the same year he participated in the Ecumenical World Conference for Practical Christianity in Stockholm. In 1927 the journal, *Die Christliche Welt,* reported that Wobbermin had received a call to lecture at the University of Chicago, but there is no information available to determine why he refused this call to return to the United States for a second time.

Beginning in 1933, after the Nazi seizure of power, Wobbermin turned to church-political questions in his lectures and seminars, which

---

3. This meeting occurred just a few weeks after the publication of Wobbermin's translation of James's *Varieties of Religious Experience.* Wobbermin wrote in the introduction to the second edition that "the hours that brought me into personal contact and conversation with William James will always be unforgettable to me." Wobbermin, cited in Klünker, *Psychologische Analyse und theologische Wahrheit,* 15.

he always ended with the "Heil Hitler" exclamation and salute.[4] His publications during this period were also devoted to political questions within the church, including his public debate with Rudolf Bultmann on the Aryan Paragraph and the place of Jews or "non-Aryans" within the German churches.[5] In 1934 he published *Deutscher Staat und evangelische Kirche*, which would be the last of his books published by the Göttingen publisher Vandenhoeck & Ruprecht.[6]

In 1937 he accepted a call to occupy the chair previously held by Schleiermacher, Kaftan, and Titius at Berlin, and six months later he was made emeritus professor. While in Berlin he planned a major work on Schleiermacher's German nationalism, but this work was never begun.[7] Wobbermin died in Berlin on October 15, 1943.

---

4. Ibid., 19.
5. See Appendix 2.
6. Klünker, *Psychologische Analyse und theologische Wahrheit*, 21.
7. Ibid., 22.

Bibliography

Allen, William Sheridan. *The Nazi Seizure of Power: The Experience of a Single German Town, 1922-1945*. Rev. ed. New York: F. Watts, 1984.
Allison, Henry E. *Lessing and the Enlightenment: His Philosophy of Religion and Its Relation to Eighteenth-Century Thought*. Ann Arbor: University of Michigan Press, 1966.
Anselm. *Proslogion*. Edited by M. J. Charlesworth. Oxford: Clarendon, 1965.
"Apologia Confessionis." In *BSLK*, 141-404.
"Apology of the Augsburg Confession." In *BOC*, 107-294.
Ashcraft, Morris. *Rudolf Bultmann*. Makers of the Modern Theological Mind. Waco, TX: Word Books, 1972.
"Aufruf der 93 an die Kulturwelt." In *Die protestantischen Kirchen Europas im Ersten Weltkrieg: Ein Quellen- und Arbeitsbuch*, edited by Gerhard Besier, 78-83. Göttingen: Vandenhoeck & Ruprecht, 1984.
"Aufruf deutscher Kirchenmänner und Professoren: An die evangelischen Christen im Ausland." In *Die protestantischen Kirchen Europas im Ersten Weltkrieg: Ein Quellen- und Arbeitsbuch*, edited by Gerhard Besier, 40-45. Göttingen: Vandenhoeck & Ruprecht, 1984.
"The Augsburg Confession." In *The Book of Concord: The Confessions of the Evangelical Lutheran Church*, translated and edited by Theodore G. Tappert, 23-96. Philadelphia: Fortress, 1959.
"The Augsburg Confession." In *BOC*, 27-105.
"Die augsburgische Konfession." In *BSLK*, 31-137.
Aune, Michael B. "Discarding the Barthian Spectacles, Part I: Recent Scholarship on the History of Early 20th Century German Protestant Theology." *Dialog* 43 (2004): 223-32.
———. "Discarding the Barthian Spectacles, Part II: Rereading Theological Directions, 1910-1914." *Dialog* 44 (2005): 56-68.
———. "Discarding the Barthian Spectacles, Part III: Rewriting the History of Protestant Theology in the 1920s." *Dialog* 45 (2006): 389-405.
———. "Discarding the Barthian Spectacles, Conclusion: Might We Be 'Liberals' After All?" *Dialog* 46 (2007): 153-65.
Baird, William. *History of New Testament Research*. 2 vols. Minneapolis: Fortress, 1992-2002.
Barth, Karl. "Antwort an D. Achelis und P. Drews." *ZThK* 19 (1909): 479-86.
———. *Die Auferstehung der Toten*. Munich: C. Kaiser, 1926.
———. "Der christliche Glaube und die Geschichte." *SThZ* 29 (1912): 1-18, 49-72.
———. *Church Dogmatics*. Vol. 1, *The Doctrine of the Word of God*, Part 1. 2nd ed. Translated by G. W. Bromiley. Edited by G. W. Bromiley and T. F. Torrance. London and New York: T & T International, 2004.

Bibliography

———. "Concluding Unscientific Postscript on Schleiermacher." In Karl Barth, *The Theology of Schleiermacher: Lectures at Göttingen, Winter Semester 1923-24*, edited by Dietrich Ritschl. Translated by Geoffrey W. Bromiley, 261-79. Grand Rapids, MI: Eerdmans, 1982.

———. "Evangelical Theology in the 19th Century." In Karl Barth, *The Humanity of God*, translated by John Newton Thomas and Thomas Wieser, 11-33. Richmond, VA: John Knox, 1960.

———. *Gesamtausgabe*. Edited by Hinrich Stoevesandt. Vol. 2, *Akademische Werke 1923/24*, Part 11, *Die Theologie Schleiermachers: Vorlesung Göttingen Wintersemester 1923/24*. Edited by Dietrich Ritschl. Zurich: Theologischer Verlag, 1978.

———. *Gesamtausgabe*. Edited by Hinrich Stoevesandt. Vol. 5, *Briefe*, Part 1, *Karl Barth – Rudolf Bultmann Briefwechsel, 1911-1966*. 2nd ed. Edited by Bernd Jaspert. Zurich: Theologischer Verlag, 1994.

———. *Karl Barth – Rudolf Bultmann Letters, 1922-1966*. Edited by Bernd Jaspert. Translated and edited by Geoffrey W. Bromiley. Grand Rapids, MI: Eerdmans, 1981.

———. *Die kirchliche Dogmatik*. Vol. 1, *Die Lehre vom Wort Gottes: Prolegomena zur kirchlichen Dogmatik*, Part 1. 5th ed. Zollikon-Zurich: Evangelischer Verlag, 1947.

———. "Moderne Theologie und Reichgottesarbeit." *ZThK* 19 (1909): 317-21.

———. "Nachwort." In *Schleiermacher-Auswahl: Mit einem Nachwort von Karl Barth*, edited by Heinz Bolli. Gütersloh: Mohn, 1980.

———. *Nein! Antwort an Emil Brunner*. Theologische Existenz heute 14. Munich: C. Kaiser, 1934.

———. *Protestant Theology in the Nineteenth Century: Its Background and History*. New ed. Translated by Brian Cozens and John Bowden. Grand Rapids, MI: Eerdmans, 2002.

———. *Die protestantische Theologie im 19. Jahrhundert: Ihre Vorgeschichte und ihre Geschichte*. 3rd ed. Zurich: Evangelischer Verlag, 1960.

———. *The Resurrection of the Dead*. Translated by H. J. Stenning. New York: F. H. Revell, 1933.

———. "Rudolf Bultmann: An Attempt to Understand Him." In *Kerygma and Myth: A Theological Debate*, vol. 2. Edited by Hans-Werner Bartsch. Translated by Reginald H. Fuller, 83-132. London: S. P. C. K., 1962.

———. *Rudolf Bultmann: Ein Versuch, ihn zu verstehen*. Theologische Studien 34. Zollikon-Zurich: Evangelischer Verlag, 1952.

———. *The Theology of Schleiermacher: Lectures at Göttingen, Winter Semester of 1923/1924*. Edited by Dietrich Ritschl. Translated by Geoffrey W. Bromiley. Grand Rapids, MI: Eerdmans, 1982.

———. *The Word of God and the Word of Man*. Translated by Douglas Horton. New York: Harper, 1957.

———. *Das Wort Gottes und die Theologie: Gesammelte Vorträge*. Munich: C. Kaiser, 1925.

Barth, Karl, Eduard Thurneysen and Georg Merz. "Abschied von *Zwischen den Zeiten*." *ZZ* 6 (1933): 536-54. Reprinted in *Anfänge der dialektischen Theologie*, edited by Jürgen Moltmann. 2 vols. 2:313-31. Theologische Bücherei: Neudrucke und Berichte aus dem 20. Jahrhundert 17. Munich: C. Kaiser, 1962-1963.

Berkhof, Hendrikus. *200 Jahre Theologie: Ein Reisebericht*. Neukirchen-Vluyn: Neukirchener Verlag, 1985.

Bibliography

———. *Two Hundred Years of Theology: Report of a Personal Journey*. Translated by John Vriend. Grand Rapids, MI: Eerdmans, 1989.

Besier, Gerhard, ed. *Die protestantischen Kirchen Europas im Ersten Weltkrieg: Ein Quellen- und Arbeitsbuch*. Göttingen: Vandenhoeck & Ruprecht, 1984.

Birkner, Hans-Joachim. "Liberale Theologie." In *Kirchen und Liberalismus im 19. Jahrhundert*, edited by Martin Schmidt and Georg Schweiger, 32–42. Göttingen: Vandenhoeck & Ruprecht, 1976.

———. "Über den Begriff des Neuprotestantismus." In *Beiträge zur Theorie des neuzeitlichen Christentums*, edited by Hans-Joachim Birkner and Dietrich Rössler, 1–15. Berlin: de Gruyter, 1968.

Birkner, Hans-Joachim and Dietrich Rössler, eds. *Beiträge zur Theorie des neuzeitlichen Christentums*. Berlin: de Gruyter, 1968.

Blanke, Horst Walter and Jörn Rüsen, eds. *Von der Aufklärung zum Historismus: Zum Strukturwandel des historischen Denkens*. Historisch-politische Diskurse 1. Paderborn: F. Schöningh, 1984.

Bousset, Wilhelm. "Die Bedeutung der Person Jesu für den Glauben: Historische und rationale Grundlagen des Glaubens." In *Fünfter Weltkongress für Freies Christentum und Religiösen Fortschritt: Protokoll der Verhandlungen*, edited by Max Fischer and Friedrich Michael Schiele, 291–305. Berlin-Schöneberg: Protestantischer Schriftenvertrieb, 1910.

———. *Kyrios Christos: Geschichte des Christusglaubens von den Anfänge des Christentums bis Irenaeus*. 6th ed. Göttingen: Vandenhoeck & Ruprecht, 1967.

———. *Kyrios Christos: A History of the Belief in Christ from the Beginnings of Christianity to Irenaeus*. Translated by John E. Steely. Nashville, TN: Abingdon, 1970.

Braaten, Carl E. "Christ, Faith, and History: An Inquiry into the Meaning of Martin Kähler's Distinction between the Historical Jesus and the Biblical Christ Developed in Its Past and Present Contexts." Th.D. diss., Harvard University, 1959.

———. Introduction to *The So-called Historical Jesus and the Historic, Biblical Christ*, by Martin Kähler. Translated and edited by Carl E. Braaten. Philadelphia: Fortress, 1964.

Brachmann, Wilhelm. *Glaube und Geschichte: Eine religionswissenschaftliche Untersuchung über den deutschen Protestantismus*. Frankfurt: Moritz Diesterweg, 1942.

Brunner, Emil. *Erlebnis, Erkenntnis und Glaube*. 2nd and 3rd eds. Tübingen: Mohr Siebeck, 1923.

———. *Die Mystik und das Wort: Der Gegensatz zwischen moderner Religionsauffassung und christlichem Glauben dargestellt an der Theologie Schleiermachers*. Tübingen: Mohr Siebeck, 1924.

———. *Natur und Gnade: Zum Gespräch mit Karl Barth*. 4th and 5th eds. Zurich: Zwingli-Verlag, 1935.

———. *Truth as Encounter*. New ed. Philadelphia: Westminster, 1964.

———. *Wahrheit als Begegnung: Sechs Vorlesungen über das christliche Wahrheitsverständnis*. Berlin: Furche-Verlag, 1938.

Brunner, Emil and Karl Barth. *Natural Theology: Comprising "Nature and Grace" by Emil Brunner and the Reply "No!" by Karl Barth*. Translated by Peter Fraenkel. London: G. Bles, Centenary, 1946.

Buder, Eberhard. "Fides iustificans und fides historica." *EvTh* 13 (1953): 67–83.

Bultmann, Rudolf. "Der Arier-Paragraph im Raume der Kirche." *ThBl* 12 (1933): 359–70. Reprinted in Liebing, 32–45.

Bibliography

———. "Autobiographical Reflections." In Rudolf Bultmann, *Existence and Faith: Shorter Writings of Rudolf Bultmann*, translated by Schubert M. Ogden, 283–88. New York: Meridian, 1960.

———. *Faith and Understanding*. Edited by Robert W. Funk. Translated by Louise Pettibone Smith. Fortress Texts in Modern Theology. Philadelphia: Fortress, 1987.

———. "Geschichtliche und übergeschichtliche Religion im Christentum." In *GuV*² 1:65–84.

———. "Historical and Supra-historical Religion in Christianity." In Rudolf Bultmann, *Faith and Understanding*, edited by Robert W. Funk. Translated by Louise Pettibone Smith, 95–115. Fortress Texts in Modern Theology. Philadelphia: Fortress, 1987.

———. "Is Exegesis Without Presuppositions Possible?" In *NT&M*, 143–53.

———. "Ist voraussetzungslose Exegese möglich?" In *GuV*¹ 3:142–50.

———. *Jesus*. Berlin: Deutsche Bibliothek, 1926.

———. *Jesus and the Word*. Translated by Louise Pettibone Smith and Erminie Huntress. New York: Scribner, 1934.

———. "Karl Barth, *Die Auferstehung der Toten*." In *GuV*¹ 1:38–64.

———. "Karl Barth, *The Resurrection of the Dead*." In Rudolf Bultmann, *Faith and Understanding*, edited by Robert W. Funk. Translated by Louise Pettibone Smith, 66–94. Fortress Texts in Modern Theology. Philadelphia: Fortress, 1987.

———. *Karl Barth – Rudolf Bultmann Letters, 1922–1966*. Edited by Bernd Jaspert. Translated and edited by Geoffrey W. Bromiley. Grand Rapids, MI: Eerdmans, 1981.

———. "Liberal Theology and the Latest Theological Movement." In Rudolf Bultmann, *Faith and Understanding*, edited by Robert W. Funk. Translated by Louise Pettibone Smith, 28–52. Fortress Texts in Modern Theology. Philadelphia: Fortress, 1987.

———. "Die liberale Theologie und die jüngste theologische Bewegung." In *GuV*² 1:1–25.

———. "Neues Testament und Mythologie: Das Problem der Entmythologisierung der neutestamentlischen Verkündigung." In *Kerygma und Mythos*. Vol. 1, *Ein theologisches Gespräch*. 4th ed. Edited by Hans-Werner Bartsch, 15–48. Theologische Forschung: Wissenschaftliche Beiträge zur kirchlich-evangelischen Lehre. Hamburg: H. Reich, 1960.

———. "Neues Testament und Rassenfrage." *ThBl* 12, no. 10 (October 10, 1933): 294–96. Reprinted in Liebing, 16–19.

———. "New Testament and Mythology: The Problem of Demythologizing the New Testament Proclamation." In *NT&M*, 1–43.

———. "On the Problem of Demythologizing (1952)." In *NT&M*, 95–130.

———. "On the Problem of Demythologizing (1960)." In *NT&M*, 155–63.

———. "The Primitive Christian Kerygma and the Historical Jesus." In *The Historical Jesus and the Kerygmatic Christ: Essays on the New Quest of the Historical Jesus*, translated and edited by Carl E. Braaten and Roy A. Harrisville, 15–42. Nashville, TN: Abingdon, 1964.

———. *Theologische Enzyklopädie*. Edited by Eberhard Jüngel and Klaus W. Müller. Tübingen: Mohr Siebeck, 1984.

———. *Das Verhältnis der urchristlichen Christusbotschaft zum historischen Jesus*. 2nd ed. Sitzungsberichte der Heidelberger Akademie der Wissenschaften, Philosophisch-Historische Klasse 3. Heidelberg: Carl Winter Universitätsverlag, 1962.

———. "Welchen Sinn hat es, von Gott zu reden?" In *GuV*¹ 1:26–37.

Bibliography

———. "What Does It Mean to Speak of God?" In Rudolf Bultmann, *Faith and Understanding*, edited by Robert W. Funk. Translated by Louise Pettibone Smith, 53–65. Fortress Texts in Modern Theology. Philadelphia: Fortress, 1987.

———. *What is Theology?* Edited by Eberhard Jüngel and Klaus W. Müller. Translated by Roy A. Harrisville. Fortress Texts in Modern Theology. Minneapolis: Fortress, 1997.

———. "Zum Problem der Entmythologisierung (1952)." In *Kerygma und Mythos*. Vol. 2, *Diskussionen und Stimmen zum Problem der Entmythologisierung*, edited by Hans-Werner Bartsch, 179–208. Theologische Forschung: Wissenschaftliche Beiträge zur kirchlich-evangelischen Lehre. Hamburg: H. Reich, 1952.

———. "Zum Problem der Entmythologisierung (1960)." In *GuV*² 4:128–37.

Cappelørn, Niels Jørgen et al., eds. *Schleiermacher und Kierkegaard – Subjektivität und Wahrheit: Akten des Schleiermacher-Kierkegaard-Kongresses in Kopenhagen, Oktober 2003*. Kierkegaard Studies 11. Schleiermacher-Archiv 21. Berlin: de Gruyter, 2006.

Carlston, Charles E. "Biblicism or Historicism? Some Remarks on the Conflict between Kähler and Herrmann on the Historical Jesus." *BR* 13 (1968): 26–40.

Chapman, Mark D. *Ernst Troeltsch and Liberal Theology: Religion and Cultural Synthesis in Wilhelmine Germany*. Christian Theology in Context. Oxford: Oxford University Press, 2001.

———. "The Past, Present and Future of Liberal Theology." In *The Future of Liberal Theology*, edited by Mark D. Chapman, 3–17. Burlington, VT: Ashgate, 2002.

Chapman, Mark D., ed. *The Future of Liberal Theology*. Burlington, VT: Ashgate, 2002.

Chemnitz, Martin. *Loci theologici*. 3 vols. Frankfurt: Joannes Spies, 1591.

———. *Loci theologici*. Translated by J. A. O. Preus. 2 vols. St. Louis: Concordia, 1989.

Childers, Thomas. *The Nazi Voter: The Social Foundations of Fascism in Germany, 1919–1933*. Chapel Hill: University of North Carolina Press, 1983.

Clayton, John Powell. *Ernst Troeltsch and the Future of Theology*. Cambridge: Cambridge University Press, 1976.

———. "Tillich, Troeltsch and the Dialectical Theology." *MoTh* 4 (1988): 323–44.

"Confessio Augustana." In *BSLK*, 32–137.

Copernicus, Nicholas. *On the Revolutions of the Heavenly Spheres*. Translated by A. M. Duncan. New York: Barnes and Noble, 1976.

Crouter, Richard E. "Schleiermacher: Rethinking Kierkegaard's Relationship to Him." In *Kierkegaard and His German Contemporaries*, edited by Jon Stewart, 197–232. Kierkegaard Research: Sources, Reception and Resources 6, Tome 2 – Theology. Burlington, VT: Ashgate, 2007.

Dalferth, Ingolf Ulrich. "Volles Grab, leerer Glaube? Zum Streit um die Auferweckung des Gekreuzigten." *ZThK* 95 (1998): 379–409.

Davaney, Sheila Greeve. *Historicism: The Once and Future Challenge for Theology*. Guides to Theological Inquiry. Minneapolis: Fortress, 2006.

de Boor, Werner. "Der letzte Grund unseres Glaubens an Gott in der Theologie W. Herrmanns. 1. Stück: Religion als Erleben Gottes." *ZThK* NF 6 (1925): 437–53.

———. "Der letzte Grund unseres Glaubens an Gott in der Theologie W. Herrmanns. 2. Stück: Das innere Leben Jesu." *ZThK* NF 7 (1926): 37–61.

DeVries, Dawn. "The Word of God in the Theology of Friedrich Schleiermacher." In *Papers of the Henry Luce III Fellows in Theology*. Vol. 4, 45–69. Pittsburgh, PA: Association of Theological Schools in the United States and Canada, 2000.

Dillenberger, John and Claude Welch. *Protestant Christianity: Interpreted Through Its Development*. 2nd ed. New York: Macmillan, 1988.

Bibliography

Dilthey, Wilhelm. *Gesammelte Schriften*. Edited by Karlfried Gründer and Frithjof Rodi. Vol. 1, *Einleitung in die Geisteswissenschaften: Versuch einer Grundlegung für das Studium der Gesellschaften und der Geschichte*. 9th ed. Edited by Bernhard Groethuysen. Göttingen: Vandenhoeck & Ruprecht, 1990.

———. *Gesammelte Schriften*. Edited by Karlfried Gründer and Frithjof Rodi. Vol. 7, *Der Aufbau der geschichtlichen Welt in den Geisteswissenschaften*. 8th ed. Edited by Bernhard Groethuysen. Göttingen: Vandenhoeck & Ruprecht, 1992.

———. *Gesammelte Schriften*. Edited by Karlfried Gründer and Frithjof Rodi. Vols. 12–13, *Leben Schleiermachers*. Edited by Martin Redeker. Göttingen: Vandenhoeck & Ruprecht, 1979–1985.

———. *Gesammelte Schriften*. Edited by Karlfried Gründer and Frithjof Rodi. Vol. 26, *Das Erlebnis und die Dichtung: Lessing, Goethe, Novalis, Hölderlin*. Edited by Gabriele Malsch. Göttingen: Vandenhoeck & Ruprecht, 2005.

———. *Selected Works*. Edited by Rudolf A. Makkreel and Frithjof Rodi. Vol. 1, *Introduction to the Human Sciences*. Princeton, NJ: Princeton University Press, 1989.

———. *Selected Works*. Edited by Rudolf A. Makkreel and Frithjof Rodi. Vol. 3, *The Formation of the Historical World in the Human Sciences*. Princeton, NJ: Princeton University Press, 2002.

———. *Selected Works*. Edited by Rudolf A. Makkreel and Frithjof Rodi. Vol. 5, *Poetry and Experience*. Princeton, NJ: Princeton University Press, 1985.

Dorrien, Gary. *Theology without Weapons: The Barthian Revolt in Modern Theology*. Louisville, KY: Westminster John Knox, 2000.

Drews, Arthur. *The Christ Myth*. Translated by C. Delisle Burns. Westminster College – Oxford Classics in the Study of Religion. Amherst, NY: Prometheus, 1998.

———. *Die Christusmythe*. 4th ed. Jena: E. Diederichs, 1910.

Duke, James O. and Robert F. Streetman, eds. *Barth and Schleiermacher: Beyond the Impasse?* Philadelphia: Fortress, 1988.

Dunkmann, Karl. *Systematische Theologie*. Vol. 1, *Religionsphilosophie: Kritik der religiösen Erfahrung als Grundlegung christlicher Theologie*. Gütersloh: C. Bertelsmann, 1917.

Engel, Mary Potter and Walter E. Wyman, Jr., eds. *Revisioning the Past: Prospects in Historical Theology*. Minneapolis: Fortress, 1992.

Ericksen, Robert P. *Theologians under Hitler: Gerhard Kittel, Paul Althaus, and Emanuel Hirsch*. New Haven, CT: Yale University Press, 1985.

Erikson, Erik H. *Young Man Luther: A Study in Psychoanalysis and History*. Austin Riggs Monograph 4. London: Faber and Faber, 1958.

Evang, Martin. "Rudolf Bultmanns Berufung auf Friedrich Schleiermacher vor und um 1920." In *Rudolf Bultmanns Werk und Wirkung*, edited by Bernd Jaspert, 3–24. Darmstadt: Wissenschaftliche Buchgesellschaft, 1984.

Feuerbach, Ludwig. *The Essence of Christianity*. Translated by George Eliot. Buffalo, NY: Prometheus, 1989.

———. *The Essence of Faith according to Luther*. Translated by Melvin Cherno. New York: Harper & Row, 1967.

———. *Gesammelte Werke*. Edited by Wolfgang Harich and Werner Schuffenhauer. Vol. 5, *Das Wesen des Christentums*. Berlin: Akademie-Verlag, 1973.

———. "Das Wesen des Glaubens im Sinne Luthers." In *Ludwig Feuerbach's sämmtliche Werke*. Vol. 1, *Erläuterungen und Ergänzungen zum Wesen des Christentums*, 259–325. Leipzig: O. Wigand, 1846.

Bibliography

Fischer, Max and Friedrich Michael Schiele, eds. *Fünfter Weltkongress für Freies Christentum und Religiösen Fortschritt: Protokoll der Verhandlungen*. Berlin-Schöneberg: Protestantischer Schriftenvertrieb, 1910.

"The Formula of Concord." In *BOC*, 481–660.

Forstman, Jack. *Christian Faith in Dark Times: Theological Conflicts in the Shadow of Hitler*. Louisville, KY: Westminster John Knox, 1992.

Fresenius, Wilhelm. "Die Bedeutung der Geschichtlichkeit Jesu für den Glauben." *ZThK* 22 (1912): 244–68.

Fülling, Erich. *Geschichte als Offenbarung: Studien zur Frage Historismus von Herder bis Troeltsch*. Studien der Luther-Akademie, Neue Folge 4. Berlin: A. Töpelmann, 1956.

Fürst, Walther, ed. *"Dialektische Theologie" in Scheidung und Bewährung, 1933–1936: Aufsätze, Gutachten und Erklärungen*. Theologische Bücherei: Neudrucke und Berichte aus dem 20. Jahrhundert 34. Munich: C. Kaiser, 1966.

Gadamer, Hans-Georg. *Gesammelte Werke*. 5th ed. Vol. 1, *Wahrheit und Methode*. Tübingen: Mohr Siebeck, 1986.

———. *Truth and Method*. 2nd rev. ed. Translated by Joel Weinsheimer and Donald G. Marshall. New York: Continuum, 1997.

Gay, Peter. *Weimar Culture: The Outsider as Insider*. New York: Harper & Row, 1968. Reprint, New York: Norton, 2001.

Gemmer, Anders and August Messer. *Sören Kierkegaard und Karl Barth*. Stuttgart: Strecker und Schröder, 1925.

Gerhard, Johann. *Locorum theologicorum*. 9 vols. Jena: Tobiae Steinmanni, 1610–1622.

Gerrish, B. A. *Continuing the Reformation: Essays on Modern Religious Thought*. Chicago: University of Chicago Press, 1993.

———. "Doctor Martin Luther: Subjectivity and Doctrine in the Lutheran Reformation." In B. A. Gerrish, *Continuing the Reformation: Essays on Modern Religious Thought*, 38–56. Chicago: University of Chicago Press, 1993.

———. "Ernst Troeltsch and the Possibility of a Historical Theology." In *Ernst Troeltsch and the Future of Theology*, edited by John Powell Clayton, 100–35. Cambridge: Cambridge University Press, 1976.

———. "Friedrich Schleiermacher." In B. A. Gerrish, *Continuing the Reformation: Essays on Modern Religious Thought*, 147–77. Chicago: University of Chicago Press, 1993.

———. "Jesus, Myth, and History: Troeltsch's Stand in the 'Christ-Myth' Debate." *JR* 55 (1975): 13–35.

"Gesetz zur Wiederherstellung des Berufsbeamtentums." *Reichsgesetzblatt*, part 1, no. 34 (1933): 175–77.

Gestrich, Christof. "Luther und Melanchthon in der Theologiegeschichte des 19. und 20. Jahrhunderts." In *LuJ* 66 (1999): 29–53.

Geyer, Hans-Georg. "Die dialektische Theologie und die Krise des Liberalismus." In *Die Krise des Liberalismus zwischen den Weltkriegen*, edited by Rudolf von Thadden, 155–70. Göttingen: Vandenhoeck & Ruprecht, 1978.

Glaue, Paul. "Wobbermin, Georg." In *RGG*[1] 5:2110.

Goethe, Johann Wolfgang von. *Goethe's Collected Works*. Edited by Thomas P. Saine and Jeffrey L. Sammons. Vols. 4–5, *From My Life*. Translated by Thomas R. Heitner and Thomas P. Saine. New York: Suhrkamp, 1987.

———. *Goethe's Collected Works*. Edited by Thomas P. Saine and Jeffrey L. Sammons. Vol. 11, *The Sorrows of Young Werther, Elective Affinities, Novella*. Translated by Victor Lange and Judith Ryan. Edited by David E. Wellbery. New York: Suhrkamp, 1988.

Bibliography

———. *Goethes Werke*. Edited by Friedmar Apel et al. Vol. 4, *Die Leiden des jungen Werthers*. Jubiläumsausgabe. Frankfurt: Insel, 1998.

———. *Goethes Werke*. Edited by Friedmar Apel et al. Vol. 5, *Dichtung und Wahrheit*. Jubiläumsausgabe. Frankfurt: Insel, 1998.

Gogarten, Friedrich. "Between the Times." In *The Beginnings of Dialectic Theology*, edited by James M. Robinson. Translated by Keith R. Crim and Louis De Grazia, 277–82. Richmond, VA: John Knox, 1968.

———. "Historicism." In *The Beginnings of Dialectic Theology*, edited by James M. Robinson. Translated by Keith R. Crim and Louis De Grazia, 343–58. Richmond, VA: John Knox, 1968.

———. "Historismus." *ZZ* 2 (1924): 7–25. Reprinted in *Anfänge der dialektischen Theologie*, edited by Jürgen Moltmann. 2 vols. 2:171–90. Theologische Bücherei: Neudrucke und Berichte aus dem 20. Jahrhundert 17. Munich: C. Kaiser, 1962–1963.

———. "Zwischen den Zeiten." *ChW* 34, no. 24 (1920): 374–78. Reprinted in *Anfänge der dialektischen Theologie*, edited by Jürgen Moltmann. 2 vols. 2:95–101. Theologische Bücherei: Neudrucke und Berichte aus dem 20. Jahrhundert 17. Munich: C. Kaiser, 1962–1963.

Gorringe, Timothy. "Karl Barth and Liberal Theology." In *The Future of Liberal Theology*, edited by Mark D. Chapman, 163–69. Burlington, VT: Ashgate, 2002.

Graf, Friedrich Wilhelm. "Kulturprotestantismus: Zur Begriffsgeschichte einer theologiepolitische Chiffre." In *Kulturprotestantismus: Beiträge zu einer Gestalt des modernen Christentums*, edited by Hans Martin Müller, 21–77. Gütersloh: Mohn, 1992.

———. "Liberale Theologie." *EKL* 3:86–98.

———. "What Has London (or Oxford or Cambridge) to Do with Augsburg? The Enduring Significance of the German Liberal Tradition in Christian Theology." In *The Future of Liberal Theology*, edited by Mark D. Chapman, 18–38. Burlington, VT: Ashgate, 2002.

Graf, Friedrich Wilhelm, ed. *Liberale Theologie: Eine Ortsbestimmung*. Troeltsch-Studien 7. Gütersloh: Gütersloher Verlagshaus, 1993.

———. *Profile des neuzeitlichen Protestantismus*. 2 vols. Gütersloh: Mohn, 1990.

Graf, Friedrich Wilhelm and Klaus Tanner. "Philosophie des Protestantismus: Immanuel Kant (1724–1804)." In *Profile des neuzeitlichen Protestantismus*, edited by Friedrich Wilhelm Graf. 2 vols. 1:86–112. Gütersloh: Mohn, 1990.

Grau, Rudolf Friedrich. "Vom christlichem Glauben." *BGl* NF 10 (1889): 441–68.

Greive, Wolfgang. *Der Grund des Glaubens: Die Christologie Wilhelm Herrmanns*. Forschungen zur systematischen und ökumenischen Theologie 36. Göttingen: Vandenhoeck & Ruprecht, 1976.

Greshake, Gisbert. *Historie wird Geschichte: Bedeutung und Sinn der Unterscheidung von Historie und Geschichte in der Theologie Rudolf Bultmanns*. Koinonia 3. Essen: Ludgerus, 1963.

Grin, Edmond. "Une Théologie de la Synthèse: La Dogmatique du Professeur Wobbermin." *RThPh* NS 15 (1927): 279–301.

"Gutachten der theologischen Fakultät der Universität Marburg zum Kirchengesetz über die Rechtsverhältnisse der Geistlichen und Kirchenbeamten." *ThBl* 12, n. 10 (October 10, 1933): 289–94. Reprinted in Liebing, 9–15.

Haendler, Klaus. "Offenbarung – Geschichte – Glaube: Bemerkungen zum Glaubensbegriff Melanchthons." In *Reformatio und Confessio: Festschrift für D. Wilhelm Maurer zum*

65. Geburtstag am 7. Mai 1965, edited by Friedrich Wilhelm Kantzenbach and Gerhard Müller, 63–83. Berlin: Lutherisches Verlagshaus, 1965.

———. *Wort und Glaube bei Melanchthon: Eine Untersuchung über die Voraussetzungen und Grundlagen des melanchthonischen Kirchenbegriffes*. Quellen und Forschungen zur Reformationsgeschichte 37. Gütersloh: Mohn, 1968.

Hägglund, Bengt. "Martin Kählers teori om det överhistorika in kristendomen." *SvTK* 48, no. 4 (1972): 153–63.

Härle, Wilfried. "Der Aufruf der 93 Intellektuellen und Karl Barths Bruch mit der liberalen Theologie." *ZThK* 72 (1975): 207–24.

Harnack, Adolf. *Das Wesen des Christentums: Sechzehn Vorlesungen vor Studierenden aller Facultäten im Wintersemester 1899/1900 an der Universität Berlin gehalten*. Leipzig: J. C. Hinrichs, 1901.

———. *What is Christianity?* Translated by Thomas Bailey Saunders. New York: Harper, 1957.

Harrisville, Roy A. and Walter Sundberg. *The Bible in Modern Culture: Baruch Spinoza to Brevard Childs*. 2nd ed. Grand Rapids, MI: Eerdmans, 2002.

Hart, John W. *Karl Barth vs. Emil Brunner: The Formation and Dissolution of a Theological Alliance, 1916–1936*. Issues in Systematic Theology 6. New York: Peter Lang, 2001.

Harvey, Van A. *The Historian and the Believer: The Morality of Historical Knowledge and Christian Belief*. Urbana: University of Illinois Press, 1966. Reprint, 1996.

Harvey, Van A. and Schubert M. Ogden. "How New is the 'New Quest for the Historical Jesus'?" In *The Historical Jesus and the Kerygmatic Christ: Essays on the New Quest for the Historical Jesus*, translated and edited by Carl E. Braaten and Roy A. Harrisville, 197–242. Nashville, TN: Abingdon, 1964.

———. "Wie neu ist die 'Neue Frage nach dem historischen Jesus'?" *ZThK* 59 (1962): 46–87.

Heidegger, Martin. *Being and Time*. Translated by John Macquarrie and Edward Robinson. The Library of Philosophy and Theology. London: SCM Press, 1962.

———. *Sein und Zeit*. 7th ed. Tübingen: M. Niemeyer, 1953.

Heinzelmann, Gerhard. "Die Erfahrungsgrundlage der Theologie." *ZSTh* 5 (1928): 737–57.

Helmreich, Ernst Christian. *The German Churches under Hitler: Background, Struggle, and Epilogue*. Detroit, MI: Wayne State University Press, 1979.

Henke, Peter. "Die Bedeutung der Befindlichkeit für den christlichen Glauben." *ZMR* 62 (April 1978): 123–33.

Hermann, Rudolf. *Christentum und Geschichte bei Wilhelm Herrmann: Mit besonderer Berücksichtigung der erkenntnis-theoretischen Seite des Problems*. Leipzig: A. Deichert, 1914.

Herms, Eilert and Joachim Ringleben, eds. *Vergessene Theologen des 19. und frühen 20. Jahrhunderts: Studien zur Theologiegeschichte*. Göttinger theologische Arbeiten 32. Göttingen: Vandenhoeck & Ruprecht, 1982.

Herrin, Burley F. "The Contributions of Kähler's *The So-called Historical Jesus and the Historic, Biblical Christ*." *LexTQ* 31 (Summer 1996): 171–77.

Herrmann, Wilhelm. "Die Bedeutung der Geschichtlichkeit Jesu für den Glauben: Eine Besprechung des gleichnamigen Vortags von Ernst Troeltsch." In Wilhelm Herrmann, *Schriften zur Grundlegung der Theologie*, edited by Peter Fischer-Appelt. 2 vols. 2:282–89. Theologische Bücherei: Neudrucke und Berichte aus dem 20. Jahrhundert 36. Munich: C. Kaiser, 1966–1967.

Bibliography

———. *The Communion of the Christian with God Described on the Basis of Luther's Statements*. 2nd ed. Translated by J. S. Sandys Stanyon. Edited by R. W. Stewart. New York: Putnam, 1906.

———. *Gesammelte Aufsätze*. Edited by F. W. Schmidt. Tübingen: Mohr Siebeck, 1923.

———. "Der geschichtliche Christus der Grund unseres Glaubens." In Wilhelm Herrmann, *Schriften zur Grundlegung der Theologie*, edited by Peter Fischer-Appelt. 2 vols. 1:149–85. Theologische Bücherei: Neudrucke und Berichte aus dem 20. Jahrhundert 36. Munich: C. Kaiser, 1966–1967.

———. "Grund und Inhalt des Glaubens." In Wilhelm Herrmann, *Gesammelte Aufsätze*, edited by F. W. Schmidt, 275–94. Tübingen: Mohr Siebeck, 1923.

———. *Die mit der Theologie verknüpfte Not der evangelischen Kirche und ihrer Ueberwindung*. Religionsgeschichtliche Volksbücher für die deutsche christliche Gegenwart, 4. Reihe, 21. Heft. Tübingen: Mohr Siebeck, 1913.

———. *Schriften zur Grundlegung der Theologie*. Edited by Peter Fischer-Appelt. 2 vols. Theologische Bücherei: Neudrucke und Berichte aus dem 20. Jahrhundert 36. Munich: C. Kaiser, 1966–1967.

———. "Soll es eine besondere theologische Geschichtsforschung geben?" *ChW* 32 (1918): 31–32.

———. *Der Verkehr des Christen mit Gott im Anschluss an Luther dargestellt*. 4th ed. Stuttgart: J. G. Cotta, 1903.

———. "Warum bedarf unser Glaube geschichtlicher Tatsachen?" In Wilhelm Herrmann, *Schriften zur Grundlegung der Theologie*, edited by Peter Fischer-Appelt. 2 vols. 1:81–103. Theologische Bücherei: Neudrucke und Berichte aus dem 20. Jahrhundert 36. Munich: C. Kaiser, 1966–1967.

Hirsch, Emanuel. *Geschichte der neuern evangelischen Theologie im Zusammenhang mit den allgemeinen Bewegungen des europäischen Denkens*. 5 vols. Gütersloh: C. Bertelsmann, 1949–1954.

Hofmann, Arne. *Wir sind das alte Deutschland, das Deutschland wie es war: Der "Bund der Aufrechten" und der Monarchismus in der Weimarer Republik*. Moderne Geschichte und Politik 11. Frankfurt: Peter Lang, 1998.

Holl, Karl. *Was verstand Luther unter Religion?* Tübingen: Mohr Siebeck, 1917.

———. "Was verstand Luther unter Religion?" In Karl Holl, *Gesammelte Aufsätze zur Kirchengeschichte*. 6th ed. Vol. 1, *Luther*, 1–110. Tübingen: Mohr Siebeck, 1932.

———. *What Did Luther Understand By Religion?* Edited by James Luther Adams and Walter F. Bense. Translated by Fred W. Meuser and Walter R. Wietzke. Philadelphia: Fortress, 1977.

Howard, Thomas A. *Religion and the Rise of Historicism: W. M. L. de Wette, Jacob Burkhardt and the Theological Origins of Nineteenth-Century Historical Consciousness*. Cambridge: Cambridge University Press, 2000.

Hübbinger, Gangolf. *Kulturprotestantismus und Politik: Zum Verhältnis von Liberalismus und Protestantismus im wilhelminischen Deutschland*. Tübingen: Mohr Siebeck, 1994.

Husserl, Edmund. *Ideas: General Introduction to Pure Phenomenology*. Translated by W. R. Boyce Gibson. The Muirhead Library of Philosophy. New York: Humanities Press, 1969.

———. *Ideen zu einer reinen Phänomenologie und phänomenologische Philosophie*. Halle: M. Niemeyer, 1913.

Bibliography

———. *Logical Investigations*. Translated by J. N. Findlay. 2 vols. International Library of Philosophy. New York: Routledge, 2001.
———. *Logische Untersuchungen*. 4th and 5th eds. 2 vols. Tübingen: M. Niemeyer, 1968.
Iggers, Georg C. *The German Conception of History: The National Tradition of Historical Thought from Herder to the Present*. Rev. ed. Middletown, CT: Wesleyan University Press, 1983.
Irle, Günter. "Theologie als Wissenschaft bei Georg Wobbermin." Diss., University of Marburg, 1973.
Jacobs, Manfred. "Liberale Theologie." In *TRE* 21:47–68.
James, William. *Die religiöse Erfahrung in ihrer Mannigfaltigkeit: Materialien und Studien zu einer Psychologie und Pathologie des religiösen Lebens*. Translated by Georg Wobbermin. Leipzig: J. C. Hinrichs, 1907.
———. *Varieties of Religious Experience: A Study in Human Nature, Being the Gifford Lectures on Natural Religion Delivered at Edinburgh in 1901–1902*. New York: Longmans, Green, 1902.
Jaspert, Bernd. "Rudolf Bultmanns Wende von der liberalen zur dialektischen Theologie." In *Rudolf Bultmanns Werk und Wirkung*, edited by Bernd Jaspert, 25–43. Darmstadt: Wissenschaftliche Buchgesellschaft, 1984.
Jones, Garaint Vaughan. "Bultmann and the Liberal Theology – II." *ET* 67 (1956): 313–17.
"Journey Together Faithfully." Accessed July 15, 2008. Online: http://www.elca.org/What-We-Believe/Social-Issues/Social-Statements-in-Process/JTF-Human-Sexuality/Resources.aspx.
Jüngel, Eberhard. "Von der Dialektik zur Analogie: Die Schule Kierkegaards und der Einspruch Petersons." In Eberhard Jüngel, *Barth-Studien*, 127–79. Ökumenische Theologie 9. Zurich and Cologne: Benzinger; Gütersloh: Mohn, 1982.
———. *Paulus und Jesus: Eine Untersuchung zur Präzisierung der Frage nach dem Ursprung der Christologie*. 3rd ed. Hermeneutische Untersuchungen zur Theologie 2. Tübingen: Mohr Siebeck, 1967.
Kähler, Martin. *The So-called Historical Jesus and the Historic, Biblical Christ*. Translated and edited by Carl E. Braaten. Fortress Texts in Modern Theology. Philadelphia: Fortress, 1964. Reprint, 1988.
———. *Der sogenannte historische Jesus und der geschichtliche, biblische Christus*. 2nd ed. Leipzig: A. Deichert, 1896.
———. *Die Wissenschaft der christlichen Lehre von dem evangelischen Grundartikel aus im Abrisse dargestellt*. 3rd ed. Leipzig: A. Deichert, 1905. Reprint, Neukirchen-Vluyn: Neukirchener Verlag, 1966.
Kant, Immanuel. *Critique of Pure Reason*. Translated and edited by Paul Guyer and Allen W. Wood. The Cambridge Edition of the Works of Immanuel Kant. Cambridge: Cambridge University Press, 1998.
———. *Critique of the Power of Judgment*. Edited by Paul Guyer. Translated by Paul Guyer and Eric Matthews. The Cambridge Edition of the Works of Immanuel Kant. Cambridge: Cambridge University Press, 2000.
———. *Gesammelte Schriften*. Edited by the Königliche Preußischen Akademie der Wissenschaften. Werke VI, *Die Religion innerhalb der Grenzen der bloßen Vernunft; Die Metaphysik der Sitten*. Edited by Georg Wobbermin and Paul Natorp. Berlin: G. Reimer, 1907.

Bibliography

———. *Kritik der reinen Vernunft*. Edited by Raymund Schmidt. Jubiläumsausgabe. Philosophische Bibliothek 37a. Hamburg: F. Meiner, 1993.

———. *Kritik der Urteilskraft*. Edited by Heiner F. Klemme. Philosophische Bibliothek 507. Hamburg: F. Meiner, 2001.

———. *Lose Blätter aus Kants Nachlaß*. Edited by Rudolf Reicke. 3 vols. Königsberg: F. Beyer, 1889-1898.

———. *Notes and Fragments*. Edited by Paul Guyer. Translated by Curtis Bowman, Paul Guyer, and Frederick Rauscher. The Cambridge Edition of the Works of Immanuel Kant in Translation. Cambridge: Cambridge University Press, 2005.

———. *Die Religion innerhalb der Grenzen der bloßen Vernunft*. Edited by Bettina Stangneth. Philosophische Bibliothek. Hamburg: F. Meiner, 2003.

———. *Religion within the Boundaries of Mere Reason*. Translated and edited by Paul Guyer, Allen W. Wood, and George Di Giovanni. Cambridge Texts in the History of Philosophy. Cambridge: Cambridge University Press, 1998.

Käsemann, Ernst. "Das Problem des historischen Jesus." *ZThK* 51 (1954): 125-53.

———. "The Problem of the Historical Jesus." In Ernst Käsemann, *Essays on New Testament Themes*, translated by W. J. Montague, 15-47. Studies in Biblical Theology 41. London: SCM Press, 1964.

Kattenbusch, Ferdinand. *Die deutsche evangelische Theologie seit Schleiermacher*. 6th ed. Gießen: A. Töpelmann, 1934.

Kierkegaard, Søren. *Gesammelte Werke*. Translated by Hermann Gottsched and Christoph Schrempf. 12 vols. in 8. Jena: E. Diederichs, 1913-1925.

———. *Gesammelte Werke*. Translated and edited by Emanuel Hirsch et al. 36 vols. Düsseldorf: E. Diederichs, 1950-1969. Reprint, Gütersloh: Mohn, 1979-1986.

Klünker, Wolf-Ulrich. *Psychologische Analyse und theologische Wahrheit: Die religionspsychologische Methode Georg Wobbermins*. Göttinger theologische Arbeiten 33. Göttingen: Vandenhoeck & Ruprecht, 1985.

Knape, Joachim. "Melanchthon und die Historien." *ARG* 91 (2000): 111-26.

Koch, Traugott. "Christologie jenseits der Alternative von 'historischem Jesus' und 'dogmatischem' Christus." In *Liberale Theologie: Eine Ortsbestimmung*, edited by Friedrich Wilhelm Graf, 83-92. Troeltsch-Studien 7. Gütersloh: Gütersloher Verlagshaus, 1993.

König, Gisbert. "Die systematische Funktion der historischen Forschung bei Wilhelm Herrmann, Ernst Troeltsch und Karl Barth." Diss., University of Bonn, 1979.

Koepp, Wilhelm. *Einführung in das Studium der Religionspsychologie*. Tübingen: Mohr Siebeck, 1920.

"Die Konkordienformel." In *BSLK*, 735-1100.

Kruhöffer, Gerald. "Der geschichtliche Christus: Die Offenbarung Gottes in ihrer Beziehung auf die Wirklichkeit des Menschen nach der Theologie Wilhelm Herrmanns." Diss., University of Göttingen, 1969.

Krumwiede, Hans Walter. *Glaube und Geschichte in der Theologie Luthers: Zur Entstehung des geschichtlichen Denkens in Deutschland*. Forschungen zur Kirchen- und Dogmengeschichte 2. Göttingen: Vandenhoeck & Ruprecht, 1952.

Leipold, Heinrich. *Offenbarung und Geschichte als Problem des Verstehens: Eine Untersuchung zur Theologie Martin Kählers*. Gütersloh: Mohn, 1962.

"The Leipzig Interim." In *S&C*, 183-96.

Lessing, Eckhard. *Geschichte der deutschsprachigen evangelischen Theologie von Albrecht Ritschl bis zur Gegenwart*. 2 vols. Göttingen: Vandenhoeck & Ruprecht, 2000-2004.

Bibliography

Lessing, Gotthold Ephraim. "On the Proof of the Spirit and of Power." In *Gotthold Ephraim Lessing, Philosophical and Theological Writings*, translated and edited by H. B. Nisbet. Cambridge Texts in the History of Philosophy. Cambridge: Cambridge University Press, 2005.

———. "Ueber den Beweis des Geistes und der Kraft." In *Gotthold Ephraim Lessings Sämtliche Schriften*, edited by Karl Lachmann. 23 vols. 13:1–8. Leipzig: G. J. Göschen, 1886–1924.

Liebing, Heinz, ed. *Die Marburger Theologen und der Arierparagraph in der Kirche: Eine Sammlung von Texten aus den Jahren 1933 und 1934*. Marburg: N. G. Elwert, 1977.

Link, Hans-Georg. *Geschichte Jesu und Bild Christi: Die Entwicklung der Christologie Martin Kählers in Auseinandersetzung mit der Leben-Jesu-Theologie und der Ritschl-Schule*. Neukirchen-Vluyn: Neukirchener Verlag, 1975.

Livingston, James C. *Modern Christian Thought*. Vol. 1, *The Enlightenment and the Nineteenth Century*. Upper Saddle River, NJ: Prentice Hall, 1997.

Lohff, Wenzel. "Wobbermin, Georg." In *RGG³* 6:1788–89.

Lübbe, Hermann. "Liberale Theologie in der Evolution der modernen Kultur." In *Liberale Theologie: Eine Ortsbestimmung*, edited by Friedrich Wilhelm Graf, 16–31. Troeltsch-Studien 7. Gütersloh: Gütersloher Verlagshaus, 1993.

Luther, Martin. "A Brief Instruction on What to Look for and Expect in the Gospels." In *LW* 35, 113–24.

———. "Diui Pauli apostoli ad Romanos Epistola." In *WA* 56, 3–528.

———. "Die ein und dreissigste Predigt (1538)." In *WA* 47, 86–93.

———. "Eyn kleyn unterricht, was man ynn den Euangelijs suchen und gewartten soll." In *WA* 10.I.1, 8–18.

———. "Der große Katechismus." In *BSLK*, 545–733.

———. "The Large Catechism." In *BOC*, 377–480.

———. "Lectures on Genesis." *LW* 5.

———. "Lectures on Romans: Glosses and Scholia." *LW* 25.

———. "The Magnificat, Translated and Expounded." In *LW* 21, 297–358.

———. "Das Magnificat verdeutschet und ausgelegt." In *WA* 7, 538–604.

———. "Temporal Authority: To What Extent It Should Be Obeyed." In *LW* 45, 81–129.

———. "Von weltlicher Oberkeit, wie weit man ihr Gehorsam schuldig ist." In *WA* 11, 229–81.

———. "Vorlesung über 1. Mose." *WA* 43.

Macintosh, Douglas Clyde. Foreword to *The Nature of Religion*, by Georg Wobbermin. Translated by Theophil Menzel and Daniel Sommer Robinson. New York: T. Y. Crowell, 1933.

McCormack, Bruce. *Karl Barth's Critically Realistic Dialectical Theology: Its Genesis and Development, 1909–1936*. New York: Oxford University Press, 1995.

McGrath, Alister. "Justification and Christology: The Axiomatic Correlation between the Historical Jesus and the Proclaimed Christ." *MoTh* 1 (October 1984): 45–54.

Melanchthon, Philipp. *The Loci Communes of Philipp Melanchthon*. Translated by Charles Leander Hill. Boston: Meador, 1944.

———. "Loci praecipui theologici." In *Melanchthons Werke in Auswahl*. Edited by Robert Stupperich. Vol. 2, Part 2, *Loci praecipui theologici von 1559 (2. Teil) und Definitiones*, edited by Hans Engelland, 353–780. Gütersloh: C. Bertelsmann, 1953.

———. "Loci theologici." *CR* 21.

———. "Loci theologici germanice." *CR* 22.

Bibliography

———. *Melanchthon on Christian Doctrine: Loci Communes, 1555*. Translated and edited by Clyde L. Manschreck. A Library of Protestant Thought. New York: Oxford University Press, 1965.

Mencke, Martin. *Erfahrung und Gewißheit des Glaubens: Das Gewißheitsproblem im theologischen Denken Martin Kählers*. Forum Systematik: Beiträge zur Dogmatik, Ethik und ökumenischen Theologie 6. Stuttgart: W. Kohlhammer, 2001.

Meyer, Wilhelm. "Religionspsychologie: Historismus und Psychologismus in der evangelisch-protestantischen Theologie seit Schleiermacher." In *Luther, Kant, Schleiermacher in ihrer Bedeutung für den Protestantismus: Forschungen und Abhandlungen. Georg Wobbermin zum 70. Geburtstag (27. Oktober 1939) dargebracht von Kollegen, Schülern und Freunden*, edited by Friedrich Wilhelm Schmidt, Robert Winkler, and Wilhelm Meyer, 48–56. Berlin: A. Collignon, 1939.

Michalson, Gordon E. *The Historical Dimensions of a Rational Faith: The Role of History in Kant's Religious Thought*. Washington, D. C.: University Press of America, 1977.

———. *Lessing's "Ugly Ditch": A Study of Theology and History*. University Park: Pennsylvania State University Press, 1985.

Michel, Karl-Heinz. *Glaubensdokument contra Geschichtsbuch? Die Schriftlehre Wilhelm Herrmanns*. Monographien und Studienbücher. Wuppertal: R. Brockhaus, 1992.

Moltmann, Jürgen, ed. *Anfänge der dialektischen Theologie*. 2 vols. Theologische Bücherei: Neudrucke und Berichte aus dem 20. Jahrhundert 17. Munich: C. Kaiser, 1962–1963.

Morgan, Marcia. "Adorno's Reception of Kierkegaard: 1929–1933." *Søren Kierkegaard Newsletter* 46 (Sept 2003). Accessed July 15, 2008. Online: http://www.stolaf.edu/collections/kierkegaard/newsletter/issue46/46002.htm.

Morgan, Robert. "Ernst Troeltsch and the Dialectical Theology." In *Ernst Troeltsch and the Future of Theology*, edited by John Powell Clayton, 33–77. Cambridge: Cambridge University Press, 1976.

Müller, Hans Martin, ed. *Kulturprotestantismus: Beiträge zu einer Gestalt des modernen Christentums*. Gütersloh: Mohn, 1992.

Mundle, Wilhelm. *Der Glaube an Christus und der historische Zweifel: Eine biblisch-theologische Untersuchung*. Metzingen: Brunquell-Verlag, 1950.

Newhall, Jannette Elthina. "The Influence of William James on Georg Wobbermin's Psychology and Philosophy of Religion." Diss., Boston University, 1931.

Niebuhr, H. Richard. *The Meaning of Revelation*. Library of Theological Ethics. Louisville, KY: Westminster John Knox, 2006.

Norden, Günther van. *Der deutsche Protestantismus im Jahr der nationalsozialistischen Machtergreifung*. Gütersloh: Mohn, 1979.

Oakes, Guy. "Rickert's Theory of Historical Knowledge." In Heinrich Rickert, *The Limits of Concept Formation in the Natural Sciences: A Logical Introduction to the Historical Sciences*, edited and translated by Guy Oakes, vii–xxx. Abr. ed. Texts in German Philosophy. Cambridge: Cambridge University Press, 1986.

Ollig, Hans-Ludwig. *Der Neukantianismus*. Stuttgart: Metzler, 1979.

Orth, Ernst Wolfgang and Helmut Holzhey, eds. *Neukantianismus: Prospektiven und Probleme*. Studien und Materialen zum Neukantianismus 1. Würzburg: Königshausen & Neumann, 1994.

Ott, Heinrich. *Die Frage nach dem historischen Jesus und die Ontologie der Geschichte*. Theologische Studien 62. Zurich: EVZ-Verlag, 1960.

Bibliography

Pannenberg, Wolfhart. "Heilsgeschehen und Geschichte." *KuD* 5 (July 1959): 218–37, 259–88.

———. "Redemptive Event and History." In Wolfhart Pannenberg, *Basic Questions in Theology: Collected Essays*, translated by George H. Kehm. 2 vols. 1:15–80. Philadelphia: Fortress, 1970–1971.

Paulsen, Friedrich. *Kant, Der Philosoph des Glaubens*. Berlin: Reuther & Reichard, 1899.

Paulus, Rudolf. *Das Christusproblem der Gegenwart: Untersuchung über das Verhältnis von Idee und Geschichte*. Tübingen: Mohr, 1922.

———. "Geschichtliche und übergeschichtliche Grundlagen des Glaubens: Eine Studie zum Christusproblem in der heutigen Theologie." *ZThK* NF 3 (1922): 188–202, 266–94.

———. *Gott in der Geschichte? Ein Vortrag, mit einem Nachwort über "Glaube und Geschichte."* Tübingen: Mohr Siebeck, 1920.

———. "Zum Problem 'Glaube und Geschichte' (Traub – Troeltsch – Wobbermin – Windisch – Roessingh)." *ZThK* NF 7 (1926): 378–99.

Peukert, Detlev J. K. *The Weimar Republic: The Crisis of Classical Modernity*. Translated by Richard Deveson. New York: Hill and Wang, 1992.

Pfleiderer, Georg. *Theologie als Wirklichkeitswissenschaft: Studien zum Religionsbegriff bei Georg Wobbermin, Rudolf Otto, Heinrich Scholz und Max Scheler*. Beiträge zur historischen Theologie 82. Tübingen: Mohr Siebeck, 1992.

———. "Wobbermin, Georg." In *RGG*[4] 8:1672.

Quenstedt, Johann Andreas. *The Nature and Character of Theology: An Introduction to the Theology of J. A. Quenstedt from "Theologia didactico-polemica sive systema theologicum."* Edited and translated by Luther Poellot. St. Louis: Concordia, 1986.

———. *Theologia didactico-polemica sive systema theologicum*. Leipzig: T. Fritsch, 1715.

Rand, Calvin. "Two Meanings of Historicism in the Writings of Dilthey, Troeltsch, and Meinecke." *JHI* 25 (1964): 503–18.

Reid, David. "Translator's Note." In Ernst Troeltsch, *The Absoluteness of Christianity and the History of Religions*, translated by David Reid, 21–24. Research in Theology. Richmond, VA: John Knox, 1971.

Reischle, Max. "Der Streit über die Begründung des Glaubens auf den 'geschichtliche' Jesus Christus." *ZThK* 7 (1897): 171–264.

Rickert, Heinrich. *Die Grenzen der naturwissenschaftlichen Begriffsbildung: Eine logische Einleitung in die historischen Wissenschaften*. 5th ed. Tübingen: Mohr Siebeck, 1929.

———. *The Limits of Concept Formation in the Natural Sciences: A Logical Introduction to the Historical Sciences*. Abr. ed. Edited and translated by Guy Oakes. Texts in German Philosophy. Cambridge: Cambridge University Press, 1986.

Robinson, James M., ed. *The Beginnings of Dialectic Theology*. Translated by Keith R. Crim and Louis de Grazia. Richmond, VA: John Knox, 1968.

———. *A New Quest of the Historical Jesus and Other Essays*. Philadelphia: Fortress, 1983.

Rohls, Jan. *Protestantische Theologie der Neuzeit*. 2 vols. Tübingen: Mohr Siebeck, 1997.

Ruddies, Hartmut. "Karl Barth im Kulturprotestantismus: Eine theologische Problemanzeige." In *Wahrheit und Versöhnung: Theologische und philosophische Beiträge zur Gotteslehre*, edited by Dietrich Korsch and Hartmut Ruddies, 193–231. Gütersloh: Mohn, 1989.

Bibliography

———. "Liberale Theologie: Zur Dialektik eines komplexen Begriffs." In *Liberale Theologie: Eine Ortsbestimmung*, edited by Friedrich Wilhelm Graf, 176–203. Troeltsch-Studien 7. Gütersloh: Gütersloher Verlagshaus, 1993.

Runge, Carl-Ludwig. *Geschichte und Historie bei Martin Kähler*. Neustrelitz: O. Wagner, 1927.

Rupp, George. *Culture-Protestantism: German Liberal Theology at the Turn of the Twentieth Century*. AAR Studies in Religion 15. Missoula, MT: Scholars Press, 1977.

Rust, Hans. "Historismus." In *RGG²* 2:1938–40.

Schleiermacher, Friedrich. *The Christian Faith*. Edited by H. R. Mackintosh and J. S. Stewart. Edinburgh: T. & T. Clark, 1928. Reprint, 1989.

———. *Der christliche Glaube nach dem Grundsätzen der Evangelischen Kirche im Zusammenhange dargestellt (1830/1831)*. 7th ed. 2 vols. in 1. Edited by Martin Redeker. De Gruyter Studienbuch. Berlin: de Gruyter, 1960. Reprint, 1999.

———. *Friedrich Schleiermacher's sämmtliche Werke*. Div. 1, vol. 6, *Das Leben Jesu: Aus Schleiermachers handschriften Nachlasse und Nachschriften seiner Zuhörer*. Edited by K. A. Rutenik. Berlin: G. Reimer, 1864.

———. *The Life of Jesus*. Edited by Jack C. Verheyden. Translated by S. Maclean Gilmour. Lives of Jesus Series. Philadelphia: Fortress, 1975.

———. *On the Glaubenslehre: Two Letters to Dr. Lücke*. Translated by James Duke and Francis Fiorenza. AAR Texts and Translations 3. Atlanta: Scholars Press, 1981.

———. *On Religion: Speeches to Its Cultured Despisers*. Translated by John Oman. Louisville, KY: Westminster John Knox, 1994.

———. *On Religion: Speeches to Its Cultured Despisers*. 2nd ed. Translated and edited by Richard Crouter. Cambridge Texts in the History of Philosophy. Cambridge: Cambridge University Press, 1996.

———. "Über die Religion: Reden an die Gebildeten unter ihren Verächtern." In *Friedrich Daniel Ernst Schleiermacher Kritische Gesamtausgabe*, edited by Hans-Joachim Birkner et al. Vol. 1, pt. 2, *Schriften aus der Berliner Zeit, 1796–1799*, edited by Günter Meckenstock, 185–326. Berlin: de Gruyter, 1984.

———. "Über die Religion: Reden an die Gebildeten unter ihren Verächtern." In *Friedrich Daniel Ernst Schleiermacher Kritische Gesamtausgabe*, edited by Hans-Joachim Birkner et al. Vol. 1, pt. 12, *Über die Religion (2.-) 4. Auflage, Monologen (2.-) 4. Auflage*, edited by Günter Meckenstock, 1–321. Berlin: de Gruyter, 1995.

"Die schmalkaldische Artikel." In *BSLK*, 405–68.

Schmid, Heinrich. *The Dogmatics of the Evangelical Lutheran Church*. 3rd ed. Translated by Charles A. Hay and Henry E. Jacobs. Minneapolis: Augsburg, 1961.

———. *Die Dogmatik der Evangelisch-lutherischen Kirche dargestellt und aus den Quellen belegt*. Erlangen: C. Heyder, 1843.

Schmid, Johannes Heinrich. *Erkenntnis des geschichtlichen Christus bei Martin Kähler und bei Adolf Schlatter*. Theologische Zeitschrift Sonderband 5. Basel: F. Reinhardt, 1978.

Schmidt, Friedrich Wilhelm, Robert Winkler, and Wilhelm Meyer, eds. *Luther, Kant, Schleiermacher in ihrer Bedeutung für den Protestantismus: Forschungen und Abhandlungen. Georg Wobbermin zum 70. Geburtstag (27. Oktober 1939) dargebracht von Kollegen, Schülern und Freunden*. Berlin: A. Collignon, 1939.

Schmidt, Martin and Georg Schweiger, eds. *Kirchen und Liberalismus im 19. Jahrhundert*. Göttingen: Vandenhoeck & Ruprecht, 1976.

Bibliography

Scholder, Klaus. *The Churches and the Third Reich*. Translated by John Bowden. 2 vols. Philadelphia: Fortress, 1988.

———. *Die Kirchen und das Dritte Reich*. 2 vols. Frankfurt: Ullstein, 1977–1985.

Schröter, Fritz. *Glaube und Geschichte bei Friedrich Gogarten und Wilhelm Herrmann*. Köthen-Anhalt: Greiner, 1932.

Schultz, Werner. *Schleiermacher und der Protestantismus*. Theologische Forschung: Wissenschaftliche Beiträge zur kirchlich-evangelischen Lehre 14. Hamburg-Bergstedt: H. Reich, 1957.

Schweitzer, Albert. *Geschichte der Leben-Jesu-Forschung*. 2nd ed. Tübingen: Mohr Siebeck, 1926.

———. *The Quest of the Historical Jesus*. 1st complete ed. Edited by John Bowden. Translated by W. Montgomery et al. Minneapolis: Fortress, 2001.

Semler, Johann Salomo. *Versuch einer freiern theologischen Lehrart*. Halle: C. H. Hemmerde, 1777.

Siegmund-Schultze, F[riedrich]. *Schleiermachers Psychologie in ihrer Bedeutung für die Glaubenslehre*. Tübingen: Mohr Siebeck, 1913.

"The Smalcald Articles." In *BOC*, 295–328.

Sockness, Brent W. *Against False Apologetics: Wilhelm Herrmann and Ernst Troeltsch in Conflict*. Beiträge zur historischen Theologie 105. Tübingen: Mohr Siebeck, 1998.

———. "The Ideal and the Historical in the Christology of Wilhelm Herrmann: The Promise and the Perils of Revisionary Christology." *JR* 73 (July 1992): 366–88.

Spengler, Oswald. *The Decline of the West*. Translated by Charles Francis Atkinson. New York: A. A. Kopf, 1926.

———. *Der Untergang des Abendlandes: Umrisse einer Morphologie der Weltgeschichte*. Munich: C. H. Beck, 1923. Reprint, 1980.

Spieckermann, Ingrid. *Gotteserkenntnis: Ein Beitrag zur Grundfrage der neuen Theologie Karl Barths*. Beiträge zur evangelischen Theologie 97. Munich: C. Kaiser, 1985.

Starbuck, Edwin D. *The Psychology of Religion: An Empirical Study of the Growth of Religious Consciousness*. New York: Scribner's, 1908.

Stephan, Horst. *Geschichte der evangelischen Theologie seit dem deutschen Idealismus*. Die Theologie im Abriß 9. Berlin: A. Töpelmann, 1938.

Stephan, Horst and Martin Schmidt. *Geschichte der deutschen evangelischen Theologie seit dem deutschen Idealismus*. 2nd rev. ed. Sammlung Töpelmann: 1. Reihe, Die Theologie im Abriß 9. Berlin: A. Töpelmann, 1960.

Sticht, Friedrich Wolfgang. *Die Bedeutung Wilhelm Herrmanns für die Theologie Rudolf Bultmanns*. Berlin: Ernst Reuter Gesellschaft, 1965.

Strauss, David Friedrich. *The Life of Jesus Critically Examined*. Edited by Peter Hodgson. Translated by George Eliot. Lives of Jesus Series. Philadelphia: Fortress, 1973. Reprint, Ramsey, NJ: Sigler, 1994.

Strecker, Georg. "The Historical and Theological Problems of the Jesus Question." Translated by Neil R. Parker. *TJT* 6, no. 2 (1990): 201–23.

Tillich, Paul. *Dynamics of Faith*. New York: Harper, 1957.

———. Foreword to *The So-called Historical Jesus and the Historic Biblical Christ*, by Martin Kähler. Translated and edited by Carl E. Braaten. Fortress Texts in Modern Theology. Philadelphia: Fortress, 1964. Reprint, 1988.

———. *Systematic Theology*. Vol. 1. Chicago: University of Chicago Press, 1967.

"The Torgau Articles." In Jacobs, 75–98.

"The Torgau Articles." In *S&C*, 93–104.

Bibliography

Troeltsch, Ernst. "Ein Apfel vom Baume Kierkegaards." *ChW* 35 (1921): 186–89. Reprinted in *Anfänge der dialektischen Theologie*, edited by Jürgen Moltmann. 2 vols. 2:134–40. Theologische Bücherei: Neudrucke und Berichte aus dem 20. Jahrhundert 17. Munich: C. Kaiser, 1962–1963.

———. "An Apple from the Tree of Kierkegaard." In *The Beginnings of Dialectic Theology*, edited by James M. Robinson. Translated by Keith R. Crim and Louis De Grazia, 311–16. Richmond, VA: John Knox, 1968.

———. *Die Bedeutung der Geschichtlichkeit Jesu für den Glauben*. Tübingen: Mohr Siebeck, 1911.

———. *The Christian Faith*. Edited by Gertud von le Fort. Translated by Garrett E. Paul. Fortress Texts in Modern Theology. Minneapolis: Fortress, 1991.

———. *Gesammelte Schriften*. Vol. 3, *Der Historismus und seine Probleme*. Aalen: Scientia, 1961.

———. *Glaubenslehre*. Edited by Gertrud von le Fort. Berlin: Duncker and Humboldt, 1925. Reprint, Aalen: Scientia, 1981.

———. "Die Krisis des Historismus." *NeRu* 33 (1922): 572–90.

"Variata." In Jacobs, 103–47.

Verheule, Anthonie F. "'Historie' en 'Geschichte.'" *KeTh* 22 (1971): 232–47.

———. *Wilhelm Bousset, Leben und Werk: Ein theologiegeschichtlicher Versuch*. Amsterdam: Van Bottenburg, 1973.

Vollmann, William T. *Uncentering the Earth: Copernicus and "The Revolutions of the Heavenly Spheres."* Great Discoveries. New York: Norton, 2006.

Ward, Keith. "The Importance of Liberal Theology." In *The Future of Liberal Theology*, edited by Mark D. Chapman, 29–53. Burlington, VT: Ashgate, 2002.

Wehrung, Georg. *Geschichte und Glaube: Eine Besinnung auf die Grundsätze theologischen Denkens*. Gütersloh: C. Bertelsmann, 1933.

Weinhardt, Joachim. *Wilhelm Herrmanns Stellung in der Ritschlischen Schule*. Beiträge zur historischen Theologie 97. Tübingen: Mohr, 1996.

Welch, Claude. *Protestant Thought in the Nineteenth Century*. 2 vols. New Haven, CT: Yale University Press, 1972–1985.

Wendland, Johannes. "Schrift und Erfahrung, die beiden zusammenhängenden Prinzipien des Protestantismus." In *Luther, Kant, Schleiermacher in ihrer Bedeutung für den Protestantismus: Forschungen und Abhandlungen. Georg Wobbermin zum 70. Geburtstag (27. Oktober 1939) dargebracht von Kollegen, Schülern und Freunden*, edited by Friedrich Wilhelm Schmidt, Robert Winkler, and Wilhelm Meyer, 530–64. Berlin: A. Collignon, 1939.

Werblowsky, R. J. Zwi. "Die Krise der liberalen Theologie." In *Die Krise des Liberalismus zwischen den Weltkriegen*, edited by Rudolf von Thadden, 147–54. Göttingen: Vandenhoeck & Ruprecht, 1978.

Wesseling, Klaus-Gunther. "Wobbermin, Ernst Gustav Georg." *BBKL*, 13:1455–62. Accessed July 15, 2008. Online: http://www.bautz.de/bbkl/w/wobbermin.shtml.

Willey, Thomas E. *Back to Kant: The Revival of Kantianism in German Social and Historical Thought, 1860–1914*. Detroit, MI: Wayne State University Press, 1978.

Winkler, Robert. "Wobbermin, Georg." In *RGG*² 5:1996.

Wirsching, Johannes. *Gott in der Geschichte: Studien zur theologiegeschichtlichen Stellung und systematischen Grundlegung der Theologie Martin Kählers*. Forschungen zur Geschichte und Lehre des Protestantismus, 10. Reihe 26. Munich: C. Kaiser, 1963.

Bibliography

Wittkau-Horgby, Annette. *Historismus: Zur Geschichte des Begriffs und des Problems.* Sammlung Vandenhoeck. Göttingen: Vandenhoeck & Ruprecht, 1992.

Wobbermin, Georg. *Altchristliche liturgische Stücke aus der Kirche Ägyptens, nebst einem dogmatischen Brief des Bischofs Serapion von Thmuis.* Leipzig: J. C. Hinrichs, 1899.

———. "Die anthropologische Gedanken in der Theologie Luthers und Schleiermachers." *NLA* 2 (1933): 25–26.

———. "Aufgabe und Bedeutung der Religionspsychologie." In *Fünfter Weltkongress für Freies Christentum und Religiösen Fortschritt: Protokoll der Verhandlungen*, edited by Max Fischer and Friedrich Michael Schiele, 245–61. Berlin-Schöneberg: Protestantischer Schriftenvertrieb, 1910.

———. *Bishop Sarapion's Prayer-Book: An Egyptian Pontifical Dated Probably about A.D. 350–356.* Translated by John Wordsworth. London: Society for Promoting Christian Knowledge, 1899.

———. *Christian Belief in God: A German Criticism of German Materialistic Philosophy.* Translated by Daniel Sommer Robinson. New Haven, CT: Yale University Press, 1918.

———. *Deutscher Staat und evangelische Kirche.* Göttingen: Vandenhoeck & Ruprecht, 1934.

———. "Deutschland, Nordamerika und England als christliche-evangelische Kulturstaaten." *DE* 5 (1914): 671–74.

———. "The Doctrine of Grace in Evangelical German Theology from Schleiermacher Onwards." In *The Doctrine of Grace*, edited by William Thomas Whitley, 291–320. London: SCM Press, 1932.

———. *Den evangeliska teologins kris och dess övervinnande.* Translated by Gösta Wahlström. Uppsala: Lindblad, 1931.

———. "Die Frage nach Gott in Luthers großem Katechismus." In *Festgabe für D. Dr. Julius Kaftan zu seinem 70. Geburtstage dargebracht von Schülern und Kollegen*, edited by Arthur Titius, Friedrich Niebergall, and Georg Wobbermin, 418–35. Tübingen: Mohr Siebeck, 1920.

———. *Geschichte und Historie in der Religionswissenschaft: Über die Notwendigkeit, in der Religionswissenschaft zwischen Geschichte und Historie strenger zu unterscheiden, als gewöhnlich geschieht.* 2. Ergänzungsheft zur Zeitschrift für Theologie und Kirche. Tübingen: Mohr Siebeck, 1911.

———. "Gibt es eine Linie Luther-Schleiermacher?" *ZThK* NF 12 (1931): 250–60.

———. "Historische und systematische Theologie." *ZThK* NF (1920): 393–416.

———. "Im Kampf gegen Historismus und Psychologismus: Aus dem Vorwort zur schwedischen Ausgabe meiner *Richtlinien evangelischer Theologie zur Ueberwindung der gegenwärtigen Krisis*." *ThBl* 10 (1931): 257–58.

———. *Die innere Erfahrung als Grundlagen eines moralischen Beweises für das Dasein Gottes: Eine methodologische Studie.* Berlin: C. Vogt, 1894.

———. Introduction to *Die religiöse Erfahrung in ihrer Mannigfaltigkeit*, by William James. 2nd ed. Translated by Georg Wobbermin. Leipzig: J. C. Hinrichs, 1914.

———. "Ist Schleiermacher wirklich ausgeschöpft?" *ChW* 41 (1927): 99–104.

———. "Karl Barths Anspruch, als Papst aller evangelischen Kirchen zu gelten: Englisch-deutsche Erklärung von 36 deutschen Theologen vom Dezember 1935." In Georg Wobbermin, *Arthur Titius – Ökumenische Theologie zur Befriedung der Kirche: Eine Gedenkrede*, 20–23. Berlin: A. Collignon, 1937.

Bibliography

———. "Luther, Kant, Schleiermacher und die Aufgabe der heutigen Theologie." *ZThK* NF 5 (1924): 104–20.

———. "Luthers trinitarischer Monotheismus." *ZThK* NF 9 (1928): 237–52.

———. *The Nature of Religion*. Translated by Theophil Menzel and Daniel Sommer Robinson. New York: T. Y. Crowell, 1933.

———. "Nochmals die Arierfrage in der Kirche." *DtPfrBl* 38 (1934): 9–10. Reprinted in Liebing, 51–52.

———. "Psychologie und Erkenntniskritik der religiösen Erfahrung." In *Weltanschauung, Philosophie und Religion in Darstellungen von Wilhelm Dilthey und Anderen*, edited by Max Frischeisen-Köhler, 341–63. Berlin: Reichl, 1911.

———. "Psychologismus." In *RGG*² 4:1646.

———. "Religionspsychologie." In *RGG*² 4:1921–27.

———. "Religionspsychologische Arbeit und systematische Theologie." *ARPs* 2, no. 3 (1921): 200–5.

———. "Die religionspsychologische Methode in der systematischen Theologie: Wider Friedrich Traubs Einwendungen dagegen." In *Festgabe für Wilhelm Herrmann zu seinem 70. Geburtstage dargebracht von Schülern und Kollegen*, edited by Martin Rade and Horst Stephan, 314–50. Tübingen: Mohr Siebeck, 1917.

———. Review of *Die Mystik und das Wort*, by Emil Brunner. *ThLZ* 49 (1924): 241–44.

———. Review of *Die Mystik und das Wort*, by Emil Brunner, 2nd ed. *ThLZ* 55 (1930): 185–88.

———. *Richtlinien evangelischer Theologie zur Überwindung der gegenwärtigen Krisis*. Göttingen: Vandenhoeck & Ruprecht, 1929.

———. "Schleiermacher, Friedrich Daniel Ernst." In *RGG*² 5:170–9.

———. "Schleiermacher in der Theologie des englischen Sprachgebiets." *CuW* 8 (1932): 388–89.

———. "Schleiermacher in der Zeit seines Werdens: Aus Anlaß von Georg Wehrungs gleichnamigem Buch." *ChW* 42 (1928): 848–50.

———. *Schleiermacher und Ritschl in ihrer Bedeutung für die heutige theologische Lage und Aufgabe*. Sammlung gemeinverständlicher Vorträge und Schriften aus dem Gebiet der Theologie und Religionsgeschichte 125. Tübingen: Mohr Siebeck, 1927.

———. *Schleiermachers Hermeneutik in ihrer Bedeutung für seine religionswissenschaftliche Arbeit*. Berlin: Weidmann, 1930.

———. "Schleiermachers protestantische und vaterländische Sendung." *DtCh* 3 (1938), no. 2.

———. "Der Streit um Schleiermacher in seiner Bedeutung für die heutige Gesamtlage der evangelischen Theologie." *ZEvRU* 39 (1928): 280–94.

———. *Systematische Theologie nach religionspsychologischer Methode*. Vol. 1, *Die religionspsychologische Methode in Religionswissenschaft und Theologie*. Leipzig: J. Hinrichs, 1913.

———. *Systematische Theologie nach religionspsychologischer Methode*. Vol. 2, *Das Wesen der Religion*. Leipzig: J. Hinrichs, 1921.

———. *Systematische Theologie nach religionspsychologischer Methode*. Vol. 3, *Wesen und Wahrheit des Christentums*. Leipzig: J. Hinrichs, 1925.

———. *Theologie und Metaphysik: Das Verhältnis der Theologie zur modernen Erkenntnistheorie und Psychologie*. Berlin: A. Duncker, 1901.

———. "Wie gehören für Luther Gott und Glaube zuhaufe?" *ZThK* NF 9 (1928): 51–60.

Bibliography

———. *Wort Gottes und evangelischer Glaube.* Göttingen: Vandenhoeck & Ruprecht, 1931.

———. *Zum Streit um die Religionspsychologie.* Berlin-Schöneberg: Protestantischer Schriftenvertrieb, 1913.

———. "Zum Streit um Schleiermacher." *ChW* 41 (1927): 1145–46.

———. "Zwei theologische Gutachten in Sachen des Arier-Paragraphen – kritisch beleuchtet." *ThBl* 12, no. 12 (December 12, 1933): 356–69. Reprinted in Liebing, 28–31.

Wolfes, Matthias. *Protestantische Theologie und moderne Welt: Studien zur Geschichte der liberalen Theologie nach 1918.* Theologische Bibliothek Töpelmann 102. Berlin: de Gruyter, 1999.

Wyman, Walter E., Jr. "Revelation and the Doctrine of Faith: Historical Revelation within the Limits of Historical Consciousness." *JR* 78 (1998): 38–63.

Yasukata, Toshimasa. *Lessing's Philosophy of Religion and the German Enlightenment: Lessing on Christianity and Reason.* American Academy of Religion Reflection and Theory in the Study of Religion Series. Oxford: Oxford University Press, 2002.

Zahrnt, Heinz. *The Question of God: Protestant Theology in the Twentieth Century.* Translated by R. A. Wilson. New York: Harcourt, Brace & World, 1969.

———. *Die Sache mit Gott: Die protestantische Theologie im 20. Jahrhundert.* Munich: R. Piper, 1966.

Index of Names

Althaus, Paul, 13
Anselm, 98, 136
Augustine, 91 n.
Aune, Michael, 2, 6, 9, 116, 160

Barth, Karl, 1–2, 11, 12–13, 45, 77, 83 n., 89 n., 94 n., 100, 109 n., 115, 117–118, 133, 139–151, 157–158, 160, 162, 169 n., 170, 177
Bauer, Walter, 172 n.
Birkner, Hans-Joachim, 4
Bodelschwingh, Friedrich von, 169 n.
Bousset, Wilhelm, 15, 27, 33 n., 61–71, 113 n.
Brandt, Wilhelm, 172 n.
Brunner, Emil, 80 n., 85 n., 117–118, 143, 145 n., 147, 149 n., 150, 157–158
Bultmann, Rudolf, 11, 12, 45, 58 n., 60 n., 61 n., 99, 100 n., 109 n., 114, 116, 145 n., 151–158, 169–176, 180

Calvin, John, 88 n., 140 n.
Chapman, Mark, 3 n., 160

Deißman, Adolf, 169 n., 172 n.
Deißner, Kurt, 172 n.
Dilthey, Wilhelm, 110 n., 178
Drews, Arthur, 10, 16–17, 62, 76 n., 105

Feuerbach, Ludwig, 121 n.
Fitzer, Johannes Gottfried, 172 n.
Frank, Franz Hermann Reinhold, 148 n.
Fresenius, Wilhelm, 27 n.
Fries, Jakob Friedrich, 66

Gadamer, Hans-Georg, 25 n., 110 n.

Gerrish, B. A., 16, 60, 88 n., 113 n., 115
Goethe, Johann Wolfgang von, 64 n., 65 n., 110 n., 140
Gogarten, Friedrich, 2 n., 117 n., 145 n., 147, 157, 158 n.
Graf, Friedrich Wilhelm, 4–5, 169
Gunkel, Hermann, 62 n.

Hall, G. Stanley, 79 n.
Harnack, Adolf, 59 n., 62 n., 86, 169 n., 178
Hegel, Georg Wilhelm Friedrich, 110 n.
Heidegger, Martin, 11, 13, 99–100, 151, 152, 157
Heim, Karl, 172 n.
Herrmann, Wilhelm, 15, 21 n., 27, 47–61, 71, 73, 142 n., 169 n.
Hirsch, Emanuel, 13, 145 n.
Hofmann, Johann Christian Konrad von, 148 n.
Holl, Karl, 119, 123 n., 128, 131 n.
Husserl, Edmund, 150

James, William, 10, 78, 79 n., 133 n., 179
Jeremias, Joachim, 172 n.
Jones, Geraint Vaughan, 156
Jülicher, Adolf, 172 n.
Jüngel, Eberhard, 58 n., 145 n.
Juncker, Alfred, 172 n.

Kaftan, Julius, 59 n., 78 n., 178, 180
Kaftan, Theodor, 169 n.
Kähler, Martin, 15, 18, 21 n., 26, 27, 34–47, 49, 50, 52, 54, 55, 59 n., 60, 61, 71, 72 n., 86, 91, 92, 114, 152
Kant, Immanuel, 11, 12, 30 n., 63, 66, 69, 113, 115, 118–119, 128–132, 135, 136 n., 140 n., 150, 161

Index of Names

Käsemann, Ernst, 36 n., 157 n.
Kierkegaard, Søren, 99, 144 n.
Klünker, Wolf-Ulrich, 9, 78 n., 118 n.

Lessing, Eckhard, 4
Lessing, Gotthold Ephraim, 27–34, 63, 66, 71, 74 n., 81 n.
Leuba, James, 79 n.
Lietzmann, Hans, 172 n.
Lohmeyer, Ernst, 172 n.
Loofs, Friedrich, 169 n.
Lueken, Wilhelm, 172 n.
Lütgert, Wilhelm, 172 n.
Luther, Martin, 11, 12, 84, 88–90, 92 n., 94 n., 96, 101–103, 114, 115–116, 118, 119–128, 129 n., 131 n., 134, 135, 136, 140 n., 142 n., 143–144, 146, 147, 150–151, 155 n., 161, 165, 176

Melanchthon, Philipp, 11, 12, 91 n., 92–93, 101–102, 114, 119 n., 122, 140 n., 144, 146, 163–165

Newhall, Jannette Elthina, 10
Niebuhr, H. Richard, 19 n.

Oepke, Albrecht, 172 n.

Pannenberg, Wolfhart, 38 n., 97 n.
Pfleiderer, Georg, 9

Rickert, Heinrich, 21–23, 80 n.
Ritschl, Albrecht, 62, 86, 136 n., 148
Rupp, George, 1, 27 n.

Schleiermacher, Friedrich, 10–11, 12, 58 n., 62, 78–80, 82–83, 87–88, 92 n., 99, 100, 114, 115–119, 128 n., 132–143, 144 n., 145, 146–152, 157 n., 161, 180
Schlier, Heinrich, 172 n.
Schmidt, Karl Ludwig, 172 n.
Schmitz, Otto, 172 n.
Schniewind, Julius, 172 n.
Schweitzer, Albert, 17 n., 36 n.
Semler, Johann Salomo, 3 n.

Sockness, Brent, 49, 50 n., 53–54
Soden, Hans von, 172 n.
Soden, Hermann von, 178
Starbuck, Edwin, 79 n.
Stephan, Horst, 3, 5–8, 13
Strauss, David Friedrich, 107 n.

Tillich, Paul, 34, 83 n.
Troeltsch, Ernst, 2 n., 62 n., 82, 86 n., 117, 145 n., 149 n., 179
Tucholsky, Kurt, 64

Wehrung, Georg, 3, 13
Welch, Claude, 2 n., 51
Windisch, Hans, 172 n.
Wolfes, Matthias, 2–10, 116, 143 n., 160, 161, 169–171, 177
Wundt, Wilhelm, 79 n., 80 n., 169 n.

Topical Index

Bible. *See* Scripture

Christ. *See* Jesus Christ
Confessions, 7, 91–93, 102, 124 n., 166–167, 172, 174–175

dialectical theology, 1, 3, 11, 13, 77, 85 n., 115–118, 128, 133, 139–151, 155–157, 160, 170

existentialism, existential theology, 11, 97, 99–100, 81 n., 144, 146, 151–152, 156–157, 176
experience, religious, 5, 11–12, 25, 49, 50 n., 51–52, 61, 71–74, 76–77, 79 n., 80–82, 84–85, 87, 89–90, 99–104, 110–114, 118, 121–125, 126, 133–139, 141, 142 n., 144, 146, 147–148, 152, 156, 158, 160–161

faith
    as assent (*assensus*), 90, 92, 94 n., 101, 120–121, 146, 163, 166–167
    and certainty, 15, 47–48, 50, 52, 54, 60, 61, 63, 87 n., 102, 132,
    as decision, 99, 101, 103, 144, 146
    Easter faith (*see also* Jesus Christ, resurrection of), 73, 112, 138 n., 153
    as *fides qua creditur* (*see also* subjectivism) and *fides quae creditur* (*see also* objectivism), 11, 51 n., 84 n., 88, 89, 103, 117, 136 n., 139, 144, 147–148, 150–151, 156, 161

faith (*continued*)
    as *fides historica*, 11, 12, 91–94, 98–99, 101, 103, 112, 114, 146, 154, 163–168
    as *fides implicit*, 92 n., 101, 103, 120, 121, 146
    as *fides iustificans*, 11, 12, 91–94, 96, 103, 113–114, 154, 163–168
    as gift, 50, 90, 92–93, 102, 114, 125, 164, 168
    justification by, 11, 15, 35, 38, 41 n., 50, 85, 114, 120, 151 n., 163–168
    as knowledge (*notitia*), 91, 93 n., 101, 103, 120, 122 n., 146, 163–168
    as obedience, 90, 92, 98, 99, 101, 103, 146
    object of, 35, 38–39, 40, 48, 55, 58, 60, 87, 90, 98, 112 n., 120, 144–146, 155 n., 156
    as trust (*fiducia*), 88, 91 n., 93 n., 101, 120–121, 124 n., 135, 144–146, 155 n., 163–168

Geschichte. See under history
God, 50, 70, 74, 82, 84, 88–89, 90–93, 102, 108, 120, 121 n., 122 n., 123–127, 139 n., 148, 153, 173–174, 175
    existence of, 88–89, 101, 120–122, 126, 129–132, 134–135, 144, 148, 161
    as object of faith, 70, 84, 87 n., 88–90, 101, 103–104, 120–122, 123 n., 131, 143, 144, 155 n., 156
    revelation of. *See* revelation

God (*continued*)
　as "whence" of the feeling of absolute dependence, 83, 87 n., 135–136, 140–141
　Word of. *See* Word of God
gospel (*see also* Scripture and Word of God), 58, 65, 94 n., 124–125, 175
gospels, 36–37, 43, 49, 62, 65–66, 107–109
grace, justification by. *See under* faith

historical-critical method, 15–16, 18–19, 20–26, 33–49, 52–63, 65–69, 71–73, 76, 85 n., 86–87, 92, 93, 95, 98–99, 103–105, 111–112, 149 n., 152, 154–155
historical Jesus, quests for. *See* Jesus Christ as historical figure
historicism (*Historismus*), 79, 85–87, 117, 149, 156, 170
Historie. *See under* history
History
　effect (*Wirkung*) and efficacy (*Wirksamkeit*) of, 19, 21, 24–26, 46–47, 56, 60–61, 72, 73, 75, 91, 93, 103, 153 n.
　as *Geschichte/geschichtlich* (historic), 16–28, 31–35, 39–42, 43–44, 45–46, 52, 55–56, 57–59, 63–70, 71, 74 n., 75, 76–77, 79–80, 81–82, 85, 91–94, 97–98, 100, 103–105, 107, 111–114, 116, 117, 123 n., 137–138, 147, 152–154
　as *Historie/historisch* (historical), 16–21, 23–28, 31–33, 39, 43–44, 48, 51, 55 n., 56, 57, 59, 63, 67–68, 69 n., 71–72, 73, 75, 76–77, 91–93, 103, 104, 107 n., 112 n., 113, 152–154
　knowledge of, 16, 22, 28, 30, 41, 43, 48, 62, 74–76, 80, 91–93, 106–107, 164–168

Jesus Christ
　historic picture of, 15–17, 20, 24, 25–26, 35–36, 39–47, 48 n., 49–61, 67–70, 71–77, 104–105, 106, 112–114, 127, 131, 132, 137–139

Jesus Christ (*continued*)
　as historical figure, 15, 16, 19, 35, 36–40, 43, 47, 49, 54, 59, 60, 62, 63, 66, 67, 75–76, 85, 104, 105, 152, 157 n., 160
　inner life of, 48 n., 49–58, 60, 62
　resurrection of, 28–29, 57, 58–59, 60 n., 73, 106–111, 153–154
　as revelation of God, 4, 7, 8, 20, 39, 48, 52, 74, 97–98, 101, 104, 112, 113, 114, 131, 132, 139, 144, 147, 153, 161
justification. *See under* faith

liberal theology, 1–13, 16 n., 45, 63, 65, 85 n., 95, 115–118, 139, 142 n., 145 n., 146, 149 n., 152, 154–157, 160–162, 169
life of Jesus. *See* Jesus Christ as a historical figure

method, historical critical. *See* historical-critical method
method, religio-psychological. *See* religio-psychological method

National Socialism, 10, 13, 170, 176, 177, 179
neo-orthodoxy. *See* dialectical theology

objectivism, objectivity, 11, 82, 83 n., 84–85, 87, 88, 89, 90, 92, 98, 101, 103, 111, 114, 116, 117, 118, 120, 121–122, 125–126, 131–132, 134–139, 140–141, 146–151, 156, 157–158, 161

proclamation, 39, 40, 42, 46, 49, 50, 53, 58, 87 n., 94 n., 124–125, 127, 137, 141, 153, 173, 175
psychologism (*Psychologismus*), 85, 87, 117, 148–149, 156, 170
psychology
　empirical, 78 n., 79–80, 117, 149 n.
　of religion (*see also* religio-psychological method), 10, 11, 78, 79 n., 80–81, 83, 87, 90, 99, 100, 149 n., 179

reason, 28–33, 63–66, 68–70, 81, 92 n., 113 n., 120–121, 123, 129–132, 149
religio-psychological circle, 11, 24, 34 n., 61, 73 n., 77, 81–83, 98, 100–102, 103–104, 114, 117 n., 124, 127, 136, 138–139, 141, 144–145, 147, 151, 156, 161, 176
religio-psychological method, 10, 11, 24, 68 n., 77, 78–84, 103, 115, 116, 119, 121, 123, 128, 133–134, 136 n., 137, 143, 147, 149, 152, 155, 161–162
resurrection. *See under* Jesus Christ
revelation (*see also* Word of God and *under* Scripture), 4, 7–8, 20, 30, 35, 39, 41, 48, 52, 53, 63, 70, 74–75, 81, 89, 90, 92 n., 93, 94–95, 97–98, 100–101, 104, 111 n., 112–114, 124, 127, 131–132, 138–139, 141, 144, 147–148, 150, 153, 161

Scripture
  authority of, 15, 30, 35, 95–96, 100, 124, 127, 141, 147–148, 172
  as historical source, 15, 20, 35, 37–42, 44–45, 53, 72, 93, 97–98, 100–101, 103, 114, 138, 147, 166
  as revelation, 33, 35, 93, 95, 97–98, 100–101, 112, 114, 124, 127, 132, 138–139, 141, 147–148
  as testimony, 33, 48 n., 49, 96, 98, 100–101, 114, 127, 138, 147
subjectivism, subjectivity, 4, 11, 51 n., 80 n., 82, 83 n., 84–85, 88–90, 92, 101, 103, 110–111, 114, 116, 118, 121–126, 129–132, 134–139, 140–141, 144–150, 156–158, 161

theology. *See* dialectical theology, liberal theology, and religio-psychological method

Word of God, 1, 90, 94 n., 95–97, 100–101, 102, 124, 138, 141, 143–144, 146, 163–164

www.ingramcontent.com/pod-product-compliance
Lightning Source LLC
Chambersburg PA
CBHW060605230426
43670CB00011B/1976